HANSARD SOCIE
POLITICS AND GU

Edited by
F. F. Ridley

HANSARD SOCIETY SERIES IN POLITICS AND GOVERNMENT

Edited by
F. F. Ridley

The Hansard Society Series in Politics and Government brings to the wider public the debates and analyses of important issues first discussed in the pages of its journal, *Parliamentary Affairs*

The Quango Debate

Edited by
F. F. Ridley and David Wilson

OXFORD UNIVERSITY PRESS
in association with
THE HANSARD SOCIETY FOR
PARLIAMENTARY GOVERNMENT

Oxford University Press, Walton Street, Oxford OX2 6DP
Oxford New York
Athens Auckland Bangkok Bombay
Calcutta Cape Town Dar es Salaam Delhi
Florence Hong Kong Istanbul Karachi
Kuala Lumpur Madras Madrid Melbourne
Mexico City Nairobi Paris Singapore
Taipei Tokyo Toronto
and associated companies in
Berlin Ibadan

Oxford is a trade mark of Oxford University Press

Published in the United States
by Oxford University Press Inc., New York

© Oxford University Press, 1995

First published in Parliamentary Affairs, 1995
New as paperback, 1995

A catalogue for this book is available from the British Library

Library of Congress Cataloging in Publication Data
(Data available)

ISBN 0-19-922238-X

Printed in Great Britain
by Headley Brothers Limited, The Invicta Press,
Ashford, Kent and London

CONTENTS

CONTRIBUTORS TO THIS VOLUME

John Chumrow is Chairman of Waltham Forest Housing Action Trust

Alistair Graham is Chief Executive of Calderdale and Kirklees Training and Enterprise Council

Paul Hirst is Professor of Social Theory at Birkbeck College, University of London

Brian Hogwood is Professor of Government, Strathclyde University

Rt Hon David Hunt MP is Chancellor of the Duchy of Lancaster and Minister of Public Services and Science

Philip Hunt is Director of the National Association of Health Authorities and Trusts

Helen Johnson is a Senior Lecturer in the Centre for Educational Management, Roehampton Institute

F. F. Ridley is Professor of Political Theory and Institutions and Associate of the Institute of Public Administration and Management, University of Liverpool

Kathryn Riley is Professor and Director of the Centre for Educational Management, Roehampton Institute

Eric Sorensen is Chief Executive of the London Docklands Development Corporation

John Stewart is Professor of Local Government, University of Birmingham

Tony Stott is Senior Lecturer in Public Administration, De Montfort University, Leicester

Stuart Weir is Senior Research Fellow in the Human Rights Centre, University of Essex

David Wilson is Professor of Public Administration and Head of the Department of Public Policy and Managerial Studies, De Montfort University, Leicester

Preface

This is the first in a new series on current issues in government and politics — British or comparative. Although originated in a special issue of *Parliamentary Affairs: Journal of Comparative Politics*, it is not a collection of essays linked only by reference to quangos but, we hope, a coherent work, articles commissioned to cover all major concerns of the current quango debate, in perspectives of theory and practice and from different political standpoints, a good mix of well qualified contributors whose names or responsibilities readers will recognise.

Quangos are certainly a current issue. Hardly a week passes without a relevant news item or polemic. 'Quango, quango, quango' could have been our title. The debate, of course, is complicated by the different interests of those engaged in it. The argument is partly about principles. Are quangos a more effective way of organising some of the functions of the state than traditional forms of public administration? Can this be democratic, if different from traditional forms of representative government? But there are also questions of practice. Are quangos currently efficient (or at least no worse than central or local government)? Are they currently managed in a democratically acceptable fashion (or at least no less democratically than central or local government)? If there are faults, and there undoubtedly are, just as there are achievements, are the reason intrinsic, i.e. in the nature of the system, thus inevitable, or accidental, e.g. teething troubles or political abuse?

While the debate is sometimes objective, however different its participants' views, it is often politically motivated. The Quango Hunt was effectively started by Mrs Thatcher (without whom right-wing pamphleteers would have remained just that). The lady had many strengths but perhaps lacked the historical sense that tides which turn in your favour will turn against you in due course. So the Quango Hunt is now Labour horsemen hunting the Conservative's quango foxes. Tory quango appointments and examples of quango mismanagement are weapons in the now seemingly permanent electoral battle. In the process, sensible discussion of quangos as parts of the modern state is distorted by the bugles of the huntsmen and the baying of the hounds.

Revolutionary changes are taking place in the British state system: executive agencies, market testing and contracting out, Citizen's Charters and performance indicators, senior civil servants appointed on contract, perhaps from outside, and much else. 'Reinventing Government' is a fair description. Quangos are not new in themselves (Arts Council, BBC, University Grants Committee — indeed Labour's postwar nationalisations) but their place in this government's move to dismantle the administrative state, central and local government, makes them part of that revolution. Evolution sets in, however, after mutations occur, a gradual process of improvement. While the Conservatives remain in office, at least until the next general election, perhaps beyond, quangos will undoubtedly be reformed. If Labour comes to office, despite all polemics, reform seems as likely as counter-revolution (arguments for alternatives to 'representative' central and local government, possibly on a functional base, were after all part of the 1970s debate).

Quangoland in one form or another is quite likely to stay. Whether or not, it will certainly remain a current political issue over the next years. The present articles offer a wider survey and a wider span of views than any book presently available. Together, they enable the reader, student or citizen (not that the two are distinct groups), to understand the sprawling and confusing assembly of quangos that are part of the new British state and to consider the place quangos might have, reformed, in whatever state system one hopes to see after the next general election.

F. F. Ridley

> again, the tendency is common to all countries. But some go much further than others.

Quangos in the Skeletal State

BY DAVID WILSON

QUANGOS (quasi-autonomous non-governmental organisations) have become high profile in recent years. Spending on the 'unelected state' has mushroomed and ministerial patronage has increased. A new political lexicon has been born incorporating terms such as quangocrats, quangowatch and quangoland. The nature of public accountability has invariably been at the heart of debate about quangos, but all too frequently battle lines have been drawn rather simplistically and sweeping generalisations about the desirability or otherwise (usually otherwise) of quangos have emerged. This collection of essays on quangos provides contributions from a wide range of perspectives with the aim of introducing an element of sophistication into what has hitherto been a highly polarised debate. The purpose of this article is to provide an analysis of some of the most salient issues associated with the role of non-elected government bodies in what is becoming an increasingly skeletal state.

Context

There is no widely accepted agreement about the numbers of quangos. In 1993, according to official figures in the Cabinet Office's *Public Bodies*, there were some 1,389 Non-Departmental Public Bodies (NDPBs) operating in Britain, spending between them £15,410m and employing 111,300 staff. Most significant were the 358 'executive' bodies which spent the bulk of this money. While such bodies have long been used as vehicles for the delivery of government policy (e.g. University Grants Commission, Arts Council), recent years have witnessed new initiatives. The National Health Service Trusts, the Higher Education Funding Council (HEFC), The Further Education Funding Council (FEFC), the National Curriculum Council (NCC) and, from 1 April 1994, the Funding Agency for Schools (FAS), all represent recent government developments which, it is often claimed, run services without any local democratic accountability. The above examples certainly illustrate the trend in government to substitute appointed boards for elected authorities, with resulting confusion in accountability. From the centre's perspective, however, such bodies represent a vehicle for the incorporation of 'New Public Management', with its alternative modes of accountabilty, into government.

Debate about the role of quangos was quickened by the publication in 1994 of the Public Accounts Committee (PAC) Report, *The Proper*

Conduct of Public Business, but despite the political capital made out of this report by the Opposition in the context of corruption in quangos, an analysis of the 23 'instances of failure' shows that the majority of cases, far from occurring in quangos, were found in 'old-style' government departments.[1] While few would argue that everything is perfect in the quango garden, it is important not to let the anti-quango political bandwaggon roll on uncritically. The massive waste of public money by the West Midland Health Authority (£10M) and the Wessex Regional Health Authority (£20M) reported by the Public Accounts Committee was extensively publicised but both elected local government and central government have had their share of financial scandals recently. Analytical objectivity is essential if debate is to be moved on from the popular and superficial. In its 'attack on sleaze' in government, announced at the 1994 Conservative Party Conference, quangos were targeted for especial attention.

Definitions

The definitional complications of the term 'quasi-government' are manifold. Essentially, the word 'quango' is an umbrella beneath which a tremendous variety of organisations shelter. As Pliatzky reminds us, while quango 'is a catchy word, the adjectives quasi-autonomous and non-governmental are unfortunately inaccurate in this context'.[2] To quote from the Pliatzky report on non-departmental public bodies written in 1980, 'The special feature common to these bodies is that they are *non-departmental* and, so far from their being altogether *non-governmental*, one of the reasons given for concern about them is that they may represent not only a spread of patronage but a concealed growth of government which does not show up in the size of the civil service. Moreover, the description quasi-autonomous is not generally apposite and would be particularly misleading in relation to tribunals if it were to imply that they had less than full judicial independence.'[3] The government's definition of a NDPB excludes the newly created NHS Trusts, Training and Enterprise Councils (TECs), or the now incorporated colleges of further education and grant maintained schools. Given such definitional limitations, Davis' research in the West Midlands adopted NESPOs (Non-Elected Public Service Organisations) as a more satisfactory way forward.[4] This embraces the government's definition (i.e. NDPBs) plus NHS bodies including NHS Trusts, TECs and other non-recognised executive bodies such as governing bodies of colleges of further education. The justification is that these are public service bodies, non-elected, spending large sums of taxpayers' money. A Democratic Audit/Charter 88 report, *Ego Trip: Extra-Governmental Organisations in the UK and their Accountability*, published in 1994, identified three main categories of executive body: the government's executive NDPBs; NHS bodies; and the 'non-recognised' executive bodies, most of which operate at local level. The report observes: 'We cannot use the term "quango" to describe these bodies, as it is altogether too loose. Nor can we simply describe them as "executive bodies" without risking confusion with the government's narrower categories of "executive NDPBs" and "executive agencies". We have therefore adopted the term, "extra government organisations" or EGOs, to encompass the three categories of public agencies that we audit in this report'.[7] In this context they identified 5,521 EGOs in the UK — roughly one for every 10,000 people. Of these, 443 were at national level, 355 at regional level and 4,723 at local level. Quangos, NDPBs, NESPOs and EGOs are all variations on what has become an increasingly complex theme.

Ambiguity also characterises the diversity of quangos. Compare, for example, a local Housing Action Trust (HAT), the Apple and Pear Development Council, the UK Atomic Energy Authority and the Arts Council of Great Britain — all can be termed 'quangos' but their diversity in terms of finance, organisation, objectives and accountability is enormous. Their legal status also varies a good deal. Some bodies are non-governmental because they have a separate status in law. Some, such as TECs are established as companies limited by guarantee, with a non-executive board drawn from business and the public sector, and are subject to company law. In practice, there are wide variations in the way quangos are governed. For example, the directors of TECs bear personal fiduciary liability; the members of NHS Trust boards do not. On occasions, legislative requirements can conflict with the concept of independent public accountability. There is a further complication as Doig notes,[5] namely that 'there is no one characteristic, or lack of characteristic, that distinguishes quangos or non-departmental public bodies from other organisations in the structure of government'. For Sir Norman Chester, the growth of fringe bodies represented a 'retreat from the simple democratic principle evolved in the nineteenth century that those who perform a public duty should be fully responsible to an electorate — by way either of a minister responsible to Parliament or of a locally elected council. The essence of the fringe body is that it is not so responsible for some or all of its actions.'[6]

Accountability

Democratic accountabilty is central to contemporary debate about quangos. Direct accountability to the electorate in specific policy sectors (e.g. health and education) is missing but, arguably, other forms of accountability are not. The picture of accountability to the local community painted by advocates of elected local government often exaggerates the virtues of that particular form of government. As the last few years have shown, elected local authorities are not immune from charges of corruption, fraud and partisan patronage. Additionally, turnouts in local elections of between 40% and 50% do little to strengthen the case of those who call for elected local government to extend its functions and pull back some of those services handed over to non-elected bodies. Local election turnouts in Britain are well below those at national level and, perhaps more significantly, well below turnout in local elections in most other European countries. Some would argue with a certain force that local elections are, in any event, simply national elections writ small—essentially judgements on the performance of national governments rather than individual local authorities. As Jim Bulpitt has shown, an idealistic model of accountability via multi-functional elected local authorities can all too easily emerge, particularly given the fragmentation of provision through compulsory competitive tendering and other local service level agreements.[7]

Much recent central government activity has had as its fulcrum the citizen as consumer and in this context the government argues that the growth of quangos has in fact produced a 'democratic gain' rather than a 'democratic deficit'. Accountability, it maintains, has been strengthened by making services more responsive to consumers, which is more meaningful than giving citizens a distant and diffuse voice over the make-up of services to be provided. The government reiterates that there are now increased opportunities to complain and secure redress and hence enhance accountability. The advent of Citizen's Charters, grant-maintained schools, HATs, NHS Trusts, etc, sees the citizen essentially as a consumer. In such a context, is the traditional form of direct accountability most meaningful or can accountability emerge through, for example, contractual relationships, performance indicators and the like?

For commentators such as Graham Mather, the search for new forms of accountability should start with the contract.[8] Mather delineates four reasons why this should be so. First, the contract is a form of specification, exchange and account combined in one instrument—it therefore has both precision and transparency. Second, it is the means whereby the market economy effects its transactions. Third, modern forms of government are consciously borrowing from the new institutional economies. For example, the architect of New Zealand's radical administrative reforms, Graham Scott, argued that they were developed from 'practical experience and the literature on institutional economies, public administration, accounting, finance and management'. Fourth, Mather argues that 'it is no longer easy to draw a clear boundary between market and state. In my view it is undesirable to do so. We see in Britain a healthy constant testing and probing, both intellectual and commerical, of the borders of the state in the search for potential alternative providers.' Contract or market accountability might cut across many of the long cherished forms of electoral accountability but it has become an important strand of Conservative government policy and must be treated seriously.

Ken Young argues strongly that the actual activities, priorities and motivations of non-elected bodies need to be examined before dismissing them (simply because they are not directly elected) as inherently inferior to, or less desirable than, elected local government.[9] 'Being caught up as I am in public/private/voluntary/community partnerships in regeneration persuades me that accountability has not withered, nor is it in crisis. It has simply begun to develop along lines which complement the elective mechanisms.' Young emphasises that it is important to move debate on and to recognise the subtle complexity of accountability as regards both elected and non-elected bodies: 'What we are presented with in many of the arguments about accountability is a false dichotomy. Accountability is not an "either/or" question; it is a "how much and in what ways?" question.' Central to the contributions in this volume is a recognition of the complexity of accountability.

For example, the 'accountability' associated with elected local government needs to be set against the 'accountability' associated with the publication of accounts/scrutiny by press, public, etc, which often characterises the 'quango' sector. Junior Health Minister, Dr Brian Mahwinney, exemplified this strand of thought in a written parliamentary answer: 'Every year each National Health Service Trust issues a summary business plan and an annual report, makes its accounts publicly available and holds a public meeting. In addition, the trusts issue a strategic plan every three years. This is the minimum requirement that many Trusts exceed. It represents a high level of public accountability which requires no improvement.' Yet despite Mahwinney's statement, NHS Trusts and their boards are not covered by the Public Bodies (Admission to Meetings) Act 1960 which requires that any full meetings of authorities, at which specific action is required, be open to the public even though they can be excluded from confidential deliberations. Although applicable to other sections of the NHS, open meetings are not currently required by NHS Trusts. In practice, a good deal depends on local operating style. For example, the Chief Executive of Leicestershire Health (which assumed the joint responsibilities of the Leicestershire Health Authority and the Leicestershire Family Health Services Authority from 1 April 1994) was quoted in the *Leicester Mercury* as saying: 'There is no wish to restrict public access. Our intention is to have as much of the business as possible in the public part of our board meetings.'

Following detailed research into TECs, housing associations and NHS Trusts, John Plummer observed that there was 'great variety and inconsistency in the ways quangos are governed and a remarkable lack of clarity about how they should be governed and to whom they are accountable'.[10] Plummer argued that most of the quangos he examined saw their accountability entirely in terms of their obligations to the centre (Westminster and Whitehall) rather than to their customers or to people living in the locality. Some responsibility for this rests with the government, he maintained, because quangos 'have not been provided

with clear and workable frameworks of accountability'. Dominant
'upline' accountability should, he argues, be complemented by 'down-
line' accountability to a wider public. The current confusing and often
contradictory arrangements for accountability remain unsatisfactory
and need to be addressed by government.

Numbers and variety

Head counts of quangos are particularly difficult because, as Hood
observes, 'the "heads" involved are of enormously differing size and
importance — on a scale more like the difference between the head of an
ant and an elephant than between one human head and another.'[11]
Rather like pressure groups, there are tiny, relatively insignificant
groupings, as well as massive and extremely powerful organisations.
For Mrs Thatcher, however, numbers were important. Put simply, she
wanted a culling of the species. The variety of groups also makes
classification difficult. However, the Pliatzky Report (1980) delineated
three distinctive types — executive bodies, advisory bodies and tribunals — categories still used, along with Boards of Visitors, by the Cabinet
Office in its annual *Public Bodies* publication. The table outlines the
'official' reduction in the numbers of quangos between 1979 and 1993
as shown in *Public Bodies*.

	1979	1993
Executive Bodies	492	358
Advisory Bodies	1,485	829
Tribunals	70	68
Boards of Visitors	120	134
Total	2,167	1,389

As we saw earlier, this 'official' classification ignores quangos operating
at local level such as FE colleges, city technology colleges and grant-
maintained schools. Indeed, it is the growth in the number and
importance of local quangos that is perhaps the most significant
development in recent years. The 'official' classification also excludes
bodies such as the utility regulators (OFGAS, OFFER, etc), agricultural
marketing boards and Port and Harbour Authorities. Hence the debate
about numbers goes on incessantly. The Democratic Audit/Charter 88
report cited earlier identified 5,521 executive quangos in the United
Kingdom spending £46.6bn or 30% of all public expenditure. If
advisory bodies, tribunals and Next Steps agencies are included, the
NESPO count rises to nearly 7,000 bodies in 1992/93. With some
73,000 'quangocrats', including about 60,000 running local services,
and outnumbering the 25,000 elected councillors in principal local
authorities by over two to one, the report argued that there has been a
phenomenal proliferation of unelected extra-government organisations
in Britain. Nevertheless, the problems associated with attempting to

determine precise numbers can be illustrated by the fact that the 82 TECs in England and Wales do not appear in official statistics of NDPBs because the government views them as ['non-profit making private companies working under government contract'.] Yet they are crucially important vehicles for the delivery of government policy. They were established by the government, they are supervised by directorates within central government and they are almost entirely funded by government. Figures can conceal as much as they reveal; many bodies have simply been defined out of existence by the Cabinet Office categories. Whatever the precise figures, the size and diversity of quangos is vast. Most operate, however, in narrower, more specific areas than government departments or local authorities and enjoy an arms' length relationship with their parent body.

While quangos have become high profile in recent years, they are not new. The Crown Agents, for example, date from the mid-nineteenth century and the Horserace Totaliser Board (the Tote) originated in 1928. In the contemporary state, *Executive bodies* are by far the most important quangos. They normally employ staff and have their own budget, often very substantial. Executive organisations such as the Home-Grown Cereals Authority and the Nature Conservancy Council for England (English Nature) are justified by the rationale that certain functions can best be carried out at arm's length from central government: (i) because the work is of an executive nature which does not require ministers to be involved in day-to-day management; (ii) because the work can be more effectively carried out by a single-purpose organisation rather than by a government department with a wide range of functions; and (iii) because it is important to involve people from outside government in the direction of some organisations.

Unlike executive bodies, *Advisory bodies* do not generally employ staff or incur expenditure on their own account. They are set up by ministers to advise them and their departments on specific, often technical, matters. This category includes, for example, the Advisory Committee on NHS Drugs and the Advisory Committee on Pesticides. The major rationale for such bodies is that frequently a department's own staff is unable to provide the necessary expert advice itself, hence the desirability of enlisting outside participation from relevant specialists. *Tribunals* incorporate bodies with a licensing and appeal function. This category covers only bodies with jurisdiction in a specified field of law. In general, such tribunals (e.g. Industrial Tribunals, Lands Tribunal for Scotland) are serviced by staff from the sponsoring department. *Boards of Visitors* comprise the boards of visitors to penal establishments in Great Britain, and boards of visitors and visiting committees in Northern Ireland.

There is, then, considerable disagreement on what is, or is not, a quango with the government claiming numerical reduction and other political parties and interest groups claiming tremendous growth.

Neither is incorrect, depending on the definition of quango used. What is clear is that a massive amount of money is being spent by these non-elected organisations. It remains, however, as the chief executive of Leicestershire County Council observed recently, 'a matter of debate as to whether this shift in responsibility for delivering public services from elected to non-elected organisations is in the public interest.'

Appointments

Concern about the number of appointments in the gift of ministers has been at the heart of the 'quangowatch' industry. Parliamentary influence over appointments to chairs or boards of quangos is minimal. In effect, the matter is almost entirely one of ministerial discretion and consequently party political factors, especially since 1979, have frequently been to the fore. In a similar vein, John Stewart has argued that, at local level, 'a new magistracy is being created in the sense that a non-elected elite are assuming responsibility for a large part of local governance. They are found on the boards of health authorities and hospital trusts, Training and Enterprise Councils, the board of governors of grant-maintained schools, the governing bodies of colleges of further education and Housing Trusts.'[12] This argument depends partly, of course, on how widely 'local governance' is interpreted. The partisan background of many appointees is frequently lamented, yet this is essentially only an extension of the sovereignty of Parliament (which has become, invariably, the sovereignty of government). Majority governments can almost always convert their policy priorities into legislation; in the same way, they can use their dominance to place supporters or sympathisers on quangos. The surprise, surely, would be if this did *not* happen given that, in practical terms, the sovereignty of government is an integral part of the contemporary political scene.

'Official' figures showed that in the year 1992–93 ministers were responsible for the appointment of some 42,602 people to non-departmental public bodies, only 28% of whom were female and only a thousand of whom were from ethnic minority backgrounds (see *Public Bodies*, 1993). The Secretary of State for the Environment alone was responsible for 988 appointments. One junior minister at the Department of Trade and Industry, Lady Denton, had responsibility in 1993 for 804 public appointments. She was reported as saying: 'I can't remember knowingly appointing a Labour supporter' (*Independent on Sunday*, 23 March 1993). Again, in 1994 John Redwood, Secretary of State for Wales, was heavily criticised for appointing as chairman of the Welsh Development Agency a former Conservative Party fundraiser in Monte Carlo. Partisanship is, however, at the very core of British politics; there is arguably an element of naivety on the part of 'quango-watchers' who express surprise at such appointments.

Wales has provided much interesting material on appointments. A study by Morgan and Roberts found that 34% of Welsh Office spending

(£2.1 billion) in 1993/94 was scheduled to be dispersed by quangos.[13] The entire revenue expenditure budget for Welsh local authorities was only a shade higher at £2.5 billion. The same authors found that in 1991 the Welsh Secretary was responsible for 1,400 appointments to 80 quangos which together employed 57,311 people. The Welsh Office and its quango network, they concluded, constituted a formidable system of power, influence and patronage, a system controlled by a minority party. This is because in contemporary electoral terms Conservatism is largely absent in Wales. In the 1992 general election only six of the 38 Welsh seats were won by Conservatives, 71% of Welsh voters supporting other parties. Following the 1993 county council elections the Conservatives did not have overall control in any Welsh counties, yet through quango appointments the Conservative Party retains considerable influence over crucially important bodies such as the Welsh Development Agency and the Development Board for Rural Wales. While such appointments might be perceived as distasteful, they are hardly surprising given adversarial domestic politics. In the Wilson-Callaghan years leading trades unionists often secured similar appointments; they represent a dimension of governmental patronage which, whether desirable or otherwise, has characterised recent years.

Conclusions

During a debate on quangos in the House of Lords in January 1994 Lord Howe, for the government, denied any political bias in appointments. He then produced a crisp position statement based on ideas put forward by William Waldegrave some months earlier: 'The key point in these arguments is not whether those who run our public services are elected, but whether they are producer-responsive or consumer-responsive. You do not necessarily ensure that services respond to the public simply by giving citizens a democratic voice, which would be in any case a distant and diffuse one, in how services are delivered. Services can be responsive by giving the public choices or by instituting mechanisms which build in publicly approved standards and redress them when they are not attained.' The government argues that its reforms have strengthened the formal lines of accountability by making services directly accountable to their customers through the Citizens' Charter and other reform initiatives. Market accountability and contractual accountability are clearly very different from public accountability. Contributors to this volume will debate the extent to which these are mutually exclusive or whether they simply represent different elements of the same phenomenon. Given that public accountability rests both on giving an account and on being held to account, is it a fallacy that accountability to the public can be a substitute for public accountability? Questions also need to be raised about the adequacy of traditional forms of public accountability—notably the periodic election. This tends to assume a passive public, content to pass judgement only at limited intervals. It is perfectly possible to see public accountability involving far more of a continuing relationship between the public and its representatives but the tendency in the UK is to rest content with a limited concept of public accountability which focuses almost exclusively on the electoral system. Given the levels of turnout for local elections, this has something of a hollow ring to it. Traditional patterns of public accountability need attention if the concept is not to lose its cutting edge.

Turning to appointments to quangos, three areas of concern stand out: (i) efficiency—does patronage result in the best available people being appointed?; (ii) power—does patronage give ministers too much power to influence organisations?; (iii) privilege—does it enable elite groups to dominate patronage jobs? The lack of a properly publicised system of appointments and inadequate codes of practice need to be addressed but, given the diversity of quangos, it is difficult to come up with blanket solutions. As long ago as 1978, Holland and Fallon argued in a Conservative pamphlet that reforms were necessary. They maintained: (i) nomination should be much more open, with ministers more accountable to Parliament for each appointment; (ii) the number of paid public appointments that could be held by a single individual should be limited; (iii) all full-time paid appointments should be advertised and the appointment confirmed by a relevant parliamentary committee; (iv) appointments on solely political grounds should cease.[14]

Fifteen years later (*Observer*, 4 July 1993) Sir Philip Holland maintained that the only way to curb the growth of quangos was 'eternal vigilance'. He went on, 'The whole argument of bringing power closer to the people is bogus. Quangos are always in the interests of ministers and civil servants. They are not elected and are not answerable to the people.' A critique very much in the vein of John Stewart! Indeed, at the local level a 'quangowatch' industry has sprung up, with authorities adopting a range of strategies to monitor the actions of those quangos which provide local services. Councils such as Bristol, Avon, Greenwich and Leicester have been at the forefront. Some authorities have established scrutiny committees to examine how local issues relate to the services provided by the quangos. In other authorities, individual councillors take a specific brief for a quango and act as the community advocate. The list of community advocates is published locally so that local people know which councillor to go to with their concerns. In one case the council invites the chairs of various quangos to make a presentation to the policy committee. Underlying all this activity is the belief that local people have a right to know what local quangos are responsible for, how much they spend, who makes the decisions and how they can be contacted. Needless to say, the non-elected dimension of quangos is invariably highlighted by local authorities. For example, the leader of Leicester City Council, a pioneer of 'quangowatch' in the city, claimed that the local authority had good working relationships with local quangos and that the city's quango register was not a witch-hunt. He maintained that his council worked well with these unelected bodies, 'but we believe they must be accountable. I spend public money and am quite rightly accountable to the public who can vote me out of office if they are not pleased with what I do. Plus my name, address and number are in the telephone directory. But no one knows the members of these quangos, yet it is very important they do know' (*Leicester Mercury*, 12 September 1994).

By 1996, according to a *Guardian* forecast using official statistics, some 7,710 quangos could be spending some £54 billion of public money — nearly a quarter of all government expenditure (19 November 1993). Certainly, their influence is expanding at every level of government. One reason for this is that they have turned out to be a convenient vehicle for bypassing an often hostile and recalcitrant local government system. Locally non-elected bodies have enabled central government to retain considerable leverage even when the local electorate has expressed alternative preferences. In other words, quangos are a manifestation of the reality that central government is invariably sovereign. Given that governments will want to place people sympathetic to their policies in organisations that are responsible for delivering policy, a central issue becomes how these processes are opened up for public scrutiny to ensure greater operational transparency. National registers and codes of practice could, for example, be useful ways forward. This, however, needs to be part of a broader constitutional debate about accountability and scrutiny in an increasingly fragmented state.

1 J. Harrow and R. Gillett, 'The Proper Conduct of Public Business, *Public Policy and Management*, 14/2, 1994, pp.4–6.
2 L. Pliatzky, 'Quangos and Agencies' *Public Administration*, 70/4, 1992, p.556.
3 *Report on Non-Departmental Public Bodies* (HMSO, Cmnd 7797, 1980).
4 H. Davis, *A First Guide to Appointed Local Executive Bodies in the West Midlands*, Birmingham City Council and the University of Birmingham Partnership Paper, 1993.
5 A. Doig, 'The Machinery of Government and the Growth of Governmental Bodies,' *Public Administration*, 57, 1979, p.311.
6 Sir N. Chester, 'Fringe Bodies, Quangos and All That,' *Public Administration*, 57, 1979, p.54.
7 J. Bulpitt, Review in *Public Administration*, 71/4, 1993, pp.621–23.
8 G. Mather, 'The Market, Accountability and the Civil Service', PAC Conference, York, September 1994.
9 K. Young, 'Rethinking Accountability', QMC Public Policy Seminar, April 1994.
10 J Plummer, *The Governance Gap: Quangos and Accountability*, LGC Communications and Joseph Rowntree Foundation, 1994, p.4.
11 C. Hood, 'The World of Quasi-Government', PSA Annual Conference 1979.
12 J. Stewart, 'The Rebuilding of Public Accountability', *European Policy Forum*, December 1992, p.7.
13 K. Morgan and E. Roberts, *The Democratic Deficit: A Guide to Quangoland*, Papers in Planning Research, University of Wales, Cardiff, 1993.
14 P. Holland and M Fallon, *The Quango Explosion*, Conservative Political Centre, 1978, p.25.

Worthwhile Bodies

BY RT HON DAVID HUNT

I WELCOME the opportunity to contribute to this volume on quangos. In the daily business of politics there is often little time to take a longer look at an issue, still less to commit thoughts to print some four months before publication! But there are few things more reliable in political life than the long-running nature of the debate over what is and is not a quango, on whether quangos are a good thing, and if not, in what numbers they should be culled. Quango counts have been published which claim that there are more than five (sometimes more than seven) thousand of these strange and terrifying creatures, active in all areas of the public sector and controlling vast amounts of public money. I welcome the opportunity to set the record straight.

It is difficult to follow custom and to begin at the beginning. The habit of counting quangos and public bodies grew up in the 1970s. Sir Philip Holland has been a vigilant hunter of the species for more than two decades, and closed in on his quarry from the right long before a school of marksmen appeared on the left. He has shown in *The Hunting of the Quango* how quango-trapping became an international sport, energetically pursued as far afield as the United States and Australia.

The species nevertheless survives and indeed flourishes in some habitats, but there is still remarkably little consensus on how to identify or count it, let alone how to trap and extinguish it. Not many people know, for example, that the count of 7,700 sometimes cited by the critics of the government includes an estimate that there will be 5,000 grant-maintained schools by 1996. At the start of 1994 there were in fact 1,023, but I am happy to share their expectations for the prosperity of the sector!

Boards and commissioners responsible for various public service functions have a long history. There have always been suspicions as to the accountability of boards as an instrument of government. J. S. Mill wrote: 'As a general rule, any executive function, whether superior or subordinate, should be the appointed duty of some given individual. It should be apparent to the world who did everything, and through whose fault anything was left undone. Responsibility is null when nobody knows who is responsible. Nor, even when real, can it be divided without being weakened.'[1] Such criticism may have been one reason why in the nineteenth century the trend was to absorb boards into ministerial departments.

One of the paradoxes about the present attack from the left on quangos is that Labour governments have played a large part in the proliferation of the species. The absorption of thousands of municipal and privately owned units into state industries and the state health service created by the Attlee government presented the public sector with formidable problems of control of the giant units so created. In that programme of transformation there was an inbuilt tension between national direction and ownership on the one hand, and the local responsiveness of local units on the other.

It was the Labour Party that decided that the National Health Service should not be the province of locally elected government. Nye Bevan had a struggle to remove the provision of health care from the direct influence of local politics, but that is what he did. 'A patchwork of local paternalism is', he said, 'the enemy of intelligent planning. Warm gushes of self-indulgent emotion are an unreliable source of driving power in the field of health organization.'[2] This left a permanent tension in the management of local accountability in the service. As Sir Kenneth Stowe said prophetically in 1989: 'The burden of ultimate responsibility for health services and their institutions will, of course, remain with the central Department of State in some degree under any conceivable programme of "modernisation", especially while the most costly services of all are financed mainly and directly by the Exchequer. But the centre cannot manage what it does not truly own, and/or cannot grasp because of its size and complexity.'[3]

I shall return to the Health Service and to the issue of accountability later, but it may help to look at questions of enumeration and definition first. The first comprehensive list of public bodies was Philip Holland's *Quango, Quango, Quango*, the fruit of his detailed research in these then uncharted waters. Answers to Parliamentary Questions which he put between 1974 and 1979 revealed that, although departments did keep tabs on what tended to be described as 'fringe bodies' (generally speaking what would now be described as executive NDPBs) and were also able to list the appointments for which their ministers were responsible, there was no central list of such bodies. There were not even classifications of the various types of bodies which were then in existence. Philip Holland's pamphlet identified a grand total of 3,068 quangos split into the categories of 'main', advisory, state industry, academic and judicial.

Official publications such as *A Directory of Paid Public Appointments Made by Ministers*, which appeared in 1976 and 1978, did not offer a definition of what constituted a public body. The 1973 publication *Councils Committees and Boards: A Handbook of Advisory Consultative Executive and Similar Bodies in British Public Life*. This contained details of some 1,300 bodies, some of them only very distantly connected with the functions of central government, the figure including trade associations, professional bodies and the like which were not dependent on public funds but which occasionally acted in an advisory capacity to the government.

Non-Departmental Public Bodies

The government's count was put on a more systematic basis after the 1979 election. Mrs Thatcher commissioned a review of Non-Departmental Public Bodies with the aim of rationalising them and reducing their numbers. In January 1980 Sir Leo Pliatzky produced what is still the definitive work in the field, with the publication of the _Report on Non-Departmental Public Bodies_ (Cmnd 7797). The Pliatzky report defines Non-Departmental Public Bodies as bodies having a role in the processes of government of the United Kingdom but which are not government departments or part of one, and accordingly operate to a greater or lesser extent at arm's length from ministers. An NDPB has formal terms of reference including defined membership, a chairman and records of its proceedings, and some or all of its members are appointed by ministers. Most executive NDPBs are set up in statute and employ their own staff, who generally are not civil servants.

That report identified 2,117 such bodies falling into the categories of executive NDPBs, advisory NDPBs and tribunals. To these are also added the Boards of Visitors to penal institutions, bringing the total to 2,167. There has been much debate over whether the number of quangos has grown or reduced since 1979, and the different view points turn entirely on questions of definition. Pliatzky's clear classifications have been obscured somewhat in the current debate, and it is important that spotters of trends should compare like with like.

Democratic Audit and Charter 88 have published a report, _Ego Trip_, which put out an estimate of 5,521 'extra governmental organisations'. The count includes such bodies as Training and Enterprise Councils, which are private sector companies, and grant-maintained schools, which become self-governing only after a ballot. It also includes some 2,300 Housing Associations, which are non profit-making organisations run by unpaid committees of volunteers, overwhelmingly drawn from the local community. Such bodies are not included in the Cabinet Office count of Non-Departmental Public Bodies. None of their members are appointed by ministers; private companies and the voluntary sector are not part of the public sector; and they are part of a decentralisation, not a centralisation of power.

Even higher projections of the number of quangos have been produced. In November 1993, _The Guardian_ announced that there would be a grand total of 7,700 appointed bodies in existence by 1996. This relies on the forecast of growth of grant maintained schools mentioned above. Philip Holland incidentally accepts that neither NHS bodies nor grant-maintained schools should be 'hunted as quangos': '... It would be grossly unfair to include all grant-maintained schools, or all NHS hospital trusts, as Quangos, when their raison d'être is precisely to devolve powers out of the hands of Whitehall and towards local managers and the parents and patients they work for.'[4] Other quango count include Next Steps Agencies which, with a few exceptions, are not legally independent or distinct from their departments or controlled by boards. They remain directly accountable to ministers, and their function and objectives are listed with contact addresses in the quarterly *Next Steps Briefing Note* as well as the *Civil Service Year Book*.

Some of the argument about definition and numbers is therefore rhetorical. It suits those who wish to argue that there has been a growth in the 'non-elected state' to produce large looking numbers. The Cabinet Office has kept *Public Bodies* on track by following Pliatzky's definitions. It makes good practical sense to keep to bodies whose creation and termination are under the control of ministers and to which their powers of appointment are relevant. Trends in the growth and numbers of NDPBs are therefore recorded separately from trends within the health service, although the total of ministerial appointments is aggregated.

Far from growing, as critics misguidedly claim, the number of NDPBs, by Pliatzky's definition, has been steadily falling since his review. This stems from a strict policy of questioning the creation of new bodies, and reviewing every five years the continuing need for existence of all significant spending bodies. The discipline of prior options is now being applied, so that in each case both the continuing need for the body and the reasons for retaining it in the public sector are examined.

The 1994 edition of *Public Bodies* contained information on 1,345 NDPBs. In other words, their numbers have fallen by 38% since 1979. It also listed 770 health service bodies, not listed in comparable form in 1979. Some 325 of the 1,389 bodies have substantial executive functions and budgets to support them. Of the remaining NDPBs, 814 are advisory, 71 are tribunals and 135 are boards of visitors, none of which has a large budget. It is worth taking a brief look at what these various bodies actually do. On inspection, It is hard to sustain the view that they are a wicked and secretive arm of the state. In fact, their functions and purposes are so diverse that it is hard to construct sensible generalisations of any kind.

As Pliatzky explains, none of these bodies can be described as quangos (quasi-autonomous non-governmental organisations) because they patently are governmental bodies. Nor is the term 'quasi-autonomous' generally apposite, especially in the case of tribunals, which enjoy full judicial independence. The label nevertheless sticks, and many members of the public would be surprised to know that they have not only visited a quango but enjoyed their visit enormously. Among the executive NDPBs are such household names as the Royal Botanic Gardens at Kew, the British Museum and many other museums and galleries; and a series of national monuments such as Stonehenge are run by English Heritage — a quango of which one can be a card-carrying member at a

bargain price! Others may have cause to thank the Advisory Concilia-
tion and Arbitration Service for the resolution of disputes that affected
them as employees, employers or travelling members of the public, or
the Health and Safety Commission for their vigilance in protecting
health and safety at work.

Other executive NDPBs are distributors of public funds. They account
for the bulk of the £18.5bn expenditure attributed to NDPBs in Public
Bodies. Most people agree with the use of public money to support
medical and other scientific research, legal aid, social housing, further
and higher education, the arts or sport. They might also agree that the
distributors of such money should stand at one remove from politics
and the political process, and should rely on expert advice and membership from their respective fields. This was what Jenny Lee had in mind
when she set up the Arts Council, and it remains the principle on which
the Medical Research Council (spending £185m), the Legal Aid Board
(£1,278m) and the Housing Corporation (£1,843m), to name but a few,
are run.

The advisory bodies support and advise ministers on a wide range of
matters which require highly specific or technical expertise. They often
consist of acknowledged experts in their fields. A good example from
my own department, the Office of Public Service and Science, is the
Advisory Committee on Human Genome Research. The chairman and
twelve members provide first-class advice on what are very important
issues in a highly complex field where matters of medicine, ethics and
science meet. The fact that they are unpaid, as are many of the members
of advisory NDPBs, demonstrates how the government obtains a vast
amount of high quality advice at little cost. There are plenty of other
examples, such as the Department of Health's Expert Advisory Committee on AIDS, the Parliamentary Boundary Commissions for England
and Wales, sponsored by the Home Office, or the Department of Trade
and Industry's Advisory Committee on Deregulation.

The tribunal systems have quasi-judicial functions in various special-
ised fields of law or service delivery. Tribunals resolve conflicts in these
areas between the citizen and the state, or between individuals, and
relieve the court system of some of its burden. They include the Social
Security Appeals Tribunal, the Pensions Appeal Tribunal and the Rent
Assessment Panels. Some of these are standing tribunals while others
are constituted on an ad hoc basis from a pool of chairmen and
members. Tribunals undertake vital work and are an efficient means of
resolving disputes. It is sometimes forgotten that tribunals do a vast
amount of good work in assuring the judicial functions of the state have
been fairly and accurately performed. '*Public Bodies 1994*', lists the
thousands of cases heard. For example, in 1993/4 the Social Security
Appeals Tribunal heard a total of 70,211 cases and the Industrial
Tribunals received a total of 71,661 cases.

Largely because of growth in the number and budgets of the bodies I have described as distributors, expenditure by executive NDPBs grew substantially between 1979 and 1993. That this increase in expenditure took place at the same time as reductions in the number of NDPBs, and while staff numbers in executive NDPBs were virtually halved, points to significant efficiency savings. Thanks to these savings, more of those funds reach the places where they are most usefully spent, with less loss in administration.

Oversight and control

FINANCIAL MANAGEMENT. There are various mechanisms for oversight of the financial affairs of NDPBs and the ways in which public bodies are held accountable for their actions. It is worth mentioning here that there exists a financial management and control framework within which executive NDPBs operate. This is currently being revised with the intention of making the relationship between government departments and the NDPBs they sponsor more strategic in line with the Next Steps principles which have been increasingly applied to executive NDPBs since April 1990. NDPBs are encouraged to focus on results and essential activities and to privatise or contract out those activities which do not need to be carried out in the public sector and so to improve efficiency and effectiveness. This is something which the public sector must take very seriously in order to get the best possible value for money for the tax payer. Together with other initiatives which I will come to later, it demonstrates the importance placed on sound and responsible public sector management.

APPOINTMENTS. Criticism has been focused on appointments to NDPBs. There have been accusations of political and actual nepotism. The Labour Party has even suggested that General Sir Peter de la Billière was appointed to the board of the Imperial War Museum not because he is a general but because he is connected with a company which once made a political donation. Just as obtusely, a member of the royal family serving on the Overseas Trade Board has been attacked on the same basis. The unsensational truth is that ministers make appointments to all public bodies on the basis of the most appropriate person for the job. Many of those who serve with distinction on the boards of public bodies are also sought after by private companies or have been appointed in order to bring their business experience into public service. The main consideration in making an appointment is, rightly, to ensure that the correct balance of necessary skills, experience and expertise is available to enable the relevant body to carry out its functions as effectively as possible.

The Cabinet Office produces a *Guide on Public Appointments Procedures*. Last revised in 1992, it sets out the mandatory central requirements for advising ministers on appointments and provides advice on other related matters. By May 1994 several factors made it appropriate to consider whether the guidance was adequate. A number of departments had significantly improved their procedures for making appointments and provided useful examples of good practice to disseminate through government. The Public Appointments Unit in the Cabinet Office had also made improvements to the quality of information held on its central list of candidates and was, as a result, better placed to offer advice to departments with vacancies to fill. Additionally, there was a desire to ensure that the momentum of the Prime Minister's initiative on equal opportunities, announced in 1991, was sustained. Finally, it was becoming clear in the light of public comment that we needed to underline the fact that appointments to public bodies are made on the basis of merit and not political allegiance and that appointees are properly accountable.

It was against this background that the Prime Minister, together with my predecessor as Chancellor of the Duchy of Lancaster, asked for a review of the 1992 guidance. The Public Appointments Unit was given the task of carrying out this review with the help of a working group from several departments. Recognising the lack of a clear and widely accepted definition of a 'public appointment', the working group stated in its report that the conclusion of the report would apply to 'those fixed-term non-judicial appointments made by or on the authority of Ministers to posts or offices outside the Civil Service'.

The summary of the Report of the Review of Guidance on Public Appointments, which was released in February, restates the basic aim of appointing the most appropriately qualified people for the tasks in question and ensuring that they are able to work effectively within the policy framework for the relevant body as set out by ministers or by statute. Drawing on best practice in departments, the report makes a range of recommendations for changes to appointment procedures to ensure that these aims are effectively met. In brief, these relate to greater openness, assuring high standards of probity, applying equal opportunities standards, and improving accountability and responsiveness in line with Citizen's Charter principles.

A key feature of policy developments over the last ten years has been greater openness. Increasingly, major appointments have been advertised or filled through executive search, and the process of compiling databases of names to use as sources for appointments has been amaned. Now, the lists held by departments, including that held by the Cabinet Office's Public Appointments Unit (PAU), are increasingly filled by self-nomination rather than recommendation by others. The 5,000 names on the PAU's list are not just 'the great and the good'—which was always an inaccurate description of the range of people willing to put themselves forward for public service. They are people from all walks of life, and representation includes a welcome and increasing number of women as well as those from the Black and Asian communities, though more nominations from underrepresented groups are always needed. A simple application form is all that is required.

Greater openness has extended too to the appointment process. Where a single job advertisement is not used, there may instead be nomination by other bodies—employers' organisations, trade unions or selection panels—or advertisements seeking interest in a range of posts. The aim of the PAU report is to sustain and increase these open procedures, both by increasing awareness of the options and by making it the norm, particularly in the case of paid full-time posts, that open procedures should be adopted. But the report also recognises that the approach used should be the most open possible consistent with value for money. The procedures recommended in the review are not intended to apply in the same way to all of the more than 40,000 public appointments made by or on behalf of ministers. An important test of 'proportionality' is also recommended. This recognises that with two-thirds of the appointments being unpaid and part-time, and fewer than 150 of them paid more than £50,000 a year, it would be wrong to apply the same approach in very different circumstances. What is right and value for money for a full-time post paying £50,000 may well be quite inappropriate for a part-time specialist post demanding one day a month, which an acknowledged expert is being persuaded to do through some public-spirited arm twisting.

On probity, public concern has been expressed over the relevance of political affiliation of appointees, any screening procedures used prior to appointment, and the codes of conduct required of appointees. Here I will look briefly at the matter of political affiliation as it is of particular concern to many contributors to the current debate.

The question of political affiliation has always been sensitive and one which gives rise to allegations about bias and abuse of patronage. Any changes to existing practice need to be made in a way which do not deter or prevent good people with relevant skills, experience and knowledge putting themselves forward. Government policy is quite clear and has often been restated: the political affiliation of candidates is not normally known or relevant to public appointments. But existing guidance does make it clear that some potential appointees should be debarred from appointment to some posts because they hold political office. Moreover, in a few cases political experience will be a relevant factor and those responsible for appointments may well need to take affiliation into account because they wish to achieve demonstrable political balance—an example would be the Millennium Commission. These cases are the exception, however.

Also the subject of debate is the suggestion that right across the board appointees should be required to reveal their political affiliation and that this should be published. This sometimes has a McCarthyite ring. My own view is that to reveal such information would be an unfair intrusion into people's privacy and would wrongly imply that decisions are taken on the basis of politics rather than qualification and ability. Perversely, it might increase the risk of politicising the process. Moreover, past affiliation is not necessarily an indication of present belief.

The PAU report looks at these issues carefully and points to the possible use in the future of a test of relevance in relation to such disclosure. There may well need to be an informed debate on the case for greater and more systematic disclosure of significant political office holding where it is clearly relevant to public confidence either because of the level, nature, expenditure or sensitivity of the appointment itself or because of any other important areas of public concern about the appointments process. The government's evidence to the Nolan Committee indicates that we wish to take account of the Committee's views on this before coming to a conclusion.

There is one other recommendation made in the report which I would like to mention in conclusion as it addresses a concern which is frequently voiced about the alleged 'fog' surrounding the matter of public bodies and appointments to them. Paragraph 6.iv is worth quoting in full: 'Departments should ensure that, for each public body, the identity of appointees is available on demand to anyone who wishes to know. Sponsor departments should hold copies of the information centrally and know where to direct enquiries about particular bodies. In addition, most appointments of whatever kind should be publicly announced in the local, regional or national press or publications available at these levels.'

I believe that these steps, and the others set out in the report, will do much to restore faith in the work of public bodies and the public-spirited individuals who give up so much of their time to them. The government will consider whether any further action is necessary in the light of the observations and any recommendations made is this area by the Nolan Committee.

THE CONDUCT OF PUBLIC LIFE. The Standing Committee which the Prime Minister set up in October of last year to look into standards of propriety in public life is casting a wide net. As the Prime Minister explained to the House, its investigations and conclusions will apply not only to ministers, MPs and civil servants but also to members and senior office holders of all Non-Departmental Public Bodies, NHS bodies and other bodies discharging publicly-funded functions, and non-Ministerial office holders.

At the time of going to press, the government had submitted written evidence to Lord Nolan's Committee and responded to specific questions related to public bodies and appointments to them. I have written above that we will need to look again at certain aspects of government practice with regard to appointments to public bodies in the light of the Committee's deliberations. We will be issuing a new version of the *Guidance on Public Appointments* at that time.

BEST PRACTICE IN CORPORATE GOVERNANCE. The Citizen's

Charter and Code of Practice on Access to Government Information both address matters of accountability and transparency and I look at these below. There has also been concern about an alleged dilution of the public service ethos, the standards of governance of public bodies. Such concerns have been and continue to be addressed seriously. In June 1994, the Treasury issued a Code of Best Practice for Board Members of Public Bodies. This grew out of the publication in December 1992 of the Cadbury Report on the Financial Aspects of Corporate Governance and an undertaking to the Public Accounts Committee to consider updating existing guidance on the responsibilities of NDPB board members. It is intended to improve financial management and control of public funds—about which there has been much concern of late. NHS bodies have their own codes.

The Code of Best Practice states that public bodies and their boards must at all times:
—observe the highest standards of impartiality, integrity and objectivity in relation to stewardship of public funds and management of the bodies concerned;
—in accordance with government policy on openness, comply with all reasonable requests for information from Parliament, users of services and individual citizens;
—be accountable to Parliament, users of services, individual citizens and staff for the activities of the bodies concerned, their stewardship of public funds and the extent to which key performance targets and objectives are met;
—maximise value for money through ensuring that services are delivered in the most efficient and economical way, within available resources and with independent validation of performance achieved wherever practicable.

This sets the very highest standards and stresses the importance of openness and accountability. The Minister of the sponsor department is finally accountable to Parliament for the policies and performance of its public bodies, and the Code of Best Practice also calls for a clear statement of the respective roles of the sponsor department and individual public bodies.

The Code goes on to make two important recommendations. The first is that all public bodies should set up Audit Committees, and advice is given on how this can be achieved. The second is that all boards should establish a register of interests of board members which should be open for public inspection at least once a year. The Treasury has been working with departments on the production of this guidance over a long period. As I believe the rest of this article shows, we see it as one of a series of steps we are taking to encourage better financial management and control.

TRANSPARENCY. This government places a great deal of importance on transparency and we are working together with those in NDPBs and other public bodies to strengthen further and improve the information available to the public about all aspects of their operations in line with Citizen's Charter and Open Government principles. These reforms, bringing greater clarity and responsiveness across the public sector, are relevant to all service delivery.

The Office of Public Service and Science and the Treasury jointly publish *Non-Departmental Public Bodies: A Guide to Departments*. This detailed guide, intended to assist all those involved in the management of NDPBs, was last produced in March 1992 and is currently being updated to reflect changes and progress since then. The new version will include a chapter on the application of the Citizen's Charter to NDPBs. This reflects our wish for all NDPBs providing a service to the public to consider how they can implement Charter principles to improve that service and their performance more generally. The Office of Public Service has also commissioned a study of best practice on consultation and responsiveness. The outcome of the study will provide examples and lessons for the whole of the public sector and help all service providers to aim at the highest standards. Here it is worthwhile to look briefly at what the Citizen's Charter means for Non-Departmental Public Bodies and what is expected of them.

THE CITIZEN'S CHARTER. There are six Citizen's Charter principles for public services: standards; information and openness; choice and consultation; courtesy and helpfulness; putting things right; and value for money. The first two principles are perhaps the most important in the context of the current concerns about NDPBs. NDPBs are encouraged to set, monitor and publish demanding specific standards of service which the public can expect and to publish information about performance against those standards. Full and accurate information should be available on how services are run, who is in charge, what they cost and how well they perform. The fifth principle is of enormous importance to all public service providers. It is vital that any service provider should have well developed systems for dealing with complaints, providing full explanations and swift and effective remedies. Wherever possible, well publicised and easy to use complaints procedures should be backed up by an independent review system. The Citizen's Charter Complaints Task Force, due to report in 1995, has published a booklet *Effective Complaints Systems: Principles and Checklist*.

These, along with the other Charter principles, are all matters which executive NDPBs are expected to address. It may not always be appropriate for them to work up full Charters of their own. For smaller organisations, a Charter standard statement, describing how the organisation intends to put the Citizen's Charter principles into practice, would be usual. It was encouraging that the Treasury and Civil Service Committee stated, in the fifth report 1993–94: 'We believe that the

Citizen's Charter has value as an expression of a high political commitment to quality in the provision of public services which should assist further in raising the profile of service delivery within the civil service. The orientation towards the requirements of individuals whom the civil service serves is particularly welcome.' In the same week as the report was published I had confirmed to the House that the Charter Principles apply to all public services, including those delivered by public bodies.

OPEN GOVERNMENT. The Code of Practice on Access to Government Information develops the Charter principle of information and openness. It applies to information held by all government departments and public bodies within the jurisdiction of the Parliamentary Commissioner for Administration (the Ombudsman). This includes many executive NDPBs which deliver services to the public. Those covered are expected to volunteer certain information such as the facts and analysis of the facts important in framing major policy proposals and decisions. Explanatory material, including departments' internal guidance on dealing with the public and guidance on rules and procedures should also be made available, and information explaining reasons for administrative decisions should be given to those affected.

Perhaps the greatest advance, though, is the commitment to respond to requests for information from the public. There are naturally areas where confidentiality will always be required, and these are clearly set out in the Code of Practice. Should anyone be dissatisfied with the response they receive from any of those bodies within the jurisdiction of the Ombudsman, they can ask their MP to pass a complaint to him. He is able to inspect the original papers to ensure that the terms of the Code have been observed. These important commitments are set out in more detail in the text of the Code itself. The Code has only been in operation for one year, but the Ombudsman's rulings on the complaints which have so far been passed to him have shown that it can be really effective and is leading to the release of information which would formerly have remained unavailable. The success of the Code so far is a good reply to those who claim that NDPBs are shadowy, secretive bodies and that it is therefore difficult to hold them to account for their actions. The transparency born of the Code supports informed policy making and debate and efficient service delivery.

Although the Code of Practice does not apply to bodies outside the Ombudsman's jurisdiction, it represents good administrative practice. As I explain below, NDPBs are being encouraged to use it as the basis of their policy on the provision of information and to set up methods of external review, as the Ombudsman is not able to investigate complaints against them. I am pleased to say that the evidence is that this is beginning to happen. A separate Code on Access to NHS Information has been developed, whilst work on a local government code is also under way.

The 'democratic deficit'

Another important side to the debate about public bodies is concerned with the alleged rise of a 'new magistracy' and the so-called 'democratic deficit'. The contention is that functions which were formerly the domain of locally-elected representatives have been passed to quangos and thus into the hands of ministerial appointees who are not accountable for their actions. The most frequently quoted example rests on the myth that the health service was once controlled by locally-elected people. As we have seen, we owe it to Labour's Nye Bevan that this has never been the case: there have never been direct elections to NHS bodies at regional or local level, and health, rightly, was kept out of the party-political area.

Christine Hancock of the Royal College of Nursing said quite recently that placing ultimate responsibility for the healthcare with local authorities would threaten the concept of a national health service. We have, broadly, kept health policy national whilst devolving more and more operational and organisational decisions to a local level. There was once a statutory quota of local members on District Health Authorities and Family Health Services Authorities. David Wilshire MP, who had eleven years experience of local government, explained during a Commons debate (24 February 1994) that this was not a shining example of local accountability: 'Somewhere on the agenda, at item 10 or whatever, is the appointment of representatives to outside bodies . . . At that point in any AGM, councillors are press-ganged to serve on dozens, if not hundreds, of bodies . . . and no one explains the responsibilities or ever asks for a report back on what happened last year . . .' Today's reformed NHS is designed to square the circle of national ownership and local management to which Sir Kenneth Stowe referred. The reforms provide a powerful example of the greatly enhanced accountability and transparency which have been introduced as a result of public service reforms. For the first time, there is clear, published information at all levels. Strategic purchasing plans from Regional and District Health Authorities are published, allowing more informed debate about health priorities. Reports on the performance of individual local hospitals and ambulances are available; and quality standards and maximum waiting times under the Patient's Charter are produced throughout the service. National priorities, which are openly debated, can be set where necessary.

The public now need to learn how to use the information which is now available — particularly through Community Health Councils and by attending public meetings. I know that my colleague Virginia Bottomley, the Secretary of State for Health, has emphasised the role of health authority and Trust chairmen as the visible heads of their organisations. They must communicate with the public, listen to their views and ensure that services reflect local views and needs. A willingness and ability to be open and frank is one of the qualities ministers look out for in making appointments.

We can look at the specific case of NHS Trusts. They are directly accountable to health authorities and GP fundholders who purchase services through their contracts. Trusts must also publish an annual report and hold at least one meeting a year open to the public. They will also be expected to comply with the Code of Practice on Openness which is currently out for consultation and which will require them to meet all requests for information unless there are carefully defined reasons, such as patient confidentiality, for not doing so.

The function of the Trusts is not to remove health service management further from the people, but to be sure that decisions are taken much closer to the people than in the old command and control bureaucracy which stifled local initiative in the health service. Much the same can be said of the innovations in education. It is now much more common for teachers and parents to be directly involved in the decisions which affect their school. This is true of both locally-managed schools and grant-maintained schools; meanwhile, the invigorating effect of published league tables of educational attainment is transforming parently choice.

There are many other areas where there has been a shift in power, and it has been towards the people. Among the EGOs identified by Democratic Audit there is the example of the Housing Associations, whose boards of local volunteers are not appointed by ministers and often include tenant members. We have the Training and Enterprise Councils—private companies—and their Scottish equivalents, whose members are drawn from the local business community. The Tenant's Charter and the creation of the Housing Action Trusts have given tenants a greater role in the management of their estates. In each case, those working on such local bodies bring invaluable local knowledge to their work. They are members of the communities they serve. Accountability does not come much more direct than that.

National accountability

While local accountability has been improved, national accountability is also vital for bodies with a national role. NDPBs are subject to the rigours and instruments of parliamentary scrutiny and accountability. All executive NDPBs publish an annual report and accounts which enable Parliament, the taxpayer and the customer to judge whether that NDPB is securing value for money. The National Audit Office, which reports to Parliament, is either the auditor of, or has inspections rights to, all executive NDPBs. The Public Accounts Committee scrutinises their activities closely and may summon the chief executive to give evidence if necessary. The orders of reference of the House of Commons Departmental Select Committees provide for the examination of expenditure administration and policy of the departments and associated public bodies.

As well as improving local accountability, as I have explained above, the NHS reforms have also had a positive effect on its national accountability. The Chief Executive of the NHS is also its Chief Accounting Officer and answerable directly to the Public Accounts Committee for the service's stewardship of public money. In addition, the remit of the Audit Commission has been extended to the NHS, introducing a valuable independent source of rigorous scrutiny of how effectively it uses its resources.

In passing, I should also mention that the long term ESRC research programme on Whitehall includes several relevant studies of accountability and new management relationships. These will provide us with a great deal of very useful information on the changing routes of accountability and the historical background. We will then be able to have an informed debate about these matters rather than one based on myths of a golden age when, if a bedpan was dropped in an NHS hospital, the Secretary of State not only heard about it, but also lost his or her job and, the electorate having expressed its dissatisfaction, his or her seat in Parliament. As we have seen, the reality today is that there are people who are effectively and directly accountable for the quality of public services and they are responsive to the people most concerned; the users of those services.

The sheer complexity of modern government means that there are roles in the government of the country for diverse bodies. Different functions, be they executive or advisory, local or national, require different approaches. My concern, and the concern of all of my colleagues, is that in each case the most appropriate and efficient means are used to achieve the necessary end. That is why we are constantly reassessing existing bodies to ensure that their work still needs to be done and whether their current form represents the best way of getting that work done. Despite a lot of pretty vile attacks on those engaged in various forms of public service, I believe that we are getting the balance right and I know that standards of service to the public and public accountability, in its most direct and meaningful form, have been vastly improved.

The Chancellor of the Duchy of Lancaster contributed this piece, after it was written for this volume, to Lord Nolan's Committee on Standards in Public Life.

---

1   J. S. Mill *Representative Government*, ch. 14.

2   cit. Michael Foot, *Aneurin Bevan*, vol. 2, 1973.

3   Sir Kenneth Stowe, 1989 Rock Carling Lecture, cit. P. Hennessy, *Never Again* (Jonathan Cape, 1993), p.138.

4   Sir Philip Holland, *The Hunting of the Quango* (Adam Smith Institute, 1994), p.5.

The 'Growth' of Quangos: Evidence and Explanations

BY BRIAN W. HOGWOOD

IN 2008, or thereabouts, there will be a large number of news items about the growth in the number of bodies appointed by or funded by government. Many of these news items will be fuelled by what will still be called Written Answers recorded on the electronic version of *Hansard*, placed by MPs in the main party of opposition to the government in power, often at the behest of members of 'independent' think tanks established to challenge the conventional wisdom embodied in the incumbent government. This whimsical speculation is inspired by the common features behind the upsurge in interest in the late 1970s and that in the 1990s, and the distinct sense of déjà vu about much of the debate, with the common assumption that the phenomenon is a growing and worrying one.

This article first of all explores the difficulties of defining the types of body which are the focus of interest, then explores the available evidence for the direction of change since 1979, including concern about ministerial patronage, and finally explores explanations for the pattern of change since 1979.

Quangos are big, quangos are nasty: but what are they?

In Britain the term quango is now normally taken to stand for quasi-autonomous national government organisations, but what does that mean? The origin was the term, invented in the USA at the end of the 1960s as a half-joke—quasi-non-governmental organisations.[1] It referred to organisations which were in no way officially part of government, such as not-for-profit corporations, but which were effectively used by government to deliver public policy. This was taken up by the participants in a British-US research programme, contracted to QNG, hence (due to Anthony Barker) quango.

However, in entry into popular usage in the mid 1970s it was taken to refer to bodies to which the government makes public appointments, a rather different phenomenon. When the term was re-expanded, it was taken to stand for quasi-autonomous national government organisation. Sometimes it was confined to bodies with executive functions, but sometimes it is used to cover advisory committees or tribunals as well. Along the way, the useful if difficult distinction between public bodies and private bodies carrying out public functions has been lost.

The term quasi-autonomous national government organisation is not helpful as a basis for analysis for a number of reasons. 'Quasi-autonomous' implies a distinction from bodies which have real autonomy and those that have none but does not give us any guidance about identifying such bodies. 'National' is unhelpful, since many of the organisations in which we are interested operate at regional and local level, and indeed many of the concerns expressed in the mid-1990s are concerned precisely with the extent to which central government is using local-level bodies as a substitute for elected local government. Finally, 'government organisation' begs the question of how we would identify an organisation as a government one rather than a non-government organisation, and is in danger of excluding private or voluntary organisations explicitly or tacitly used by government for a particular purpose.

To such an extent had quango become useless as a description and become heavily laden with polemical implications that the originator of the term, Anthony Barker, expressed a hope that 'this now overused and misused term will have only a brief life'—but he still used it in the title of his book *Quangos in Britain*.[2] Its use in this special issue of a journal shows that it has tenacity if not clarity.

Partly as a result of the ambiguity and polemical connotations of the term, both commentators and government have attempted to devise alternatives, such as non-departmental organisation, non-departmental agency, public body, insterstitial organisation, ad hoc agency, statutory special purpose authority, administrative body, semi-autonomous authority, paragovernmental agency, parastatal agency, fringe body and intermediate body. Some offerings seem to have been produced simply to derive another catchy acronym, such as extra-government organisation (EGO), resulting in the aptly named report *Ego Trip*.[3] Like quango itself, all of these terms are ambiguous, and do not enable us to determine from the term whether particular sets of bodies will be included or not.

The government's own preferred term is Non-Departmental Public Body (NDPB), a term which includes selected executive bodies, advisory committees and tribunals. It does not cover nationalised industries, other public corporations and the National Health Service, though some information is provided about such bodies and NDPBs annually in *Public Bodies*. *Public Bodies* does not include a number of sets of organisations such as Training and Enterprise Councils (TECs), set up at the initiative of government; in other words bodies closest to the original quasi-non-governmental organisations which were the focus of research interest in the late 1960s and early 1970s. There is no operational definition of an NDPB; it is a pragmatic labelling, focusing mainly on a set of bodies to which government makes appointments, and applied inconsistently. Nevertheless, the greater availability of annual information about such bodies, if used with caution, can give us some understanding of recent trends, as will be discussed further below.

Differing definitions will produce widely varying indicators of the scale of quango activity (though sometimes the 'definition' is simply the outcome of the arbitrary choices made about what to include or leave out). This point will be explored further below.

Any attempt to define quangos by listing distinguishing characteristics will break down, since some of these characteristics will not apply to some quangos and some will be shared by other types of bodies. We can talk about relative frequencies, but it is difficult to classify bodies unambiguously by their characteristics. Further, we should ask whether we really want to carve out neatly and separately different categories rather than explore the impact of characteristics which may apply to varying extents within categories but also straddle different categories. An obvious example here would be issues of accountability of Next Steps agencies, recognised non-departmental public bodies and bodies which the government uses for delivering policy but does not count as public bodies.

Even the basic definition of what is an organisation or 'body' is problematic. Were Wages Councils 'organisations', given that they had no staff or expenditure of their own? There is also the question of the unit of analysis. Would we do better seeing Agricultural Wages Committees as a single system rather than a fluctuating number of individual committees covering varying geographical areas? Is the Commonwealth Institute one body or two (there is an Institute presence in Edinburgh)?

Some of the difficulties of definition can be seen if we explore the possibilities of distinguishing among bodies on the basis of different characteristics.

A *definition based on appointment* of board members would fail to capture bodies which the government funds, or to which it delegates regulatory responsibilities, but to which it does not make appointments. Such a definition would also have to cope with the variation in the proportion appointed by ministers, which can vary from a single appointment to the entire board. In some cases ministers may not make the nominations or appointments but may have set out the criteria for suitable appointees, as with Training and Enterprise Councils, and the department may have a formal or informal veto on the chair or other members of boards.

A *definition based on funding* would fail to capture bodies which raise their own money by fees, charges or statutory levies, but which were formed by government to carry out public purposes. An example would be the Horserace Betting Levy Board. The amount or existence of government funding may also vary across time, as in the case of nationalised industries which used to receive government funding but now are payers into the Exchequer. Further, proportion of funding does not help us with the distinction between 'quangos' and 'government',

since departments or agencies within departments vary in the proportion
of funding which they receive from the Exchequer from zero to 100%.

A *definition based on legislative basis* would fail, since not all quangos
are set up by statute or secondary legislation, and many other types of
body, including some government departments, have a statutory base.
The fact that many industries or professions are subject to self-
regulation by a body with a statutory basis can be regarded as an
advantage or a disadvantage to a definition based on legislation
depending on the degree of inclusiveness which is being sought.

A *definition based on staff status* would fall down since some quangos
are staffed by civil servants or seconded civil servants (what used to be
the largest, the Manpower Services Commission, was in this category).
Others are serviced by departmental civil servants rather than having
staff of their own. In their early years, Training and Enterprise Councilss
(TECs) were largely staffed by civil servants. Non-civil-service status
certainly does not help us with the boundary between quangos and
private bodies.

A *definition based on existence of board or committee* fails because not
all executive NDPBs have such a board and some government departments still have boards (Inland Revenue), as do many Next Step
agencies.

A *definition such as bodies delivering on behalf of government* runs into
the problem that individual garages carrying out MOT tests would be
included. There is also the problem of how many layers of distance
from a government department should be traced in tracking quangos.[4]
Do we include not just the Arts Council but Regional Arts Boards
funded by the Council, and the organisations funded in turn by the
Regional Arts Boards? Do we include not just TECs, but the training
providers working with them, not just the Housing Corporation, but
hundreds of individual Housing Associations? If we do so, we will have
to be careful about possible double counting on some indicators as
public funds flow through the system.

We may have to accept that an agreed, workable, inclusive and
exclusive definition of type of body may not be possible to achieve and
that we should be concerned primarily with the extent to which a range
of bodies exhibit varying combinations of characteristics with which we
may be concerned, and what the implications of these are for policy
delivery and accountability.

In this article the term non-departmental public body will be used as
a general inclusive one without attempting to designate its boundaries.
The term executive NDPBs will be used to refer to the government's
much narrower classification.

The difficulties of definition referred to above may leave the reader
somewhat adrift, so Figure 1 attempts for executive bodies to combine
formal organisational features with roles to produce one possible map
on which any given selection of bodies can be located. It attempts to

Figure 1   An organisational map of formal status and function

| | DEPARTMENTS | | 'NON-DEPARTMENTAL PUBLIC BODIES' | | PUBLIC CORPORA-TIONS | NHS | OTHER LISTED BODIES | 'UNRECOG-NISED' BODIES |
	MINISTERIAL	NON-MINISTERIAL	EXECUTIVE	OTHER				
NATIONAL			e.g. *HEFCE*	Advisory Committees	Nationalised Industries	e.g. Health Education Authority		e.g. SIB, BBFC, National Trust
REGIONAL INTERMEDIARY			e.g. *Regional Flood Defence Committees*	Tribunals - - - →	Other: e.g. BBC	Regional Health Authorities		e.g. Regional Arts Boards
LOCAL INTERMEDIARY			UDCs			District Health Authorities, Family HSAs	Northern Ireland Bodies carrying out local functions	TECs, LECs, Local Arts Associations
LOCAL DELIVERY UNITS			HATs	Boards of Prison Visitors		Hospital Trusts*		Universities, FE Colleges, Grant-maintained schools, Housing Associations, Voluntary Bodies

NEXT STEPS AGENCIES (box spanning MINISTERIAL / NON-MINISTERIAL across the REGIONAL INTERMEDIARY and LOCAL INTERMEDIARY rows)

LOCAL AUTHORITIES

Notes: Bodies listed in the annual government publication *Public Bodies* are shown in **Bold**, executive NDPBs are shown in ***Bold-Italic***.
*NHS Trusts are listed as NHS bodies in *Public Bodies*, but as public corporations in the annual employment count reported in *Economic Trends*

differentiate on one dimension by the government's own classification or non-classification; while in the other attempts to differentiate between national or regional bodies which are engaged in allocating funds, regulation or providing some service on a national basis, and sets of locally-based bodies which perform a distributive or mobilising role or which are final delivery units such as grant-maintained schools, hospital trusts, etc.

Any student of public administration would quickly be able to point to the difficulties of defining the content of any particular cell in an exclusive manner, but it does nevertheless provide a layout on to which the pragmatic or classificatory attempts of others can be mapped. For example, the diagram itself highlights which bodies are included and excluded from current government definitions.

Another example would be Weir and Hall who come up with a total of 5,521 bodies in contrast to the 350 government-classified executive NDPBs.[5] Some of this is their inclusion of Northern Ireland and NHS bodies listed elsewhere in *Public Bodies*. However, the bulk of the difference is from the inclusion of what are shown in Figure 1 as local delivery bodies: registered Housing Associations (which account for nearly half of the Weir and Hall total), universities and colleges, and grant-maintained schools and City Technology Colleges. They do include Training and Enterprise Councils and Local Enterprise Companies but not any of the 'non-recognised' national or regional bodies. They also exclude nationalised industries and other public corporations, which profoundly affects their findings about trends in the scale of activity of bodies.

'Growth' of quangos?

We saw in the previous section that issues of definition and coverage of bodies are related to findings about the direction and scale of change in their significance. The choice of indicators is also crucial. We may get an entirely different picture depending on whether we count the number of bodies, the size of their staff, their total expenditure, government funding, or number of appointments made by government. Findings can also be affected by the selection of the beginning and end years, and whether we look at just those beginning and end years or changes in trends within that period. It is very important to distinguish between changes at the gross level and the pattern of change to individual bodies or sets of bodies. The total number may decrease, but a substantial number of bodies can be both formed and terminated during the period, or be replaced.

An important point in the study of quangos is the extent to which apparent growth or decline in any one sector has been the result of the extension of state activities or of a rejigging of responsibilities for existing activities, such as: removal of functions from local government; transfers of functions from central government departments; restructuring within structures of appointed bodies; moves from non-departmental public bodies into central departments or local authorities.

Bearing in mind these strong caveats and the limitations both of available information and what can be reported in a section of an article, the remainder of this section examines some indicators of trends since 1979. Because of the difficulty of producing a theoretically valid, operationally practical or generally agreed definition of what the total universe of quangos is, each of a number of sub-categories is examined in the context of the contribution it makes to the overall pattern. This review concentrates on bodies which could be considered executive, rather than advisory or tribunals, though it is accepted that the conceptual boundary between these is blurred and the official classification inconsistent.

Nationalised industries and other public corporations. The decision about whether or not to include nationalised industries in an assessment of non-departmental public bodies has a profound implication for overall trends. Privatisation of state industry since 1979 has had only a relatively small impact on the total number of bodies (a decline of around 40) but has had a profound impact on staffing and expenditure, whether measured by turnover or government funding. Employment in nationalised industries fell from 1,849,000 in 1979 to only 455,000 in 1993.[6] In other public corporations the fall was from 216,000 to 77,000. The fall in employment in nationalised industries and other corporations is greater than the total employment of the entire NHS plus executive NDPBs in 1993. This decline is in part due to the reduction in the staff of those industries and corporations which still remain in state hands.

The 'other public corporations' category is a fluid one (and one which is inconsistently classified in different government documents). It includes some bodies which the literature of the 1970s regarded as classic quasi-government bodies, such as the British Broadcasting Corporation. A number of bodies formerly in the executive NDPB category were reclassified as public corporations, notably the regional water authorities and the Civil Aviation Authority. For the regional water authorities this was a temporary resting place prior to privatisation. Their reclassification poses problems for assessing trends in executive NDPBs. To leave them in gives an artificial drop between 1982 and 1983, even though they remained within the public sector for a few more years. However, to exclude them altogether from grand totals of quango activity (as do Weir and Hall) artificially exaggerates the apparent growth in that activity.

National Health Service. The justification for treating the National Health Service as a separate organisational category is not so much conceptual as pragmatic. It now forms the largest single category in terms of staffing and finance, and to include it with the executive NDPB category would drown out changes in the latter. By April 1994, not a single organisational component of the geographical structure of the NHS in England remained unaltered.

The 1982 reorganisation led to an increase in the number of appointed bodies as a larger number of District Health Authorities replaced Area Health Authorities (and reduced the link with local authorities), and Family Practitioner Committees were given separate status. Recent attention has focused on the growth in bodies resulting from the formation of Trusts. However, even before the 1994 reduction of the number of Regional and District Health Authorities, there had been a steady reduction in the number of District Authorities from 1982. The government has also announced its intention of abolishing Regional Health Authorities and providing for the merger of Family Health Service Authorities with district health authorities.

Total employees in the NHS in the UK (including Trusts) was almost the same at 1,152,000 in 1979 as the 1,158,000 in 1993, after rising to a peak in between of 1,227,000 in 1982 and 1983.[7] Public expenditure on health rose from £22.6bn in 1979 to £36.9bn in 1993 at 1993 prices adjusting for the general rate of inflation.[8]

Changes in executive NDPBs.[9] The number of bodies consistently classified by the government as executive non-departmental public bodies declined between 1979 and 1992, with most of the decline occurring in the first five years (see Table 1). However, much of this early reduction arose through consolidation (merger) of bodies rather than outright termination. There was a sharp fall in 1993–4 arising from the abolition of Wages Councils, which affects the number of bodies substantially, even though they had no funding or staffing of their own.

Total staff working in NDPBs also shows an overall decline (see Table 1). However, the noticeable decline in the number of NDPBs from 1979 to 1984 is not reflected in the staff employed. Together with the figures for expenditure discussed below, this suggests that the scale of activity of such bodies had not been cut back, despite the reduction in their numbers. Total staff did show a sharp drop in 1988 and 1989, largely as a result of the transfer of the functions of the Manpower Services Commission back to the Department of Employment.

Table 1 shows an overall upward trend in expenditure and government funding between 1979 and 1992, but with a significant dip in 1989. A major discrepancy between the author's database figures and *Public Bodies* figures for 1989 is that *Public Bodies* includes departmental expenditure on universities in 1988/89 under the University Funding Council, even though that body did not take over its formal responsibilities until 1 April 1989. The main reasons for the dip shown in 1989 and the subsequent upturn are the transfer of Manpower Services Commission activities to the Department of Employment and, in the opposite direction, the setting up of the Universities Funding Council and the Polytechnics and Colleges Funding Council, which led

1. **Changes in consistently classified executive NDPBs**
   (official *Public Bodies* figures in brackets)

	No.	Staff	Gross (000s)	Govt funding	Govt funding as % of gross
			Expenditure £bn (1991/92 prices)		
1979	458 (492)	152 (217)	11.1 (16.6)	8.3 (8.0)	74
1980	451	149	10.7	7.3	68
1981	438	146	10.7	7.4	69
1982	438 (450)	144 (205)	10.3 (14.9)	6.8 (7.0)	66
1983	423 (431)	142 (197)	11.9 (16.6)	8.4 (8.5)	71
1984	400 (402)	141 (141)	11.7 (11.6)	8.2 (8.2)	71
1985	388 (399)	139 (138)	11.9 (11.8)	7.8 (7.7)	66
1986	396 (406)	146 (146)	11.7 (11.8)	7.8 (7.7)	67
1987	382 (396)	148 (149)	12.7 (12.7)	7.9 (7.9)	62
1988	379 (390)	134 (135)	12.5 (12.5)	7.8 (7.8)	63
1989	384 (395)	117 (118)	8.8 (11.6)	5.5 (7.5)	63
1990	375 (374)	117 (118)	13.4 (13.7)	9.8 (10.0)	74
1991	368 (375)	117 (116)	14.0 (14.0)	10.8 (10.8)	77
1992	366 (369)	114 (114)	13.9 (13.8)	10.3 (10.3)	74
1993	(358)	(111)	(14.8)	(11.5)	
1994	n.a.	n.a	n.a.	n.a.	
Change 79-92	-92	-38	+£2.9bn	+£2.0bn	

Source: Author's database of public bodies. *Public Bodies* figures are from *Public Bodies 1993;* number of bodies and staffing figures are as reported in *Public Bodies*, but the expenditure figures are adjusted by the GDP deflator. Official summary figures for 1980 and 1981 do not exist.

to the transfer of expenditure from the central and local government headings.

Considering the limited immediate impact of the attempts at reducing the number of non-departmental bodies in the first two years of the Conservative government, Hood argues that 'The non-departmental body thus appears to be a remarkably tenacious form of government'.[10] It is important, however, to distinguish between the overall use of bodies of such a type and the survivability of any given organisation or set of organisations within the type. In research reported in detail elsewhere[11] I found that:

Of the 458 bodies in existence at April 1979, 195 (43% of the 1979 total) had *survived* in unchanged form to 1992. With the abolition of wages councils in 1993, the proportion of survivors has dropped dramatically.

A total of 90 bodies were *terminated* between 1979 and 1992 (that is completely wound up and not simply merged, split or transferred to other parts of the public or grant-maintained sector. The termination of 35 Wages Councils in 1993 has led to a sharp increase on terminations, so that (allowing for interim mergers and other transitions) well over a quarter of the bodies in this category existing in 1979 have now been wound up.

Between 1979 and 1992 there were 44 organisations set up as the result of organisational *innovations*, that is, established where there was no predecessor organisation.

148 of the bodies existing in 1979 had been *replaced*. Some organisations had undergone more than one succession. By far the largest category of succession was the merger of bodies, reducing the body count, though not necessarily other indicators of activity.

There were substantial *flows* to and from other parts of the public or grant-maintained sector, with the removal of the activities of the MSC and the establishment of education funding bodies being of particular note. These are discussed further below.

Changes in 'unrecognised' or 'disavowed' bodies. The government has set up a number of bodies, such as the City Technology Trust, to promote its policies, which it has chosen not to classify as executive NDPBs. The government does not consider the Training and Enterprise Councils, which it set up from 1990, to be executive NDPBs, though they have many of the attributes of the original quangos and were initially largely staffed by civil servants. These TECs, together with the Local Enterprise Companies in Scotland, would add around a hundred to the body count. *Public Bodies* does not include the Securities and Investments Board which regulates the financial sector, even though this is referred to in legislation. Another example would be the exclusion of the renamed British Board of Film Classification, even though it now has a statutory remit.

A really wide scan would take in Housing Associations, universities, Colleges of Further Education and many voluntary associations. Some indicators of this are picked up through data on executive NDPB activity because of the role of executive NDPBs in funding such bodies.

Those scrutinising *Public Bodies* for the new single industry offices which regulate privatised industries, such as Oftel, will not find them listed there as non-departmental public bodies. However, this is a trap for the unwary, since far from being unacknowledged, these are classified as (non-ministerial) government departments.

Key Trends. There have been a number of factors pointing to reductions in bodies and others pointing to increases. This section is concluded with a summary of key trends pointing in each of these directions.

Among the patterns of change associated with *reductions* in non-departmental public bodies, widely defined, are:

The substantial privatisation of nationalised industries and other public corporations, which has led to a reduction in staffing and funding greater than the entire size of the executive NDPB category as it existed in 1979.

The continuing rundown in the staffing of those nationalised industries and public corporations remaining in the public sector and the substantial reduction of government support.

The abolition of Wages Councils in 1993 (though Agricultural Wages Committees remain). This had a dramatic impact on the body count, though they had no staff or finance of their own.

The abolition of nearly all Industrial Training Boards and the transfer of their functions to industry-run organisations.

The winding-up of most New Town Development Corporations, a process which was already under way before 1979.

The dismantling of the Manpower Services Commission, the largest single body in 1979. This had an important impact on the financing total for the executive NDPB category, though the subsequent establishment of TECs and LECs, not counted by the government as executive NDPBs, led to an increase in the number of bodies with which we are interested. (It should be noted that the Manpower Services Commission operated through 125 District Manpower Committees, which were classified as advisory bodies).

Higher Education Central Institutions in Scotland (the equivalent of Polytechnics and Colleges of Education) used to be counted as executive NDPBs, since they were appointed and funded directly by the Scottish Office. A mixture of closure, merger and transfer to self-governing status has led to a reduction of 21 bodies since 1979.

Most of the key trends which have led to an *increase* in indicators of executive bodies are the result of *transfers* within the public sector rather than the state taking on additional tasks.

Museums funded by central government are now systematically classified as executive NDPBs. This has led to a substantial increase in body count. Most of the large museums were previously government departments, though some of the military museums were charities and a few were previously run by local councils abolished in the mid-1980s.

The use of executive NDPBs as the main instrument for channelling central funds to individual education establishments (other than those still in local authority control). Previously the University Grants Committee was formally an advisory committee, and its decisions on spending were counted as part of the main Department for Education and Science budget. Other bodies such as the former Polytechnics, Colleges of Further Education, and now opted-out grant-maintained schools, had been funded and controlled by local government. These funding changes make a huge difference to the funding total of the executive NDPB category, though only a minor one to body count or staffing.

The growing use of bodies to by-pass or take over local government development and housing functions, such as Urban Development Corporations and Housing Action Trusts. Although this development and the removal of education funding referred to above was in the context of Conservative government antipathy to Labour urban authorities, it can also be seen as part of a longer process by which governments of both parties have removed from local government control functions such as gas, electricity, water, health care and aspects of social security. The earlier establishment of New Town Development Corporations from the late 1940s could also be seen in this context.

The growth of NHS funding (normally seen by commentators as 'good' in the context of the NHS but 'bad' when used as an indicator of the growth of appointed bodies). This has been accompanied by an increase in the number of appointed bodies. The scale of these changes would be sufficient to swamp developments in the executive NDPB category if the NHS was grouped together with executive NDPBs.

There has been a trend to the splitting of Scottish and Welsh activities from previously British bodies, and this has led to a (small) increase in the total number of bodies.

Appointments and patronage

One of the most commented on trends since 1979 is the increase in the number of patronage jobs by the Conservative government. Your eyes no doubt slid easily over the previous sentence. However, the assumption about this 'trend' has not been adequately researched and tends to conflate unpaid appointments, appointments receiving modest per diem fees for one or a few days a year, and very substantial salaried posts. There is also a failure to track variations across time systematically.

Weir and Hall state that 'The growth of government by appointment has greatly magnified the scale of political patronage'. In support of this, they compare a 1978 estimate by Holland and Fallon of 33,411 appointments with a government estimate in *Public Bodies 1993* that ministers were responsible for 42,606 appointments.[13] However, this comparison is severely flawed. First, the two sources are not covering the same set of bodies. Secondly, Holland's various anti-quango publications of the late 1970s have a certain 'think of a number' element to them. In another of his publications, *Quango, Quango, Quango,* he estimates that there were 9,633 paid appointments and 30,890 unpaid ones, making a total of 40,523.[14] Should we taken this as evidence of a more modest but steady growth between the late 1970s and 1993? Certainly not, since, apart from differences of coverage, it does not take account of possible fluctuations in trend within the period or changes in the balance of types of appointment.

Attempts to explore this further by using government data are hampered by the fact that government did not start to publish summary data on appointments until 1987, and then only in the context of gender balance, though much of the raw material is available for individual bodies for earlier years. The summary data are limited in many ways (including serious gaps in NHS data). A major limitation is that the summaries do not distinguish between paid appointments of various types and unpaid ones. However, with appropriate care in adjusting

2. **Appointments made by central departments**

	Exec	Advis	Trib	Other NDPB	Nat Ind	Pub Corp	NHS	Total
1986	7560	13914	22106	1726	401	59	n.a.	n.a.
1987	6526	13352	22297	1723	387	61	7455	51801
1988	6489	12545	22511	1902	375	59	7609	51490
1989	6359	12141	21340	1906	330	58	7431	49565
1990	5316	11780	20712	1744	244	54	7167	47017
1991	5158	10398	19875	1768	117	45	3501	40862
1992	4343	10180	20719	1758	105	57	3846	41008
1993	4066	10022	22265	1804	98	80	4221	42556

Source: Calculated by the author from summary tables on appointments by gender in *Public Bodies* from 1986. English NHS figures for 1990 and 1991 are directly calculated from details of English NHS appointments because summary figures in *Public Bodies* do not include most appointments for NHS bodies in England.

and interpreting the data, we can learn something by compiling the information from different issues of *Public Bodies* from 1986, as shown in Table 2.

First, the table shows that there has been a decline rather than an increase in the number of appointments since 1987. Secondly, about half of the total number of appointments are to tribunals, with a further quarter to advisory committees. The number of appointments to executive NDPBs has declined dramatically since 1987, which causes problems for the growth of patronage argument. Not surprisingly, given the earlier discussion, appointments to nationalised industries have declined dramatically.

The decline on the number of appointments in the NHS may cause surprise, even when care has been taken to remove some discrepancies from the government data. Surely the growth of Trusts must have led to an increase in number of appointments? There are three important themes here. First, while the growth of Trusts has led to a new category of appointments, there has been a reduction in the number of District Health Authorities (which has continued in 1994 and will also be affected by merger of District and Family Health Authorities). Secondly, the size of the board of authorities has been reduced. Thirdly, and this is very important in the context of the patronage debate, the system has moved over the period from one in which the vast majority of members of authorities were unpaid appointments to one in which nearly all are paid part-time appointments, with the going rate for ordinary members being £5,000 a year.

This review of the appointments issue shows that while the matter is inevitably and properly one for normative comment, it is also suscept-ible to systematic analysis despite the difficulties of the data, which perhaps ought to be a prelude to some of the normative discussion based on less than sound assumptions. None of this is to detract from the importance of the broader discussion of how a 'local magistracy', much of which is not directly appointed by ministers, has taken on roles which have historically been carried out by elected local authorities or which might be thought appropriate for them to take on.

Explanations for growth — and reduction

This sections reviews possible explanations for the patterns of change in non-departmental public bodies, particularly since 1979. It draws heavily on the groups of explanations set out by Hood in 1978: random, fashion, managerial technology and various types of political explanations, and applies them to developments since that article.[15] Hood was concerned largely with explaining his perception of the growth of the use of non-departmental bodies, particularly in the context of 'keeping the centre small', the centre being central government departments. In this article we are also concerned to explain why some bodies are terminated or transferred to other forms, including in some cases into central government departments. Because the issue of patronage has already been touched on in the previous section, it is not explored further as a possible explanation for the growth of bodies.

Random. This explanation would suggest that there are no systematic patterns of particular agency forms being used for particular purposes, or being set up or terminated at particular times. It is certainly possible to cite comparisons which make it difficult to come up with explanations of agency form other than on an entirely ad hoc basis. Why, for example, is the Office of the Data Protection Registrar an executive NDPB and the Registry of Friendly Societies a non-ministerial department? However, the pattern of bodies and of their establishment and termination is not entirely random, as evidenced by the fact that we were able to identify above key trends which often affected sets of bodies rather than individual ones. Thus while ad hoc administrative history may be the only explanation for the selection of agency type in some cases, we can try to look for explanations for observable patterns, even if those explanations are partial and seem to be applicable in an inconsistent way.

Fashion. We may find it difficult to find a pattern across all bodies existing at a given time but be able to identify particular administraitve fashions which, even after they have faded from popularity, nevertheless leave the legacy in the form of bodies set up at that time. For example, 'hiving off' was in vogue in the late 1960s and 1970s following Fulton, though in practice this led to a variety of organisational forms, including units within departments and executive NDPBs. Attacks on quangos became fashionable in the late 1970s, as in 1993–94, and this led the government to set up the Pliatzky inquiry.[16] However, relatively few quangos were actually abolished in the immediate aftermath.[17] The Conservative emphasis on privatisation was responsible for the sharp reduction in nationalised industries and other public corporations and for the transfer of some NDPB activity to the private sector. From 1988, the establishment of Next Steps agencies was a major Whitehall theme and may have led to some activities being structured in agency form which might otherwise have been put into NDPBs. However, Next Steps agencies were far from the only form used by government in this period, and several major executive NDPBs were established, mostly from existing public sector activities.[18] From 1987, the Conservative emphasis is on private-sector-like forms as in the status of TECs as 'private' companies. Similarly, the move to quasi-markets in social policy areas, such as health and education, has led to a proliferation of boards of individual delivery units, often of a 'self-governing' and sometimes self-appointing form. However, these recent examples show that it may be difficult to differentiate between fashion and ideological differences.

Managerial technology. This type of explanation would account for variations in the form of body by the type of activity being performed. In general, this seems to be a very poor explanation, since it is possible to find virtually every type of activity being performed by official non-departmental bodies (regulation, grant distribution, direct service delivery) — but also being performed by ministerial departments, non-ministerial departments, Next Steps agencies and 'non-official' bodies.

There are a few cases of form relating to function. It was noted earlier that the appropriate organisational form for a gallery or museum funded by central government was an executive non-departmental body, and that there had been a systematic move in that direction.

It is also tempting to see a view that bodies which disburse funding to sets of locally based organisations are best carried out through non-departmental bodies, such as the various education funding councils, the Arts Councils, District and Regional Health Authorities, and there certainly has been a move in that direction. However, the government directly distributes funds to TECs (which could themselves be seen as intermediate bodies) and to local authorities. In the case of health, the government proposes to abolish the Regional Health Authorities in England and pull their functions into the NHS executive, which is a part of the Department of Health. Clearly, additional considerations which balance the possibility of disavowing decisions against the desire to control patterns of distribution directly are required.

Bypassing and outflanking. The desire to bypass or outflank local govenrment can be seen as an important factor in the establishment of new executive NDPBs. This can be seen in the establishment of Urban Development Corporations and Housing Action Trusts, as well as greater encouragement for a role for Housing Associations to replace local authority housing functions. All higher and further education funding has been allocated through executive NDPBs, and a growing number of grant-maintained schools are funded in this way.

However, one has to ask why the executive NDPB form was used rather than, say, handling these functions within a department, or setting up a new non-ministerial department or Next Steps agency. Here, two additional factors appear to come into play. One is that the scale of some of these activities would have swamped the core department, and the second is that the use of executive NDPBs means that the ministers are not answerable for detailed allocative decisions but can still by directives or guidance strongly influence the policy embedded in those allocations. The precedent of existing bodies such as the University Grants Committee (albeit officially an advisory body) provided a model for funding agencies for further education and schools.

Professional or industry self-control. The statutory reregulation of the financial sector is a good example of form of body being devised to enable self-regulation by a relevant group. However, dissatisfaction with some aspects of self-regulation has meant that autonomy from politicians has, despite the legal form adopted, been less than complete, and changes in both organisational structures and regulations have resulted.

Concealing the real size of the central bureaucracy. The removal of some departmental functions to English Heritage and the move of some big museums from departmental to non-departmental status had the effect of reducing the apparent size of the civil service. However, the government was also committed to reducing the number of quangos. There were some moves in the opposite direction, such as pulling functions of Manpower Services Commission back into the Department of Employment, though staff were already civil servants and some functions were shortly after pushed back out to TECs. Regional Health Authorities are to be abolished and their functions brought in to the Department of Health.

Institutionalitis. Institutionalitis refers to the practice of setting up a separate organisation for each new issue or problem which comes along. Certainly it is possible to find individual cases of new bodies resulting in this way, such as the Human Fertilisation and Embryology Authority, and the United Kingdom Eco-Labelling Board. However, this contributes only a small part of the explanation to the growth of new bodies.

The impact of political sensitivity on agency type. The problem with this criterion is that it is one that can point in two directions.[19] For some issues, such as moral ones, ministers may prefer not to have to justify particular decisions or recommendations, say about use of embryos, and this may mean the establishment of an executive NDPB. However, there are alternative forms available, such as the non-ministerial departmental form used for the tax collecting departments, and now Next Steps agencies, such as the Child Support Agency. In other cases of political sensitivy where the government does itself have priorities, however controversial, political salience or sensitivity may lead to a function being brought fully into a department, as with the regional health authorities.

Problem exhaustion. One obvious factor leading to the removal of a function from a type of body is that the problem has ceased, or that the policy function has been fulfilled, though there may be some scope for interpretation, particularly of timing. One example since 1979 is the continuing winding up of New Town Development Corporations. Some bodies may have been designed to be temporary in the first instance (and this would be a reason for choosing the executive NDPB form). An example here would be the residuary bodies set up following the abolition of the metropolitan counties and the Greater London Council in the mid-1980s; these have in their turn been wound up. This category of bodies which have both been set up and wound up in the period since 1979 also emphasises the importance of looking at developments within the period and not simply at the beginning and end if we are to get a full picture of the use made of particular types of bodies.

Can we explain anything? Overall, the findings of this section about developments since 1979 confirm Hood's conclusion that there is no single explanation for growth (to which I would add also reductions) or for why some organisational forms are used rather than others. However, there are a number of 'clues', which do not all point in the same direction. Even political explanations can point in different directions. We can say that ideological considerations have been important in shaping the pattern of bodies in the post-1979 period, but even here there have been other factors. Further these ideological considerations have led to a reduction in the body count of some types of body and a proliferation of others, rather than a reduction in the size of the state other than in industrial activities. This reinforces the point that we (still) need to develop probabilistic rather than deterministic, and multi-factor rather than single factor, explanations.

Conclusion

We now have better information about non-departmental public bodies and appointments to them than at any previous time, thanks to better (though still incomplete and inconsistent) publication of information by the government after 1979 and the efforts of MPs in asking systematic questions in Parliament. However, we (government or analysts) are little further forward in agreed definitions or terminology to describe different types of body, or even agreement about the set of organisations that are our concern. Government categorisations are not based on systematic distinctions and are at least in part motivated by a desire to keep the 'body count' down. Much of the journalistic and 'independent' coverage, by contrast, seems to be concerned to establish that the number of bodies is high and increasing and that there has been an increase in patronage. The only shared value seems to be that quangos are rather shameful, though when the details of the substantive activity or even form of particular sets of bodies is considered (Housing Action Trusts or Wages Councils) there is sometimes an inversion of justification.

Establishing *trends* for the full range of indicators across all types of body is particularly difficult. A more thoughtful analysis requires tracking of individual organisations and groups of organisations and a recognition that net figures can conceal components that can move in different directions. The selective inclusion or exclusion from analysis of different categories can paint a substantially different picture. Substantial categories of activity carried out by non-departmental bodies have been dramatically reduced: industrial activities, sectoral industrial training, new town (but not urban) development corporations, regulation of wages and prices. In others, such as education and health, there has been growth in finance in the policy area together with major reorganisations which have led to a proliferation of service delivery units with their own boards. In education, local development and housing, there has been an increase in executive non-departmental bodies to take on or displace local government activities. There have also been 'boring' changes such as the rationalisation of the status of museums and galleries, which nevertheless have an impact on the numbers.

Governments of both parties have found it useful to establish or maintain various forms of non-departmental public bodies for their own purposes. When in opposition, they have denounced the formation of bodies resulting from policy changes to which they are opposed, as well as sometimes denouncing the abolition of those that embody their own policy preferences. Governments of both parties have been criticised for using their powers of appointment for selecting or failing to select particular categories of people, or for having the power of appointment at all.

An assessment of the period since 1979 is hampered by the lack of systematic data for preceding periods. There is a general assumption in the literature that there was a pattern of continuing growth. However, this assumption is based on at best partial evidence and is crucially affected by the choice of indicators, the type of body covered and the time period selected. For example, the evidence is not available to show that the number of bodies saw a general upward trend between, say, 1949 and 1978. There is a general assumption that there was, but this tends to neglect the number of bodies which disappeared during this period.

We clearly do not have sufficient scientific understanding of the factors affecting the scale of activity of different types of non-departmental public body to make reliable predictions. Despite the lack of systematic explanations, agreed definitions or long-run data on trends, we can nevertheless safely predict that regardless of any change of government:

There will continue to be a substantial role for non-departmental public bodies, but the bodies which exist at any given time will not necessarily be the same bodies as in previous time periods even if net totals do not change much.

Some bodies will be terminated and some new ones set up.

Many existing bodies will be merged or split.

Pamphleteers and academics will intermittently write about the alleged growth of the phenomenon, but will still not be able to define a quango.

1   See A. Barker (ed.), *Quangos in Britain* (Macmillan, 1992).

2   Barker, op. cit., p.220.

3   S. Weir and W. Hall, *Ego Trip: Extra-Governmental Organisations in the United Kingdom and their Accountability* (Charter 88 Trust, 1994).

4   On 'quasi non-quasi governmental organisations', see C. Hood, The Rise and Rise of the British Quango, *New Society*, 16 August 1973.

5   Weir and Hall, *Ego-Trip*, p.9.

6   *Economic Trends*, January 1994, no. 483, p.95.

7   Ibid.

8   Calculated from *United Kingdom National Accounts*, using the GDP deflator; adjustment for increases in the costs of inputs in the NHS would give a lower increase in the volume of NHS activity. Data shown in Weir and Hall, *Ego-Trip*, p.9, Table 2 for NHS bodies seem to be seriously adrift if they are, as stated, at 1992/93 prices.

9   The research reported in this section was assisted by an ESRC research grant.

10 C. Hood, 'Axeperson, Spare That Quango . . .' in C. Hood and M. Wright (eds.), *Big Government in Hard Times* (Martin Robertson, 1981).

11 B. W. Hogwood, 'Much Exaggerated: Death and Survival in British Quangos', Political Studies Association Annual Conference, 1993.

12 Weir and Hall, op. cit. p.16.

13 P. Holland and M. Fallon, *The Quango Explosion* (Conservative Political Centre, 1978).

14 P. Holland, *Quango, Quango, Quango* (Adam Smith Institute).

15 C. Hood, 'Keeping the Centre Small: Explanations of Agency Type', *Political Studies*, 1978, 30–46.

16 Sir Leo Pliatzky, *Report on Non-Departmental Bodies* (HMSO, Cmnd 7797, 1980).

17 Hood, 'Axperson', loc. cit.

18 B. W. Hogwood, 'Whitehall Families: Core Departments and Agency Forms in Britain', European Consortium of Political Research Annual Joint Sessions of Workshops, 1994.

19 Hood, 'Keeping the Centre Small', loc. cit.

Appointed Boards and Local Government

BY JOHN STEWART

THIS article focuses on a major change in the government of local communities—the growth in the number of public bodies controlled by appointed boards, often taking over responsibilities previously carried out by local authorities. There have of course always been appointed boards operating at local level. The health service has been run by appointed boards at local level since its creation in 1947. The probation service and magistrates courts have been run by appointed boards or committees with the majority of the appointments made by the magistrates. However, under the Conservative government since 1979 a series of steps have been taken which have greatly increased the number of appointed bodies and which have removed the influence of local authorities by removing their right to make appointments to certain bodies. Local authorities no longer make appointments to District Health Authorities or to Family Health Service Agencies (the successor to Family Practitioner Committees to which they made appointments). Health Service Trusts have been created to run hospitals and community health services. Training and Enterprise Councils exercise substantial responsibilities in training and economic development. Grant-maintained schools, sixth-form colleges and Colleges of Further Education have been removed from local authorities' responsibilities and are governed by appointed boards which receive their funding from nationally-appointed bodies. Housing Associations have increasingly taken over the social housing functions previously exercised by local authorities. New Police Authorities, on which five out of seventeen members will be appointed in addition to three magistrates, will be set up as from 1 April 1995. Urban Development Corporations and Housing Action Trusts have taken over major responsibilities for redevelopment in certain urban areas

The government in its annual publication *Public Bodies* publishes statistics setting out the number and expenditure of non-departmental public bodies. These show a significant decline in the number of such bodies since 1979 and have been regularly quoted by ministers as indicating that, far from increasing, they have in fact decreased. The figures, however, exclude most of the appointed boards mentioned earlier. Those in the health service are excluded on the grounds that they are departmental (i.e. not non-departmental public bodies). Housing Associations are excluded because they are voluntary organisations. Training and Enterprise Councils are excluded because they are private companies. Many of the bodies involved in education are excluded on the grounds that they operate at local level. It is clear that the categories covered by the phrase non-departmental public bodies excludes many of the bodies which are commonly regarded as quangos. Weir and Hall, aware of the problem of the word quangos, but anxious to challenge the limited scope of the phrase 'non-departmental public bodies', adopted the initials EGO, standing for extra-governmental organisations, which they define as executive bodies of a semi-autonomous nature which effectively act as agencies for central government and carry out government policies.[1] On this basis they calculated that there were 5,521 such bodies, (with a total expenditure of £46.652 billion in 1992/3 or over a fifth of public expenditure) made up as follows:

Recognised executive NDPBs	350
'Non-recognised' NI NDPBs	8
NHS bodies	629
'Non-recognised bodies	
Grant-maintained schools	1,025
City Technology Colleges	15
Further Education Corporations	557
Higher Education Corporations	164
Registered Housing Associations	2,668
Training and Enterprise Councils	82
Local Enterprise Companies	23

These figures exclude the 1,031 advisory and quasi-government agencies as well as certain others. On the other hand, some may question the inclusion of Housing Associations. What is clear, however, is that the reason for the difference between the government's own figures and those produced by Weir and Hall lies in the exclusion from the definition of Non-Departmental Public Bodies of organisations operating at local level, whether classified as NHS bodies or listed by Weir and Hall as non-recognised bodies. Yet it is in these that the major increases have taken place. Three broad trends can be noted:

The removal of local authority representatives from boards on which they previously sat (e.g. District Health Authorities).

The removal of responsibilities from local authorities to an appointed board (e.g. Colleges of Further Education).

The separation off of activities previously under the control of a single organisation (e.g. NHS Trusts).

The bodies created vary in their status. Thus Grier and Hoggett have pointed out that: 'Several of the new bodies such as Hospital Trusts and Higher and Further Education Corporations are companies, but unlike other companies they have been created by statute. This means that they are neither regulated nor protected by the Companies Act 1985–9.

Such organisations constitute virtually a new species of corporation which is legally quite unique.'[2] The Training and Enterprise Councils are private limited companies. Housing Associations are registered charities or industrial and provident societies. Other bodies such as District Health Authorities are statutory authorities.

Of most significance for the purpose of this article is the difference in the method of appointment. There are broadly three methods of appointment: by the minister (e.g. chairs of District Health Authorities, members of Urban Development Corporations); by an intermediate body itself appointed by the minister (e.g. non-executive members of District Health Authorities; self-appointing (members of the Training and Enterprise Councils). In addition, in grant-maintained schools a minority of the governors are elected by parents or by teachers, while on joint boards (which are not included in Weir and Hall's statistics), including those set up to take over certain of the responsibilities of the Metropolitan Counties and the Greater London Council, appointments are made by local authorities through indirect election. Different methods of appointment can be combined in the same body. Thus while the chair of a District Health Authority is appointed by the Secretary of State, the other non-executive members are appointed by the Regional Health Authority and the executive members (i.e. the general managers and other chief officers) who are members of the authority's governing body are appointed by the non-executive members.

As well as differences in the method of appointment, there are significant differences in remuneration with some boards paying a parti-time salary (e.g. chairs of District Health Authorities receive between £15,330 and £20,005 per annum and members £5,000), while others (members of Training and Enterprise Councils) receive no remuneration. The complex system of appointed bodies operating at local level has grown up step by step. There is little evidence that the difference in status, method of appointment and remuneration reflects an overview of the system being created or that there was any real awareness of the scale of the change taking place. It is, however, with the overall impact of these developments and with the issues they create that this article is concerned.

Any system of government or any organisation has to differentiate its activities. Fragmentation occurs when there is differentiation without countervailing means of integration. There have been three broad trends taking place in what can best be described as the system of local governance to distinguish it from local government itself:

The separation of activities previously the responsibility of local authorities in education and in urban regeneration.

The separation of institutions from the authorities previously responsible for the institution in health and education.

The termination of local authority representation on health authorities, which was one means, however imperfect, of integration.

Method of appointment

Much of the criticism of appointed boards has centred on the appointments made. Two issues have been highlighted—political patronage and multiple appointments—both allegations made about previous Labour governments as well as about the Conservatives. Thus in 1977 it was stated that 39 members of the TUC General Council had between them 180 public appointments, and in 1978 it was pointed out that Jack Jones, the former TGWU General Secretary, held ten places on different boards and that past and present officials of the TGWU held at least 27 appointments between them.

In 1993 George Howarth, a Labour MP, prepared a report listing 32 appointments to large executive non-departmental public bodies and 13 appointments to Urban Development Corporations who had links with companies which made donations to the Conservative Party[3]. Morgan and Roberts point out that in Wales: 'The appointments process, which is seldom based upon public advertisement, has become a seething political issue on account of the type of people who have been appointed in recent years.' They go on to list a series of appointments of people mainly with Conservative Party connections, including defeated parliamentary candidates. They add: 'What is clear is that certain people hold multiple appointments and for this reason the likes of Sir Donald Walter, Dr Gwyn Jones, Mr Clyn Davies and Sir Geoffrey Inkin are variously described as the quango Kings or the inner circle that runs Wales.'[4] It has been difficult to establish the truth of allegations because of the lack of a national register of appointments, even of those made by ministers. Peter Kilfoyle MP has assembled a fairly comprehensive list by the arduous process of asking 800 parliamentary questions, which is being used to identify multiple membership and party connections where known. A list of NHS Trust chairs assembled by Alan Milburn MP was used by *The Independent* which found that of 185 Trust chairs, 62 had clear links with the Conservative Party.

The underlying problem lies in the method of appointment which gives every indication of being a system out of control. The alleged abuses are a symptom of such a situation. The lack of national registers may help explain such cases as the appointment of Clive Wilkinson, the former Labour leader of Birmingham City Council, to four positions involving six-and-a-half days a week (*The Observer*, 9 October 1994). Another example is the discovery by Alan Milburn MP of 11 people appointed both to Health Authorities and to Trusts, contrary to Department of Health policy, which department originally denied there were any such cases. Proper records would have avoided such occurrences.

It is not merely the lack of registers that indicates a system out of control. The role of the Public Appointments Unit of the Cabinet Office appears limited, dependent as it is upon departments. There appears to have been a lack of proper procedures for making such appointments; certainly there is a lack of publicly known procedures. If there were such procedures one would expect advertisements of posts, application forms, interviews, use of references, conformity to equal opportunities procedures and the possibility of external scrutiny before appointments were made. The indications are that appointments can be made in a much more informal way. Tony Lewis, at a session of the Welsh Affairs Committee on 23 November 1992, was asked about the process:

Q: 'But in fact no interview, no situation where you were asked detailed questions by a panel of people, nothing like that?'

A: 'No.'

Q: 'Just a straightforward telephone call asking you whether you would like the job and then in fact a letter confirming your appointment?'

A: 'Yes.'

The position about appointments made by intermediate bodies (e.g. Regional Health Authorities) or by self-appointing bodies is equally, if not more, unsatisfactory. Indeed, boards of Colleges of Further Education have not merely the power of appointment but have also the power by a simple resolution to remove members of the board on grounds of unfitness, a power which, it is sometimes alleged, has been used against those whose views diverge from those of the Board. Part of the problem derives from the sheer scale of what is involved. The Public Appointments Unit of the Cabinet Office states that there are 10,000 appointments made by ministers each year. On average, each minister, including Parliamentary Secretaries, would be making between 90 and 100 appointments a year if it was evenly spread. If there were proper procedures involving ministers, then much of their time would be involved interviewing suitable candidates. At other levels the problem is equally serious. All EGOs, as defined by Weir and Hall, involve 65,000–73,000 appointments. One has the impression that in, for example, Regional Health Authority appointments there is a desperate search for names, sometimes very much drawn from the chair's acquaintances. Such suggestions may or may not be correct. It is in the absence of clear publicly known procedures that one can not know whether or not there is substance in the allegations.

The growing criticism of the system of appointments is leading to attempts to improve procedures, most notably by the Welsh Office which has drawn up a register of appointments. Regional Health Authorities in England have been asked to advertise appointments. The appointments to the new Police Authorities are to be made through a procedure involving a request for nominees, scrutiny by a panel who prepare a long list for the Home Secretary from which he draws up a short list from which the councillor and magistrate members of the Police Authority make the final selection. While there are many questions to be raised about this procedure, it does show the recognition of the need for a reform of procedures. The issue is however much wider.

The flawed theory

It is often argued that the system of appointments brings to public service much needed business experience. This argument is suspect for two reasons. The first is that when one is considering the appointed bodies operating at local level, it is unlikely that the most effective businessmen will have the time or the readiness to play a major role. Indeed, there is some evidence that those making appointments have faced difficulty in obtaining the type of person that was wanted. A study of Training and Enterprise Councils found that the level of directors being appointed was falling below that intended and below that set by the original appointments.[5] The Department of Health set out to secure private sector businessmen from large undertakings. Its brochure at the 1989 CBI conference said 'if you have experience of large-scale organisations you will be particularly welcome'. In fact, another study found that: 'Just over half of the new health authority chairs and over one third of non-executive members hold company directorships, but less than one in twenty are in companies employing more than five hundred people.'[6] The first flaw in the theory lies in the failure to attract or retain the businessmen sought. It may well be that the dynamic and thrusting businessmen sought were too busy being dynamic and thrusting in their businesses to want to spend time on appointed boards.

In any event, it is at least open to question whether business experience is a useful experience in running certain public services. The task of an appointed board may well not be to manage a service but to make what can best be described as governmental decisions. Consider the role of the District Health Authority as recommended by the Audit Commission: 'The ultimate aim of commissioning is to improve the health of the population while increasing users' satisfaction with health services. Put fashionably, it is to achieve "health gain". Such a broad aim encompasses many specific outcomes, both for individuals and populations. Examples are: increased life expectancy for 70-year olds, reduction in avoidable deaths in those aged under 60, or improvement in the quality of life for sufferers from chronic diseases such as rheumatoid arthritis. Such objectives are unlikely to conflict with each other directly, but they will always be in competition for limited resources. It is therefore desirable that each DHA debate and clarify its underlying values so that its purchasing plans . . . reflect agreed strategic priorities. This process will be contentious and difficult, and it is doubtful whether the NHS is professionally, managerially or politically ready for it. But in the long run such clarity will be essential if real headway is to be made with the broad aims.'[7] The task is one of value judgement in relation to community needs, not the exercise of business skills. Of course, businessmen can have a contribution to make, but the danger is that they fail to realise the distinctiveness of public services, pointed out by William Waldegrave when Secretary of State for Health: 'Our "customers" do not come because the price of beans is less or because of the pretty girl in the advertisement; they come because they are ill, not seldom frightened, and they want help and expert care ... Without remitting for one moment the pressure to get a better management system, borrowing what is useful from business, let us watch our language a bit. It just bears saying straight out: the NHS is not a business; it is a public service and a great one.'[8] The danger is that because they have been appointed because of business experience, and because of the dominance of such appointments, the business appointees may not appreciate these points.

The issue of public accountability

The main issue raised by the growth of appointed boards at local level is the issue of public accountability. Those who exercise public power in society should be answerable for the exercise of that power. On that simple proposition rests the issue of accountability. The proposition itself is clear. In the public domain, substantive powers are exercised. Taxes are raised and expenditure incurred, constraints are imposed, and policies are developed which can affect the lives and welfare of citizens. Such powers are only justified if those who exercise them are answerable to the citizens concerned. The powers, it can be argued, do not belong to those who exercise them but belong to citizens on whose behalf they are exercised. That relationship is only justified if there is accountability. The need for accountability for public action is not disputed. What can be contested are the forms through which accountability is exercised. Accountability can be seen as involving giving an account for actions taken and being held to account for those actions. Both aspects are necessary to accountability. To hold to account needs an account of actions taken so that there is a basis for judgement. To give an account would by itself be inadequate unless there was a means of holding to account. The two aspects complement each other.[9]

Traditionally, the main means of holding to account have been the accountability of ministers through Parliament to the electorate and of local authorities to the electorate. The doctrine of ministerial accountability, which expresses that accountability at national level, is widely recognised as being under strain. The removal of responsibilities from local authorities to appointed boards places the principle as it relates to them under increased strain, putting on it a burden that it may not be able to bear. The only line of public accountability for the appointed boards is the long and often tortuous (through intermediate bodies) line of accountability to ministers. It is unrealistic to expect these to be accountable for the actions taken by the increasing number of appointed bodies. In any event, the appointed bodies considered here are those operating at local level. If it is accepted that people exercising public power or spending public money should be accountable to those on whose behalf they act, then these bodies should be accountable to local people. Yet there is no way that local people can hold a District Health Authority to account even if it is pursuing policies objected to by the great majority of local people.

Local authorities are not merely subject to election, they are subject to a wide range of statutory requirements which reinforce their account-ability. Some of these ensure that they give account of their activities or that the account of their actions can be subject to external scrutiny. Many of these requirements do not apply to appointed boards. Taking each of the provisions that apply to local authorities, the position can be summarised as follows. None of the members of these appointed bodies are liable to surcharge. Most of these bodies are not required to hold their meetings in public (the key exceptions being District Health Authorities and Family Health Service Authorities), and then only to full meetings. While these bodies are subject to the provisions of the Public Bodies Admission to Meetings Act 1960, they are not covered by the same extensions as local government in the Local Government (Access to Information) Act 1984. Health Service Trusts are required to hold one meeting a year in public. Most of these bodies are not subject to the same requirements of access to information as local authorities. Certain of these bodies (grant-maintained schools, Colleges of Further Education, and Training and Enterprise Councils) make their own arrangements for audit. The same bodies are not subject to the jurisdiction of ombudsmen and none of these bodies have monitoring officers with independent responsibility for financial and general probity.[10]

There are issues of concern, therefore, about the accountability of the appointed boards operating at local level. That these are not abstract concerns is shown by a report of the Public Accounts Committee which stated: 'In recent years we have seen and reported on a number of serious failures in administrative and financial systems and controls within departments and other public bodies, which have led to money being wasted or otherwise improperly spent. These failings represent a departure from the standards of public conduct which have mainly been established during the past 140 years.'[11] Problems arising out of the conduct of public business at the local level are not confined to appointed boards. There have been and will be problems arising in local authorities. There are, however, reasons to believe a higher proportion of the problems come to light in local authorities both because the accountability requirements are more rigorous and because on local authorities there is normally an opposition party which will seek to expose abuses. It is not just the problems relating to the conduct of public business however; it is, as already emphasised, the lack of local accountability for the policies pursued that is of concern. This can be of concern to the boards themselves.

So far this article has focused on the legal requirements. An appointed board can, if it chooses, go beyond those requirements. A study of appointed agencies and public accountability found considerable variation in practice. While some boards follow the letter of the law, others recognise the issue of public accountability and have taken what the authors describe as 'pro-active strategies' to meet that issue: 'Castle Vale Housing Action Trust board and sub-committee meetings are open to members of the public. As such, the minutes are also publicly available. But neither of these provisions are statutory obligations. If things start to go wrong there must always be the temptation, therefore, to retreat behind closed doors. As it currently operates, this HAT has been one of the more successful quangos if we use involvement of the local community in decision-making processes as a principal criterion. This sense of involvement, moreover, is fostered by a regular free door-to-door newsletter. It will shortly also be taking a unit in the shopping centre to further promote an 'open door' policy. In addition, a comprehensive register of board members' interests is publicly available, again not because of any statutory requirements but because this particular HAT has itself chosen to adopt such a practice.'[12] The authors of this study have drawn up a quango Charter and Code of Good Practice, drawing upon the best experience but lacking in many as their report shows.

This ten-point code of practice has been developed into a West Midlands Code of Good Practice by a Joint Committee representing the seven metropolitan districts, which has urged its adoption by appointed boards in the area.[13] The code comprises the following:

→ The agency should explain in a form available to the public the legislative background to its establishment, its formal status and remit, and the date on which it came into operation. A full list of board members and arrangements by which members can be contacted by the public should be published.

→ The public should be informed of how members of the agency are elected or appointed, by whom, with what selection criteria and for what period of tenure, and also how the chairman is appointed.

→ The dates and venues of meetings of the agency should be published in advance and, wherever practicable, meetings should be open to the media and public. Arrangements should be made to enable the public and media to access appropriate reports before as well as after the meeting.

↝ To ensure public accountability of financial matters, an understandable summary of annual accounts of the agency should be available to the media and public on request. Arrangements for the appointment of external auditors should be published.

→ The agency should adopt, publish and make available to the public a formal complaints procedure. In addition, the agency should publish an annual report on complaints received and dealt with.

- The agency should maintain a public register of the direct and indirect pecuniary interests of its board members, in the same way that local authorities maintain a register of interests of their elected members.
- The agency should publish an annual report outlining its achievements over the previous year and service targets for the future. This should be widely available to the public and media.
- The agency should consult with the relevant local authorities, community groups and other public agencies as appropriate in the discharge of its functions, and should annually publish its consultation arrangements.

The agency should nominate a Monitoring Officer whose duty it should be to ensure that the agency complies with the law. Such an officer shall have an independent right to report to the board of the agency on any possible breaches of law or financial irregularities. The agency should make available to the public such reports and decisions made thereon.

Some local authorities have taken action towards redressing the lack of accountability in appointed boards. A number are preparing public registers of these operating in their area with lists of their members. Stevenage District Council has set up a monitoring committee to keep its work under review. Kirklees Metropolitan District Council has set up scrutiny panels to examine issues of concern to local communities which can encompass their work. There is evidence that such developments will be welcomed by many if not all appointed boards. There have also been developments to strengthen the accountability of appointed boards operating at national level. This is in part a response to the cases highlighted by the Public Accounts Committee and in part a response to growing public concern over the issue of the accountability of the appointed boards. In the health service, following the West Midlands and Wessex Regional Health authority cases, a review of corporate governance was undertaken. The phrase corporate governance reflects the influence in that review of the Cadbury report on corporate governance in the private sector. As a result, the Department of Health now issues codes of conduct and accountability covering:

Clearer definitions of the functions of chairmen and non-executive board members which will form the basis of the appointment and induction processes.

Declaration by directors of NHS boards of private interests which are material and relevant to NHS business.

A requirement on NHS boards to establish audit and remuneration and terms of service committees.

A requirement that the standing orders of NHS boards should prescribe the terms on which committees and sub-committees of the board may hold delegated functions, including, where adopted, the schedule of decisions reserved for the board.

Clarification, by the NHS Management Executive, of the position on all financial constraints which apply to NHS authorities and Trusts.

In addition to the new codes, and in the light of the task force recommendations, the Secretary of State undertook measures to reinforce public service values in the health service:

A new obligation on health authorities to publish at least an annual report on their performance and stewardship of public finances (an annual report is already mandatory for NHS Trusts).

The publication, in annual reports, of the total remuneration from NHS sources of Chairmen, Executive board members and Non-Executive board members.

These changes, although important, do not of course meet the issue of accountability to local people but are more concerned with the procedures for accountability. The approach even to those issues is restricted by the influence of the Cadbury report which, while making an important contribution to the corporate governance of the private sector, does not necessarily cover the requirements of the public sector. Thus the Code of Practice for health authorities does not enhance open government by extending the access of the public to meetings. While requiring declarations of interest, there is no provision for making them public. Nor does it extend the scope of the Audit Commission or the National Audit Office. A review of corporate governance is also under way for Housing Associations, which, although voluntary bodies, are increasingly undertaking significant public responsibilities for social housing. A framework for local accountability for Training and Enterprise Councils has also been prepared covering key themes and is discussed by Alistair Graham in his article.

The issue of procedures to enhance accountability is being confronted in respect of the appointed bodies operating at local level. What remains unresolved, however, is the issue of the democratic deficit. William Waldegrave, when Chancellor of the Duchy of Lancaster, argued that the concern about the public accountability of appointed boards and the democratic deficit was misconceived. In a lecture on accountability in the public service, he said that there had been no weakening of public accountability because the basic accountability to Parliament remained unchanged: 'We have not in any way altered or undermined the basic structure of public service accountability to Parliament and hence to individual citizens.'[14] This statement ignores concerns about appointed boards taking over responsibilities from local authorities. The assumption that accountability to local authorities is not part of the basic structure of public service accountability and that accountability to Parliament is adequate for all local issues is a centralist view of our system of government. The heart of Waldegrave's argument is, however, that far from being weakened, accountability has been strengthened by making public services responsive to consumers. He welcomes Madsen Pirie's (of the Adam Smith Institute) contention that the key point 'is not whether those who run our public services are elected, but whether they are producer-responsive or consumer-responsive. Services are not necessarily made to respond to the public simply by giving citizens a democratic voice, and a distant and diffuse one at that, in their make-up. They *can* be made responsive by giving the public choice or by instituting mechanisms which build in publicly approved standards and redress when they are not attained.' In effect, Waldegrave's position is that the government has strengthened public accountability by 'making public services directly accountable to the customers'.

The fallacy in this argument is that responsiveness to the public as customers is seen as an alternative to accountability through elections, as though it was necessary to get rid of the latter to achieve the former. There is no need to choose between the two. There is no evidence that appointed boards provide services that are more responsive to their customers than local authorities. Indeed, many of the approaches set out in the Citizen's Charter advocated by Waldegrave were pioneered by local authorities. Service contracts specifying the standard of service to be supplied and the mechanisms for redress were pioneered by York, Islington and Lewisham amongst other authorities.

While there should be responsiveness to the user of the service, there has to be accountability to the electorate for the policy under which the service is provided. That policy necessarily sets the limits within which responsiveness will take place. It is thus wrong to believe that accountability to the customer can be a substitute for public accountability. It implies that the customer can state his or her requirement and hold those providing the service to account if they are not met, but in many services there is more than one customer whose requirements have to be balanced. Indeed, that is often the reason why the services are in the public domain. Many public services are provided free at the point of use and as a result have to be rationed, and the customer may therefore be refused a service or required to wait for a considerable period of time. In these circumstances, accountability to the customer is meaningless. Certainly, the customer should be treated with respect and the position properly explained, but those who provide the service are accountable to the wider community for the policy on which the service is allocated. In other instances, as with a planning application, decisions have to be made between different individuals and organisations. Or again, 'customers' will be instructed to take certain action, may be prosecuted or even imprisoned. Action is being taken for the community at large to whom accountability lies.

Proposals for reform

This article will concentrate on two distinct sets of reform proposals related to the issues raised earlier. The first maintains the basis for appointed boards but seeks to reform the procedures governing them; the second seeks to replace appointment by some form of directly elected control.

Proposals for reform of the procedures governing appointed boards can cover the system of appointments itself. They include proposals for publicly available registers of those appointed, setting out their names, their residence or where they can be contacted, level of payment if applicable and their membership, if any, of political parties. There could be a national register but also local registers for appointed boards operating at local level. It can be argued that the public are entitled to know such information about those who play a significant part in the government of their area. Procedures can be laid down for making appointments, whether by central government, intermediate bodies or self-appointing bodies. These would cover advertisements, standard application forms, references, interviews and observance of equal opportunities. They should be publicly known. In addition, provision can be made for external scrutiny of appointments before appointments are confirmed. This task could be undertaken by a select committee of the House of Commons at national level or by an equivalent committee of a local authority for local appointments. An alternative would be scrutiny by an independent (admittedly itself an appointed body) scrutiny board.

A code of practice could be introduced governing the procedures for accountability of appointed bodies, governing such issues as liability to surcharge; open meetings; access of the public to information; provisions for independently appointed audit; access to ombudsmen; declarations of interest; appointment of monitoring officers. Some but not all of these issues are being covered in the reviews of corporate governance and accountability mentioned earlier, but what is suggested here is a national code of practice applicable to all appointed bodies, except where a specific case is made for exemption. An additional reform would be to give local authorities powers to obtain information about the activities of appointed boards operating at local level and/or a duty to subject their activities to public scrutiny. While this would not ensure the bodies could be held to account, it would provide for their accounts, in the widest sense of the term, to be subject to local public scrutiny. Such a proposal raises issues about the accountability of local authorities and the need to strengthen that accountability given, for example, the relatively low turnout in local elections.

Clearly, the bodies governed by appointed boards differ substantially in their powers and role. The extent to which they should be subject to local democratic control and the form it should take can vary from body to body and a programme of reform would require a case by case analysis. Even where it is considered that local democratic control through elections is desirable, it can be achieved by making the local authority responsible for its activities or through separate elections. The main criterion to determine the need for local democratic control is that where an appointed body has a significant responsibility for determining local policy — albeit within a framework of national policy—then it should be subject to some form of local democratic control. The case becomes stronger where those choices involve values rather than technical considerations. The application of the criterion necessarily involves judgement of the significance of local choice. The significance of local choice is not reduced by the existence of a national framework within which local bodies act. Local authorities themselves operate within a national framework of legislation and regulation for which ministers are accountable to Parliament, while local authorities are accountable to the electorate for their decisions within that framework. Where an appointed body is merely administering national policy, it would be inappropriate for it to be accountable at local level—although it is not clear why a layer of appointees is required in such circumstances.[15] Where it is decided that the activities of a body should be made the responsibility of the local authority, it does not follow that responsibility should be exercised through the traditional working of the committee system. Local authorities have learnt to work in different ways: through contracts or through hands-off organisations. For example, they could take over the purchasing role of the District Health Authority, controlling Trusts through contracts.

Proposals for the reform of appointed bodies have been put forward by the Association of Metropolitan authorities in a discussion document entitled *Changing the Face of Quangos.* It set out a programme of reform covering the procedural issues already discussed but also recommended that 'The electoral process should be introduced into local government wherever possible. Those who hold public office should be elected to it, and removable from it by the public.'[16] Amongst their proposals are:

That the functions of District Health Authorities should be taken into local government.

That Health Service Trusts should be reformed so that membership of their boards is opened up with the non-executive membership, including elected members from the local authority and representatives of local GPs and Trust employees.

That grant-maintained and City Technology College status should be abolished and the schools returned to LEA control.

That Training and Enterprise Councils should be required to work within a policy framework established by the local authority in partnership with other local organisations; appointments to the TEC board should be made by the local authorities for the area concerned in consultation with the local business community, including the Chamber of Commerce. Where TEC membership is sufficiently broad to be genuinely representative of private sector interests, then that membership could elect the private sector nominees.

That Urban Development Corporations should be allowed to wind down, but, in the meantime, should be given a statutory duty to work in partnership with the local authority. Half of the places on the UDC board should be reserved for local government appointment.

These proposals are of course from an organisation committed to local democratic control. They are unlikely to receive support from the present government although the main opposition parties are committed to increase democratic control over quangos at local and regional level. The Conservative government has itself recognised the need to review the procedures governing appointed boards exercising public responsibilities whether at local or national level.

Conclusion

The main growth under the Conservative government in what are called quangos has been at local level, often at the expense of local authorities. Because it has happened step by step it is only recently that the full extent of this development has been appreciated. Amongst the issues raised by this development are the fragmentation of the system of local government and the method of appointment, aggravated by the number of appointments now required and by the growth of self-appointing bodies exercising public functions. The key issue raised is, however, that of public accountability. There are two sets of issues about public accountability. The first is about the ability, or rather the lack of ability, of local people to hold such bodies to account and leads to proposals for bringing them under some form of local democratic control. The second is about the limited procedures for ensuring accountability and leads to proposals for strengthening those procedures — possibly through a national code of practice. Whether such proposals are pursued or not, what is clear is the importance of appointed boards at local level as a part of the system of local governance as a field meriting continued study and research.

1   S. Weir and W. Hall, *Ego Trip*, Public Finance Foundatin, 1994.
2   A. Grier and P. Hoggett, *The Nature and Impact of Non-Elected Bodies on Local Governance*, Commission on Local Democracy, 1994.
3   G. Howarth, *Quangos and Political Donations to the Tory Party*, Knowsley North Constituency Labour Party, 1993.
4   K. Morgan and E. Roberts, *The Democratic Deficit: A Guide to Quangoland*, University of Wales, 1993.
5   R. Bennett, P. Wicks and A. McCoshan, *Local Empowerment and Business Services*, UCL Press, 1994.
6   L. Ashburner and L. Cairncross, 'Membership of the New Style Health Authorities', *Public Administration*, 1993.
7   Audit Commission, *Their Health, Your Business: The New Role of the District Health Authority*, HMSO, 1993.
8   W. Waldegrave, *The Trafford Memorial Lecture*, 1991.
9   See J. Stewart, *Accountability to the Public*, European Policy Forum, 1992.
10 See H. Davis and J. Stewart, *The Growth of Government by Appointment*, Local Government Management Board, 1993.
11 Public Accounts Committee, *The Proper Conduct of Public Business*, HMSO, 1994.
12 C. Painter, K. Isaac-Henry and T. Chalcroft, *Appointed Agencies and Public Accountability*, West Midlands Joint Committee, 1994.
13 West Midlands Joint Committee, *West Midlands Code of Practice*, WMJC, 1994.

14   W. Waldegrave, *The Reality of Reform and Accountability in Today's Public Service*, Public Finance
       Foundation, 1993.
15   See J. Stewart, *Reforming the New Magistracy*, Commission for Local Democracy, 1994.
16   Association of Metropolitan Authorities (1994), *Changing the Face of Quangos*, AMA.

London Docklands and
Urban Development Corporations

BY ERIC SORENSEN

THE setting up of the twelve Urban Development Corporations in England falls into three distinct phases. In the first phase two UDCs — London Docklands and Merseyside — were conceived in the late 1970s by Conservative Party shadow ministers before the party won power in 1979. They were a priority for the new government and were operating by the summer of 1981. There was then a gap of several years before Nicholas Ridley as Secretary of State for the Environment (1986–1989) set up a further four (Tyne and Wear, Teeside, Black Country and Trafford Park) in 1987. These were soon followed by four smaller ones in 1988/9 (Leeds, Sheffield, Bristol and Central Manchester), and a final two smaller ones in 1992/3 (Birmingham Heartlands and Plymouth). A clear pattern can be traced in the use of this particular piece of urban regeneration machinery. In the case of London and Merseyside the large areas designated as UDCs were redundant disused docklands with little sign of effective programmes to bring them back to life. There was no dispute that government financial intervention on a massive scale would be required to revive these areas. The argument was about the best form of local implementation machinery to run such a regeneration programme, and about what kind of investment ought to be promoted and supported. Even so, there were differences between London and Merseyside. In London the local authorities were strongly opposed to the use of UDC machinery because there was already the municipally-run Docklands Joint Committee (DJC) in place. For the DJC to be replaced by a quango was more than the local authorities could stand. In Merseyside there was little such dispute since no one lived in the redundant docklands areas. There was no existing regeneration programme, and greater importance was attached locally to the government funding for land reclamation and infrastructure which would accompany the setting up of a UDC. The setting up of a UDC requires the government to promote a Parliamentary Order under the Local Government Planning and Land Act 1980. This gives the opportunity for local authorities and others to petition Parliament against the making of the Order and, if Parliament judges that the petitions ought to be heard before a committee, parliamentary hearings would then follow. No such petitions were pursued in the case of Merseyside, nor for any of the later UDCs. In the London case, however, the parliamentary proceedings were intense and time-consuming, ending with clear committee support for the government's London Docklands designation proposals.

The 1987 round of four UDCs reflected both the government's growing interest in urban regeneration in the mid-1980s together with an increasing concern about the quality and ability of local authorities to deliver major programmes and involve other partners, especially the private sector. There was a growing trend to limit the expansion of local government responsibilities, and indeed to reduce them. Even so, the more dominant issue was the scale of the economic problems faced by Tyne and Wear, Teeside, Black Country and Trafford Park following the decline of traditional industries. Each of the four areas span different local authorities and there was no precedent for successful local authority led partnerships to implement regeneration programmes on this scale.

The third tranche of UDCs in 1988 — Sheffield, Leeds, Bristol and Central Manchester, together with Birmingham Heartlands and Plymouth a few years later — were clearly different in that the areas were relatively small — a few hundred rather than several thousand acres — and were contained within one local authority district. The modest scale compared with the previous UDCs and the less complex local authority picture makes the case for direct government intervention through UDC machinery that much less strong. What these designations clearly reflected was not only the wish to promote economic regeneration in a single minded way but also the lack of confidence felt by central government in local authorities' commitment and ability to draw in private-sector partners. There is no doubt, however, that UDC machinery was conceived to deal with relatively large areas of physical and economic decline, and dereliction. Such areas require substantial up-front public expenditure to kick-start the regeneration process. It should be relatively easy to achieve a degree of bipartisan spirit when such large areas are being tackled. As the UDC areas become significantly smaller, the centralist/localist arguments become sharper.

When inventing the UDC concept, the government had the advantage that a bipartisan model already existed in the New Town Development Corporation, and the legislation in the Local Government Planning and Land Act 1980 is modelled on the New Towns Acts. Not only that, there was increasing concern about the impact of population and job movement out of the inner cities in favour of the New Towns and the suburbs. The decline in population and the large scale dereliction in many cities did not make it difficult for the government to turn the New Town experiment on its head, using the administrative model represented by the New Town Development Corporation to encourage population and business to stay and grow within those cities. There were, however, important differences. Unlike the New Towns, UDCs are not developers. By assembling land, servicing it, improving transport links, they are required to attract investment. The concept of leverage —

attracting several times the value of private sector investment for a given level of public-sector pump priming—and the emphasis on developing partnerships and are central to the UDC concept. UDCs are also transient organisations with limited lives, organisations which are therefore in a hurry to achieve outputs.

The London experience

The story of regenerating London Docklands best illustrates the particular contribution of a UDC and the issues associated with this regeneration model. The Docklands experience has been one of three different regeneration models which have been tried over many years. The Port of London began to be developed in its modern form in the early 19th century. The first major enclosed dock was built in about 1800 and the last in 1925. Even as late as the early 1960s, the Port of London as a whole was handling record tonnage, but technological change began to threaten the very future of this vast area so essential to the economic life of East London. Containerisation, road traffic congestion, increasing frustration about industrial relations and working practices all combined to encourage the growth of Tilbury further down river as London's main port. The upper docks, stretching eight miles from St Katherines near the Tower of London, to the Royal Docks in Newham on the north of the river, together with the warehouses and other docks on the south of the river, rapidly and progressively closed in the period 1965–1980. It is difficult to exaggerate the economic and social trauma following the loss so quickly of two hundred years of business and social traditions for that large part of East London. It became clear in the late 1960s that the traditional port areas would not survive, and the incoming Conservative government of 1970 did what any government of that time would have done: it set up a study to advise how best to plan the future of Docklands. It could have asked the Greater London Council, set up in 1965, to prepare a plan, but the GLC was enmeshed in a massive public inquiry to consider their own strategic plan for London. Also, the London boroughs were not enthusiastic about the GLC interfering in their boroughs. This impasse was broken by direct government intervention and the appointment of Travers Morgan as consultants who carried out a two year elaborate study exploring the strategic development options for the area. A number of different strategies were offered. These included the East End Consolidated Model which acknowledged the social and economic roots of the area and proposed fostering blue-collar manual work with an emphasis on council housing. A second strategy was to turn the area into a vast recreation area with new parks exploiting the waterscape and related opportunities. A third was to encourage new businesses to invest in the area and to improve the variety of housing and other amenities and facilities. This exercise by Travers Morgan relied heavily on expert input from those experienced in the relevant fields but there was no elaborate attempt to consult with local authorities or with local communities.

The local authorities reacted strongly to their lack of involvement and were also very concerned about some of the strategic options proposed by Travers Morgan. They therefore successfully prevailed on the government to set up instead a municipally-based exercise to plan the area. Almost the last act of the 1970–1974 Conservative administration was the creation of the Docklands Joint Committee in January 1974. This committee, charged with proposing a new strategy, included the Greater London Council and the five London boroughs (Tower Hamlets, Newham, Southwark, Greenwich and Lewisham) most concerned with the traditional docklands area.

The DJC went about the work of devising an economic and development strategy for the area very differently from that of the consultants. There was widespread and intensive consultation with local communities and the aim was to achieve consensus about what should be done. Inevitably, such a consensus is likely to be formed around the traditions of an area and to coalesce around the familiar. Also, there was heavy emphasis on the needs of the area, rather than how best to create investment opportunities. Community activists, many of whom moved to the area as it became clear that Docklands was in transition, helped to foster the view that home ownership and private capital investment were inimical to people's interests. So it was that in July 1976 the DJC published a preferred strategy which emphasised public investment rather than private investment, the fostering of blue-collar job opportunities, retention of the port even though it was obvious that it was in severe economic difficulty in the up-river docks, and proposed council housing as the main social instrument, disregarding the powerful trend towards home ownership elsewhere within the country. This strategic programme was to be supported by very substantial government funding for roads, tunnels and other key infrastructure, as well as a large council housing programme.

Looking back on the DJC strategic approach, it is difficult to see how it could have had any real hope of success. Clearly, Docklands badly needed better infrastructure and much improvement to transport links. The core strategy, however, was based on fostering industrial sectors which were in structural decline and on sustaining a port at a time when the Port Authority had sought to speed up the upper docks closure in 1975 but had been persuaded by the government to delay doing so. It can only be concluded that the key dominant business force in the area had little faith in one of the key strategic tenets of the DJC strategy. The emphasis on council housing for an area which was already dominated by such housing (95% of dwellings in 1979 were in social ownership in Docklands) meant that a key social and economic trend in the country — the growth of owner-occupation — was simply ignored. This would inevitably encourage the damaging trend that those who aspired to home ownership and could afford to do so would move out of the area to seek their fortune elsewhere where there was choice and diversity in the housing stock. The DJC approach would inevitably result in an uncertain local job market for low-income tenants. It seemed to regard Docklands as a place largely dependent on public expenditure and as having little connection with the rest of London. It was an insular, inward looking strategy reflecting the views of local authorities who set limits to their horizons either deliberately or, more likely, because their mind-set prevented them from holding bigger and broader ambitions for their people.

Most damaging of all to the DJC strategy, but also reflecting simple bad luck, the government whilst appearing to support the strategy refused to fund it. It would have been highly unusual for the government to support a local authority joint committee with substantial funds in the way proposed, but it might well have been possible to devise realistic funding arrangements given the role of the Greater London Council in the Docklands Joint Committee with its strategic planning capacity and substantial resources from its own wide tax base. But whether or not the government would have been prepared to go down this novel route it was having to fight very difficult economic battles of its own. In July 1976 at just about the time that the DJC's final report was formally presented to it, it was itself engaged in very complex and difficult discussions with the International Monetary Fund. Not only was there the practical issue of the form in which the IMF might offer support to the government, there was also a fierce strategic political discussion within the government itself about what sort of economic strategy ought to be followed and whether the free trade traditions of the country ought to be replaced by a more protectionist approach.

So it was that the large ambitions of the DJC were killed by lack of government funding. It might have been better if the DJC could have demonstrated that in return for such funding a substantial number of new businesses and jobs would be attracted to the area. But it was extremely difficult to see how port and port-related activity and the supposed promotion of blue-collar job opportunities could offer a sound basis for Docklands' economic revival. The government published its own pathfinding 'Policy for the Inner Cities' White Paper in June 1977. This emphasised the quality and vibrancy of local economies as the key factor, emphasised the importance of attracting private-sector investment and the need to set up partnerships with the private sector and others. The White Paper set out a very different vision from the backward looking DJC strategy.

Nevertheless, with the modest financial support that the DJC was able to win from government and with a reordering of the municipalities' own priorities, some progress was made. Some docks were filled in, marshy areas near the docks were drained and prepared for development, some housing was constructed and one or two businesses were attracted to the area. Overall, however, in the period 1976–1980 the central flaws in the municipally based DJC model were revealed.

The growing concern about Docklands' future from the later 1960s was based on doubts about the quality and adaptability of the local economy. The fundamental problem was local economic failure, with the symptoms of business closure, job losses, population decline, derelict land and buildings. Since it is a fair bet that a change of strategic approach was necessary, a strategy which offered more of the same was almost bound to be wrong. How could such a self-defeating economic strategy have been devised? It could be that the short-sightedness of local councillors fearful of change was to blame. This is difficult if not impossible to prove. Perhaps a better way of expressing it is that councillors who were committed to the area, proud of their local roots, well aware of the two hundred years history of the port in the upper docks, were determined to fight for the economic and social heritage of the area. This is certainly praiseworthy, though it does seem to illustrate Canute-like tendencies and to ignore fundamental economic trends. The widespread consultation process underpinning the DJC strategy no doubt reinforced the conservatism of the municipal leadership and led them to concentrate on the immediate concerns of their constituents, such as better council housing, rather than promoting a wider and more ambitious economic and social vision. A successful area-based regeneration strategy requires cross-departmental analysis and implementation arrangements which both local authorities and central government departments have found difficult to set in train. Separate professionally-led departments do not easily come together to create a more rounded or holistic view and to sink their differences in a common cause.

A further fundamental difficulty faced by the DJC with its wide span of five London boroughs, together with the GLC, was the decision-making process itself. Though there were arrangements to give a core group delegated authority to make decisions, these worked poorly in practice. Decision-making processes were inherently slow and uncertain. Community groups and activists also encouraged resistance to change, stirred up fear that new infrastructure investment would mean less investment for other purposes, and fomented ideologically based opposition to capitalist entrepreneurship and home ownership.

The DJC's coalition of local authority interests provided an uneasy background for taking clear investment decisions and for presenting to investors a confident vision. A fundamental difficulty was that the DJC could not come to clear arrangements on the purchase of land from existing owners. There were particular difficulties with Port of London Authority land, and the Port was by far the largest single landowner within the Docklands area with some 2185 acres. The PLA did not have the resources to invest in pump-priming infrastructure development in order to attract developers and businesses. On the other hand, it had little incentive to sell land at all, and was extremely reluctant to sell at prices it judged did not reflect the development potential of the area. In turn, the authorities comprising the DJC did not have sufficient clarity in their powers or sufficient resources in order to break this log jam. The result was that only three or four acres of redundant PLA land were acquired by the DJC in seven years to foster the regeneration process. This was by far the most frustrating part of the DJC exercise and illustrated the consequences of the lack of clear-sighted strategy and powers to support the regeneration process.

It was these issues — the backward looking strategy, the unwieldy and slow decision making processes, the lack of powers and resources — which combined to cause a loss of credibility in the DJC. It was gradually overwhelmed by the economic changes in the area, without sufficient government support and efficient and dynamic arrangements to deliver a good strategy. Businesses gave up in disgust and moved away. In the period 1976–1981 hundreds of businesses either collapsed or moved away from London Docklands until there were only about a thousand left in 1981. The number of jobs in the area declined to 27,000 (1981) and was on a strong falling trend when the LDDC was set up. Local people, dispirited by the closing of the upper docks and by the lack of any other regeneration activity, moved away and the local population fell from 56,000 in 1976 to 39,000 in 1981. New council estates rapidly became hard to let, partly reflecting their poor, brutal design and partly the fact that there was little incentive to go and live in Docklands despite housing pressures not far away in the rest of London.

The LDDC was formally established in July 1981, covering 5,000 acres of largely redundant port land and docks. It is worth stressing how limited the powers of UDCs are compared with the very wide ranging local authority powers and responsibilities. Though UDCs are given the statutory responsibility of regenerating their areas, and though the definition of 'regeneration' is necessarily imprecise, in practice it is clear that they are land and development oriented. They are not statutory housing authorities, nor highway authorities. They have no responsibilities for education or social services, and all these and the day-to-day consumer services such as emptying dustbins and cleaning streets remain with the local authorities. Only one statutory responsibility — development control — has been transferred from the relevant local authorities to the UDCs. Thus those seeking planning permission within its area apply not to the local authority but to the UDC. Plan making powers such as drawing up Unitary Development Plans remain with the local authority. The idea, therefore, that the setting up of a UDC represents a wholesale takeover of local authority powers or a removal of democratic accountability within the UDC area is very far indeed from the truth.

The UDC derives influence from the fact that it is often, though by no means always, a major landowner within its area. In London and Merseyside, for example, a half or more of the land area came into the ownership of the respective UDCs through purchase of redundant docklands from the Port Authority. Much of that land, however, could not be put into good use and developed without prior substantial expenditure on transport and other infrastructure.

In addition to land ownership and the power of development control, UDAs have access to government grant aid, mainly used to acquire land, service it, and to provide transport and other infrastructure. In its essentials, therefore, a UDC spending programme is a relatively narrowly based one, though the outputs, particularly diverse housing investment, new businesses, new jobs, community facilities and a much improved local environment, are fundamental to broad based economic regeneration and social cohesion. With the major exception of the education service the local authority role within a UDC is a social welfare and regulatory one, and that of the UDC is regenerative.

The setting up of the LDDC did of course offer the local authorities the opportunity for a new regeneration partnership with government. The beginning of the 1980s, however, coincided with radical change in London local government, and the new generation of councillors elected in the London elections in May 1982 had a very different political agenda from that of Mrs Thatcher's government. This led to a breakdown in relations between LDDC and the London boroughs of Newham, Southwark and Tower Hamlets as the three local authorities with which the LDDC had to work constructively. The breakdown was symbolised by the refusal of the local authorities to nominate members of the LDDC board and by a policy of non-cooperation promulgated by councillors to their officers. This led to sometimes farcical procedures whereby LDDC staff and council officers had to meet in secret lest their day-to-day discussions on practical issues were discovered by the council staff's political masters.

The diversion of view between the LDDC and local authorities in the first half of the 1980s was further indicated by very different views about local planning of Docklands' areas. The LDDC published and consulted on development frameworks which informed the community about development proposals and which guided developers about its aspirations. In essence, the difference of view expressed in the frameworks on the one hand and the local authorities' local plans on the other mirrored the long-standing discussion about the strategic future of the Docklands area: should it capitalise on its port-related and manual-work heritage, with a strong emphasis on council housing, or did the future lie in trying to attract businesses in the growing sectors with greater emphasis on white-collar work and much greater housing diversity. Those two strategic options have been at issue for most of the LDDC's life.

In recent years, fortunately, there has been a growing together of the local authority and LDDC approaches and there is now a much greater commitment to partnership than there was in the early years. Partly, this reflects a growing community-oriented and training programme being promulgated by the LDDC. Partly, it reflects a recognition by the local authorities of what surely is the most hopeful strategic future for the area, one where it is essential to capitalise on growing business sectors and to bring Docklands more into the London mainstream. There is now a more obviously shared joint approach on strategic investment issues in East London, such as the Channel Tunnel Rail Link and London Transport's new Underground line—the Jubilee Line Extension.

The LDDC itself has changed through its life, trying to adapt to new issues and pressures as they emerge. The organisation has always been determinedly market oriented, willing to strike deals with all those wishing to invest in the area as long as they contributed to the broad economic and social vision. Some parameters were however fixed. For example, and in contrast to the 1970s when the local authorities and the PLA began to fill in the docks, the docks were safeguarded to capitalise on the magnificent water environment that they offered. There would be increased public access to the riverside. There would be no rigid land use zoning, though clearly some areas lent themselves to one sort of activity rather than others. For example, the 480 acres Enterprise Zone created in the northern half of the Isle of Dogs and lasting from 1982 to 1992 necessarily attracted commercial and industrial investment but not housing, which did not benefit from the tax allowances and other benefits associated with Enterprise Zone investment.

Opening up the area and making it accessible was a fundamental priority but in the early years development aspirations were relatively modest. Road proposals were on a relatively small scale and the major public transport initiative was a low capacity light railway, largely brought into being by using existing redundant railway track, supported by much improved bus services. Private house builders were reluctantly persuaded to invest in the area and they found a ready market for their projects. By the beginning of 1994, over 17,000 new homes had been built and owner occupation has risen from 5% to 45% of Docklands households.

The LDDC has also had its share of good luck. Just at the time it was getting going, radical improvements in newspaper printing technology were coming on stream. Many newspaper publishing groups finally decided to leave their traditional Fleet Street home and build new printing plants elsewhere. Docklands secured no less than five large plants, not only bringing jobs to the area but more importantly attracting a wide range of media-related businesses.

It was, however, the explosion in the London office market which has changed forever the heart of Docklands represented by the Isle of Dogs Enterprise Zone. Business expectations fuelled by GDP growth, financial services deregulation, much increased trading in financial instruments, the willingness of banks to lend to support development, all contributed to a massive growth in office development. There was fierce competition between the City of London and Docklands for offices and white-collar businesses and this led to massive over-supply. Fortunately, the market has now stabilised, and whereas a few years ago it was very difficult to see how vacant office space would ever be taken up, the trends are now very encouraging.

What seems clear, however, is that the market-led approach of the LDDC, which welcomed the massive growth of office accommodation in the later 1980s, would no doubt have met a barrage of planning restrictions under a municipal non-Enterprise Zone regime. Clearly, the office building excesses of the later 1980s and early 1990s would have been avoided; but for the medium and longer term Docklands now has an employment base which is much sounder and much more integrated with the rest of London than would otherwise have been the case. What is also insufficiently recognised is the contribution which the massive 5.5 million sq ft Canary Wharf development made to improvement in East London's infrastructure. Without the commitment of that development, the government would not have been persuaded to fund the long planned improvements in road schemes through Docklands. Without such road improvements, development on any significant scale throughout the area would have been blocked. Similarly, it was Olympia and York's (the Canary Wharf developers) willingness to fund a part of the cost of the Jubilee Line Extension which has finally enabled this long planned Underground line serving south and east London to be built. As in many other areas, part of the recent history of East London has been a succession of plans for infrastructure improvement which came to nothing. To those who casually comment that one of the failings in the London Docklands Development process has been lack of integration between infrastructure provision on the one hand and development provision on the other, one answer is to invite them to consider the paradox that it was only when the private sector committed this major development that the public authorities were prepared to release funds for infrastructure.

A central part of the regeneration debate is about how to ensure that the people benefit. Clearly, regeneration is not just for financiers and developers. It must also be for those who work in local businesses and those who live in the local communities. In a rapidly growing area such as Docklands there are, of course, new communities being created which need to be fostered and supported. The existing local community can not legitimately exercise a veto. It is inevitably a long-term programme to change expectations of communities as the job market changes. Though most of the increase in jobs in Docklands (from 27,000 in 1981 to 65,000 in 1995) has been in white-collar employment, the numbers employed in manufacturing industry are now higher than they were in the mid-1970s.

To help people's prospects, the LDDC has increasingly worked with local authorities and with Training and Enterprise Councils on training schemes to build bridges between local residents and local employment opportunities. More fundamentally, the LDDC has assisted in the investment of new and better schools as part of this long-term aim. The argument that UDCs cannot be sensitive to the needs and aspirations of local communities simply ignores the substantial commitment to better education and training, to primary health and community facilities, to improve local transport, and to housing and the local environment which the regeneration has brought.

Conclusion

A central paradox is that if Docklands regeneration were going to be successful, then, given the fact that the port with all that entailed in terms of job opportunities and conditions was moving downstream, there had to be a break with the past. Local authorities, however, who are led by representatives of the existing community, are not necessarily well placed to make that break. To try, however, to maintain ways of life and job aspirations based on economic history would have been an exercise in sentimentality, not regeneration. This issue has been particularly sharp in the East End where among communities there is a very powerful social tradition, a strong conservatism and a feeling of separateness from the rest of London. It seems inevitable, therefore, that some other organisation had to be brought in to help bring a different strategy and vision for the area. This, it should be stressed, is not to argue that the DJC strategy was wrong and that the LDDC has been right. The point is more of a comment on the ability of the local authorities as institutions to introduce required radical change on a combined and radical scale. The East London local authorities at the relevant time were diverging from national trends and concepts about how such large-scale regeneration should be tackled. While national governments, both Labour and then Conservative, talked the language of economic regeneration, private sector involvement, and partnership, such concepts found little favour amongst the Docklands local authorities. This was clearly one of the reasons why there was little commitment in central government to funding a consortium of local authorities on a sufficient scale to begin to tackle the massive programme of land assembly, reclamation and infrastructure investment. Not only that, there were no precedents for central/local cooperation on this scale, and often the way forward for central government in dealing with such regeneration and development issues has been to establish special implementation machinery. The Greater London Council could have been the strategic and powerful vehicle, with the necessary capacity to use such funds, but that authority was diverted by the GLDP and had its own problems in gaining acceptability with the London boroughs.

By the beginning of the 1980s decade, people were cynical and disillusioned by the ten years of non-success in regenerating Docklands.

There was no credibility in the market or any shared vision. Decision making had been very slow as the local authorities worked on issues through their own procedures and, worse, fought amongst themselves for the location of specific investment. Large-scale fundamental issues such as land reclamation could not be resolved satisfactorily. For Docklands, and for the other large UDCs, activity on a scale sufficient to match the issues and problems facing these areas was fundamental to success. There had to be very considerable pump priming investment, far beyond the typical London borough programme, to make any beneficial impact on the area at all. Such an infrastructure drive had to have sufficient momentum across the years in order to maintain credibility with Whitehall as the ultimate paymasters whether of local authorities or UDCs.

There is a regeneration model often put forward by community activists which professes to be community-based, sensitive to the traditions of an area, incremental, and one which promotes change at a pace which people will readily accept. It is difficult to see how such a model had any relevance to the large-scale economic failure and dereliction faced by everyone in Docklands. Examples of such community working in practice are very difficult to find. The model seems to be based on a wariness of both central and local government, even though those institutions hold the cash and have planning and implementation capacity. One way forward has been demonstrated by the City Challenge partnerships set up in recent years with government funding support to lever in investment and jobs. Leadership is not through the local authority but the authority has a very substantial part to play and its cooperation is essential. The scope of such exercises, however, is limited and the time scales are short: significant progress has to be made over a three or five year period.

In 1980 the Docklands Joint Committee and the London Docklands Development Corporation probably represented the two extremes of approach towards a large-scale economic regeneration issues. In more recent times there has been a coming together of approach represented by a shared recognition of the need for investment, new businesses and jobs, the importance of the market, the hard fight for public expenditure resources and therefore the need to create and maintain credibility, formal partnerships and shared endeavour. There are problems inherent in the UDC concept. They are transient, whereas large-scale mixed use regeneration projects take twenty years or more to come to fruition. Whilst the short life of a UDC helps to provide momentum, focus and urgency, and this seems to tune in better with the private sector timescales and horizons, it is clear that, as the UDC programme closes down, there will be much unfinished business in their regeneration areas. Making a good fist of that is the next challenge.

Housing Action Trusts: a Possible Role Model?

BY JOHN CHUMROW

HOUSING Action Trusts (HATs) are Non Departmental Public Bodies (NDPBs) set up as one of a series of government initiatives to address problems of poor housing and economic decay in urban areas. They were first proposed in a Department of the Environment (DOE) Consultation Document in 1987. There are now six in operation, the first of which is expected to complete its work in 1998 and wind itself up shortly afterwards; the remainder will continue until well into the first decade of the next century. This article covers the background to the setting up of HATs and their history to date: sets out the arguments for and against their establishment; and, as they are NDPBs or Quangos, proposes on the basis of their performance so far that they are democratic and accountable and could well serve as a role model for local authorities and other organisations set up to deal with similar problems.

Background

The intention behind the Trusts was listed in Clause 60(5) of the 1988 Housing Bill; the role of each HAT was to 'carry out a major programme of renovation, in consultation with the residents, bring empty council properties back into use, improve the way estates are looked after and generally help improve the economic, environmental and social condition of the area'. The task before the HATs reflected the cumulative problems arising from the construction processes involved in, and the quality of, social housing after the second world war. Local authorities had succeeded between the end of the war and 1980 in building a massive 4.5m units of social housing, eliminating the worst slums and helping to house many other families and those in need. Between 1955 and 1975, many of the current estates were built. High rise (classed as five storeys or more, sometimes more than 20 storeys) was the preferred structure initially, but attitudes changed after the explosion at Ronan Point in 1968. Medium rise blocks then became the favoured development, mainly of large panel construction (LPC), with common access through a walkway on each storey. The laudable aim was the elimination of traffic, but the walkway became an ideal means of burglary and escape for those tempted by the easy access.

At first the new blocks were judged favourably. The flats themselves were light and spacious, centrally heated with modern amenities, a distinct improvement on traditional terraced housing with sculleries, tin baths in the living room, freezing bedrooms and inadequate provision

© Oxford University Press

for repairs. The new blocks, however, suffered from faulty or minimal design; walls were of thin concrete, sometimes fast-setting to the detriment of durability, and roofs were usually flat with consequent problems of water ingress; heating systems often broke down; lifts were frequently out of action; sound insulation was poor. High rise and medium rise flats were often used for families with young children which created problems of wear and tear, vandalism and neighbourhood disputes. In many cases local authorities found it more and more difficult to manage the estates adequately and reserve the necessary revenue to confront the growing problems stemming from the original design and use of poor materials.

Speed had been the essence of the whole building programme. There had been no consultation with the tenants who were to be its beneficiaries. Already in 1974 the DOE recognised that most city authorities had at least three estates which were difficult to let, mainly the newest and largest, because of the physical structure, social composition and difficulties in management; local authorities, however, had no choice but to rehouse their most disadvantaged tenants on unpopular estates with ethnic minorities disproportionately affected. The general riots in Brixton and Toxteth and at Broadwater Farm estate in Haringey in the 1980s showed the inherent dangers arising from inner-city problems such as poor housing and economic deprivation; consideration was given to remedial action. Amongst a number of initiatives, the government launched an ambitious programme of estate renewal in 1985, known from 1987 as Estate Action, to address some facets of these problems. Fifty of the most difficult urban areas were targeted and an initial capital sum of £50m set aside to resolve principally major housing issues. Even though the allocation had grown sharply to £270m by 1991, it was spread over 350 schemes. Moreover, local authorities claimed the money had been taken from their capital allocations for housing and did not constitute additional finance.

Although Estate Action money was able to alleviate some problems on some estates, the DOE Consultation Document of October 1987 made it clear that 'the size of the areas involved and the extent of the problems are such that they are beyond the capacity of local authorities to tackle' and required 'novel and radical solutions beyond the normal run of local authority housing activity'. Such an argument reflected the government conviction that other ways had to be found for tackling major concentrations of run-down local authority housing by 'involvement of both private and public sector resources'.

Proposals for the establishment of six Housing Action Trusts were announced on 11 July 1988, in part III of the Housing Bill at that stage before Parliament. Individual Trusts were to be established by subordinate legislation. The aim was to address 'problems with associated run down Council Housing in a specific number of urban areas'. Three potential Trusts were identified in London; the adjacent Loughborough and Angell Town estates in Lambeth, the adjacent North Peckham and Gloucester Grove estates in Southwark and six estates in Tower Hamlets, Solander Gardens, Shadwell Gardens, Berner, Boundary, Holland and part of the Ocean Estate. Outside the capital, those areas identified included Halton Moor, Seacroft South and Gipton in Leeds; Lion Farm, Wallace Close and Titford in Sandwell; and Downhill, Town End Farm and Hylton Castle in Sunderland. A number of consultants were appointed to carry out feasibility studies on the establishment of HATs in the areas in question. The plans for Trusts in Lambeth, Southwark and Sunderland were approved, but the proposals for Tower Hamlets withdrawn on the basis that inadequate land was available to provide more housing and the disruption to the existing communities would be unacceptable. In Leeds, although the three estates recommended met the criteria for designation, the only compelling case for a Trust was judged to be in Gipton; and in Sandwell the consultants considered there was an inadequate case for the establishment of a HAT in the three estates mentioned, but advised that Windmill Lane and a wider area of the Cape Hill community should be considered. This composite judgement was announced by Nicholas Ridley, the Environment Secretary, on 16th March 1989.

The proposed legislation in the 1988 Housing Bill laid great stress on consultation with both the local authority and the tenants themselves before the establishment of a HAT. The eventual decision, however, was to be that of government alone. The establishment of the Trust would then be followed by the transfer of the land and buildings from the ownership of the local authority to the Trust until such time as redevelopment was complete and tenants could choose their future landlord. The fact that all the rights of the tenants — security of tenure, rights of succession, right to buy — were safeguarded in the bill could not allay their fears that the new organisation was a first step in the transfer of the estates to private ownership. The rent freeze promised to all tenants in any Housing Action Trust until they moved into their new properties after refurbishing or redevelopment was a further incentive, but was not enough to dispel fear of the unknown.

As a result of discussions of the bill and representations from different bodies, the government tabled a Lords' amendment which allowed a ballot of all secure tenants to take place on the proposals before any HATs could be designated. In spite of this concession, the proposals for all six areas finally identified by Nicholas Ridley were withdrawn for a variety of reasons; at Tower Hamlets the decision had already been taken, in two further areas tenants' associations refused to proceed to a vote and in only two areas, Sunderland and Southwark, was it agreed that a full consultation process should be undertaken preparatory to a confidential ballot and vote. The results were decisively against the establishment of a Trust by majorities of 70% in Sunderland, announced in April 1990, and 80% in Southwark, announced in

October that year. In Southwark, a document from the Planning Department and circulated within the council acknowledged that a HAT for the two estates of North Peckham and Gloucester Grove would be the quickest and most effective way of delivering the required development; but in spite of this apparent endorsement, the Labour group on the council voted narrowly by 15–14 to oppose the HAT some weeks before the ballot. The consultation period had already lasted nine months with the involvement of the existing tenants' associations, the DOE and the shadow chair of the HAT setting out, with the help of consultants, policies which would be followed by an eventual Trust in the field of redevelopment, housing management and economic regeneration. Public meetings were held with the participation of representatives from the local authority. The policies were set out in comprehensive documents. The nature of commitments given by the DOE and shadow chair over and above those in the primary legislation were argued extensively, particularly their validity in law. An eminent QC, engaged to advise the tenants, advised that the commitments made by government were the most far reaching he had seen outside primary legislation; but they were commitments, not guarantees. The local authority, as was expected by reason of its vote, withdrew any tacit support it had given to the consultation process and carried out aggressive lobbying against the proposed HAT inmmediately prior to, and during, the three week ballot. The result was a foregone conclusion.

But the climate was gradually changing. Tenants in the worst estates, moreover, while suspicious of the government's intentions in proposing the introduction of HATs, had an ambivalent attitude to their local councils — the devil they knew — but with whose performance in the management of their estates they were often grossly dissatisfied and from whom they felt frequently alienated by Town Hall bureaucracy. The 1987 Consultation Document from the DOE had stressed that the identification of potential HAT areas was not dependent on goverment alone; local authorities were invited, on the basis of detailed knowledge and experience of their own locality, to propose areas which they considered would benefit from a HAT approach. The final decision, however, on eventual designation would remain with the government. Labour councils, where the worst estates were situated, were reassured that funding of a HAT would not affect their normal housing subsidies. Moreover, the adversarial relationship between national and local government was also changing. Tenant groups became more aware of the safeguards written into the Act and the commitments goverment was prepared to give which could not be enshrined in primary legislation. The first breakthrough came in Hull.

Establishment of the first HATs

A section of the North Hull Estate had already benefitted from much needed improvements through Estate Action money. The balance, some

2,100 tenanted properties, built in 1920/1930s with 350 further units purchased under Right to Buy and only 38 two-storey low rise flats were sorely in need of extensive refurbishment. Help was also needed to regenerate the whole area, including the adjacent Orchard Park with many high rise blocks and social problems. Discussions on the funding of £17m for the Victoria Dock area under the Urban Programme widened to include a potential HAT for part of the North Hull Estate not covered by the Estate Action project. The marriage took two years to consummate. There was some resistance within the Hull local authority to the establishment of an NDPB to carry out housing functions which had previously been its own preserve. The North Hull Estate had no high or medium rise stock, had three shopping parades on the boundaries of the proposed HAT area as well as three churches and two community centres. It might have been considered at first sight to be a less critical area than the more obvious urban estates in the principal cities; but allied to the need for refurbishment was the problem of extensive social deprivation which the HAT programme was designed to address. All these considerations led to a meeting of minds and a joint agreement that North Hull should constitute the first of the Trusts.

The local authority and the DOE now had to convince the tenants of the benefits of a HAT. A major problem was that there had been virtually no involvement by the residents in the affairs of their area and no tenants' associations existed. An extensive consultation programme was undertaken; thirty public meetings were held in which leading tenants, council, DOE and the shadow HAT participated; detailed documentation produced setting out commitments by government and the shadow HAT; a video 'It's up to you' directed at tenants was made; and a ballot was conducted in March 1991. This achieved a favourable vote of 69% on a turnout of 75% and the HAT was designated by both Houses of Parliament four months later in July.

The Waltham Forest HAT, designated six months later in December, had a longer history. In 1985, the local council had commissioned structural surveys of all its large panel construction stock on an instruction to all local authorities from the DOE. The survey revealed serious problems on four estates built in the late 1960s and early 1970s. The estates comprised principally thirteen tower blocks of 21 storeys and 28 LPC blocks of up to eight storeys. An Estate Improvement Team set up in 1987 confirmed major structural and fabric problems and high levels of tenant dissatisfaction. Radical action was essential. Feasibility studies showed that it would be possible to rebuild the estates in phases. New build on vacant land would be followed by demolition of existing blocks, further new build would then take place on that cleared site followed by further demolition, the process continuing in four to five phases. Tenants would move only once and directly into their new homes. The council made two attempts to fund the proposal, firstly by setting up a tenant/council company to carry out the redevelopment and then leasing back the new properties to the council for twenty years. Restrictions on leaseback announced in March 1988 meant the financing of such a scheme was no longer viable. In November 1988, the establishment of a tenant-controlled Housing Association was proposed with a mix of funding methods. The essential element was to be a 'dowry' from the council to the Housing Association based on the negative value of the estates. The dowry was to be funded from capital receipts or by a special allocation from the DOE. Over the next year extensive consultation took place on the proposal. Estate Steering Groups to represent tenants, funded by the council, and outreach work teams on each estate were set up to facilitate the flow of information between the council and the wider body of tenants. In September 1989, the DOE announced it could agree neither to allow the dowry as debt nor to subsidise it; the tenants reacted angrily and organised a highly effective campaign to persuade the Secretary of State to change his mind. In November the alternative offer of a HAT was made.

Intensive negotiations began in the following month with the objective of drawing up a Tenants' Expectations Document setting out the policies the HAT would follow in the event of a 'yes' vote. Participation was similar to that in Hull, with the Joint Steering Group of tenants, the council, the DOE and from February 1991 the shadow chair and acting chief executive of the HAT. The council and the DOE shared the funding of the activities of the Joint Steering Group, the housing consultants to the tenants and the latters' legal advisers. The consultants who had drawn up the original feasibility study acted as honest brokers to all parties.

The primary legislation in the 1988 Act para 63(1) incorporated four main objectives for the HAT:

a) to secure the repair or improvement of housing accommodation for the time being held by the Trust;
b) to secure the proper and effective management and use of that housing accommodation;
c) to encourage diversity in the interests by virtue of which housing accommodation in the area is occupied and, in the case of accommodation which is occupied under tenancies, diversity in the identity of the landlords; and
d) generally to secure or facilitate the improvement of living conditions in the area and the social conditions and general environment of the area.

The consultation process addressed each of these objectives and, as far as possible, confirmed them in greater detail and the method by which they would be achieved. A parallel Joint Working Party monitored the accuracy and objectivity of all publicity material on HAT policies submitted to the tenants. For one month prior to the ballot, a one-stop shop was open on each estate staffed by a rotating number of those involved in the consultation. Models showing each phase of the redevelopment were on display. The two sets of consultant architects were in attendance to explain the continuing process of new build and demolition with all tenants remaining in their homes until the whole redevelopment was complete. Much of the original concept and design had already been formulated in the Council's two abortive schemes. Twenty fly sheets were available for each tenant to take away on every aspect of the HAT's work including the details of a new improved tenancy agreement. The ethos governing the future work of the HAT was being established. Later HATs adopted similar methods to Waltham Forest, adapted to their own circumstances. On 17th April, the Tenants' Expectations Document was signed by the Minister of Housing, Sir George Young, a tenant representative from each estate and the Shadow Chair.

The foreword from the minister is so important in defining the thoroughness with which the ground had been prepared and the level of the commitments made by him over and above the statutory guarantees in the original legislation that it is worthwhile reproducing it here:

'I am delighted to add a Preface to this document, which represents a major effort by the elected representatives of tenants on the Boundary Road, Cathall Road, Chingford Hall and Oliver Close Estates. It sets out the way in which the tenants' representatives would wish a Housing Action Trust to operate, if one is established for these estates; and the responses of the government and chairman designate.

The government has agreed to provide the resources necessary to make a Trust a success. The government's response in the document sets out clearly the government's policy intentions.

I have made it clear to the chair of the Trust that I expect the formal Statement of Proposals the Trust will have to put to the Secretary of State under the Housing Act 1988 to be based on this document and the responses he and I have given.

I therefore commend this document to the tenants of the four estates, as the basis upon which it is intended that the Trust will act if tenants support the HAT proposals in the ballot, which now needs to take place. I hope the tenants will vote in favour of the Trust and the substantial benefits it can bring them.'

Expansion of the HAT programme

The four later HATs, Liverpool, designated in February 1993, Tower Hamlets and Castle Vale, both in June 1993, and Stonebridge in July 1994 all developed their own consultation procedures, but following the same principles of comprehensive written commitments on policies to be adopted by the HAT. In Liverpool, four independent agencies appointed by the DOE had acted as consultants or tenants' friends for one year, informing tenants of what a HAT would do, organising them into representative structures and advising them during the consultation process. Between February and July 1992, the shadow chair and acting chief executive visited each one of the 71 blocks and attended residents' meetings to make themselves known and answer questions. Once the basic negotiations had taken place between the DOE and the local authority, the final form of the consultation period then reduced further to four months in the three remaining HATs, Castle Vale, Tower Hamlets and Stonebridge, an indication of the growing confidence in the process and HAT policies, reinforced by the experience gained from Trusts already in existence. There had been a further stumbling block in negotiations in the early days, namely the lack of a legislative right of tenants to return to the council; this was enacted in the Leasehold Reform, Housing and Urban Development Act 1993. By that time, however, trust in the commitments made by the Housing Minister on this subject had been sufficient to further the progress of all HATs.

Three major objectives have been achieved in all the HATs by this extensive process of consultation:

(a) The policies have been set out so clearly that there have been no significant disagreements on the progress of any of the early HATs since designation and no costly changes to their strategic plan have been necessary (although Liverpool has yet to agree options for each of its nine areas described later in this article);

(b) mutual trust has been built up between the parties involved;

(c) the leading tenants have developed a justified and growing confidence in their own abilities, both corporate and personal, whether as members of their HAT Board or on their own representative bodies.

The process, for those who participated, whether residents or non residents, was both an exhausting and rewarding experience; and as an initial experience in tenant empowerment it is salutary to compare the turnout in each of the HAT ballots and the majority achieved with the turnout in comparable council elections for the wards in which the blocks or estates are situated;

	Majority %	Turnout %	Council Turnout %
North Hull	69	75	26
Waltham Forest	81	75	41
Liverpool	82	79	37
Tower Hamlets	66	76	43
Castle Vale	92	75	34
Stonebridge	68	65	37

What were the tenants voting for? The HATs had a common set of problems identified in a number of opinion polls in each of the areas but the diversity in the nature of their housing stock and its condition, the community facilities, age, profile and ethnic mix could not be more marked. All, with the exception of North Hull which has already been described, were built in the 1960s/1970s to different systems which today show their age and deficiencies in design.

The Liverpool HAT comprises 67 of the 71 tower blocks of the whole city (the remaining four voted against a HAT) with 158 further low rise units. Ethnic minorities are only 2% of the population, 55% of the total population is over 60 and 77% over 40. Not surprisingly, health problems abound. It is perhaps remarkable that both turnout and majority were so high as there was considerable resistance in the early stages of the consultation process not so much to the HAT itself but to the upheaval which any redevelopment would occasion to many who might have preferred to live their lives out in peace. A subsequent draft strategy paper has shown the social problems to be greater than primarily thought—the fragility of an ageing population and their ability to cope with change has informed much of the Liverpool HATs recent thinking. To cope with the complexity and logistical problems of dealing with blocks either singly or in groups spread over the whole city, representing under 7% of the city's social housing stock, the HAT has divided itself into nine areas and is now formulating its redevelopment options which will go forward to the same comprehensive debate with those concerned. It will have to exercise the judgement of Solomon in reconciling the desires and expectations of existing HAT tenants with the longer-term needs of the city for which its activities are equivalent to those of a major redevelopment agency.

There are some parallels between Liverpool and Castle Vale, situated on the eastern periphery of Birmingham. Ethnic minorities represent less than 4% of the population and the age profile also tends towards the elderly. There the similarity ends, however, for Castle Vale is the only HAT contained within a single boundary area of 500 acres including 123 acres of open space. It can claim a range of community, education, health, retail and community facilities which ensure the estate is almost fully serviced and resourced. It has a magnificent wild bird sanctuary. The area is a mix of high rise blocks, maisonettes, sheltered housing and two-storey flats, houses and bungalows of which over 1,400 are owner-occupied. The tenanted properties constitute 3.4% of the total council stock in Birmingham; the population is 11,000, less than 50% of the 1969 census figure. Built likewise in the late 1960s, the owner-occupied properties and some of the high rise would provide pleasant living in a different environment. Yet, in spite of many advantages, Castle Vale has major problems. The whole area suffers from an exceptionally high crime rate, drugs, poor health standards and levels of literacy and numeracy far worse than the average for Birmingham.

The remaining two HATs, Tower Hamlets and Stonebridge, both in London, are concentrated urban estates, with a predominance of high rise blocks, both suffering equally from the design faults arising from their construction in the late 1960s and early 1970s. Tower Hamlets is the smallest of all the Trusts, with 1,400 units, but financial considerations have limited the size of this East London HAT. Both have some shops and community facilities, Stonebridge boasting a whole precinct with post office, newsagent, supermarket, chemist and even a legal practice. Ethnic minorities constitute 30% of the population in Tower Hamlets but 70% in Stonebridge, of which 60% are black and 10% Asian.

The turnout and majorities in each of the HATs bear witness to the breadth and depth of the consultation process. As confidence was established and comparisons began to be drawn between the previous philosophy of the local authority which did not involve consultation and that of the emerging HAT, tenants became more and more proactive, wishing to be involved in a process on which they recognised their growing influence.

The HAT structure

Immediately after the ballot all HATs have a similar task, the completion of the board and the recruitment of a full time executive. The Trusts are controlled by a board of eleven or twelve members including the chair; the balance is generally three to four tenants, one to two local councillors and the remainder non-residents. Tenant board members have wished to put their names forward for election only after the ballot has confirmed that a Trust will be created. The process of their election has been controlled by an independent body such as the Electoral Reform Society. The local councils propose their own members and the chairs, after consultation with the DOE, propose the non residents, all for approval by the Secretary of State. The last category cover the necessary levels of expertise in housing, finance, large scale construction projects or urban regeneration; some of them, but not all, have local experience. Some belong to voluntary bodies; a member of Age Concern sits on the Liverpool Board, a member of Open House, a mental health resource centre in Poplar, on the board at Tower Hamlets, and a member of the Commission for Racial Equality on the Waltham Forest board. The experience of these individuals and others helps greatly in solving the particular problems with which each Trust has to grapple. There is a good gender mix and, wherever possible, the board as a whole represents the ethnic balance of the tenants. Liverpool has five female, including the chair and six male members, all white of UK origin, reflecting the population of the blocks. Stonebridge has the same gender mix but there are five from ethnic minorities and the chair and deputy chair are both leading members of the Black community. There is no time or place for what are loosely known as political appointees; and in no case has a proposal for nomination to the board by the chair been rejected by the Secretary of State. Original concerns about 'non-resident majorities' on the board have been subsumed in a corporate and objective will to progress the work of the HAT according to the principles and policies set out in the pre-ballot documentation. Non-residents with their functional expertise come to recognise a different type of knowledge and expertise learned from life in the blocks, on the estates and in the local communities. In other words, the board of each HAT is a partnership where people of different origins and backgrounds learn to work together and respect one another's views. All board meetings and sub-groups of the board are open to the wider tenant body and the general public and often take place in the blocks themselves or on the estates.

The executive team mirrors the objectives of the organisation: chief executive and directors of redevelopment, housing management, community development, and finance. One of the first tasks of the executive is to draw up a Statement of Proposals distilling commitments made during the consultation process into a structured document for the board to approve after consultation with tenants, DOE, the local authority and other community bodies. It then goes to the DOE for formal approval as one of the first major documents charting the future of the HAT. Although each Statement of Proposals can vary according to the nature of the HAT and the extent of the pre-ballot consultation, the document can cover history, problems requiring solutions, how the latter will be approached, with photographic and graphic material where relevant to substantiate the arguments. Of particular importance are outline performance indicators, both quantitative and qualitative. The important factor is that the organisation is letting its customers — the tenants — know every aspect of its future objectives which in the private sector would be known only to board and senior management. Local authorities have of course recently been encouraged to strengthen their consultation process in the wider community.

HATs, however, have needed no such encouragement. While planning requirements are being addressed, the Trusts move quickly to ensure full participation by their tenant groups in all aspects of their operations. This extends far beyond the involvement of individuals, at full board or board committee level. The focal point of tenants involvement is principally the tenants' association or steering group, usually representing residents in a specific number of high and/or low rise housing units. Members from these bodies become involved not only in the recruitment of senior management but of the whole executive. They sit on panels which decide the appointment of consultants and contractors. They participate in working groups making decisions on subjects as diverse as the establishment of partnerships with the local business community to the choice of fixtures and fittings in the new homes. They carry out regular inspections of the estate management team or outside contractors in cleaning, repairs and maintenance. As tenants sometimes form up to 25% of the Trusts' staff, tenant groups can be carrying out an assessment of their own colleagues' performance and do not spare them in their judgements.

Tenants' groups need and are given resources and training to perform an ever growing number of vital functions. They are taught communications, team building, public relations, problem solving and management skills. Instruction can be for the whole group or customised if necessary. The groups are funded under the grants' procedure of Section 71 of the 1988 Housing Act and are subject to both internal and external audit, so bookkeeping and general accountancy skills also form part of their training agenda. The majority of the Trusts' meetings are open to the wider body of tenants to encourage them to participate in other committees dealing with estate based problems. Because they recognise that with authority comes responsibility, a growing number of tenants become active and enthusiastic. They had previously been ignored, their abilities underestimated and the area where they lived stigmatised. Preconceived views in the minds of employers in the region, the utilities and community at large had been a negative influence on jobs, the delivery of local services and the ability of tenants to obtain insurance. As external views change and tenants' self confidence grows, a feeling of optimism and energy replaces pessimism and passivity.

This is manifest in the fact that, with the passage of time, there is always an excess of tenants offering themselves for election to the board or their tenants' groups. The former are paid, the latter, by their own wish, unpaid so that they maintain their independence. These leading tenants take on a heavy burden which they discharge with great commitment and responsibility, attending up to twelve or fifteen different committees per month—because it is their HAT and they know they are deciding their own future.

The next formal step for each Trust is the preparation of an annual budget and three-year corporate plan. As between 75–80% of the HAT's total expenditure is accounted for by refurbishment or redevelopment, an essential element is the establishment of a master-plan for the building work, covering the total programme subdivided into the specific phases with relevant costs. This is based as far as possible on the feasibility study subsequently developed and modified in the pre ballot period and then agreed during an extensive consultation with all the interested parties. The main dialogue is between HAT, the tenants and the architects, balancing tenants' wishes, design and environmental considerations and cost. Street layout, car parking, the location of public against private gardens front and rear, flexibility of internal design to allow further choice e.g. one through-room or separate kitchen and breakfast room, sound insulation, individual heating systems and security are some of many factors uppermost in the tenants' minds as the consultation proceeds.

The Trusts' expenditure is funded principally by grant-in-aid which has to be argued through on an annual basis, the concluding debate being between the minister and DOE officials on the one hand and the chair and senior executives of the HAT on the other. Other sources of income include rental flows which comprise in addition those from commercial properties, receipts from the Right to Buy programme whereby tenants are encouraged to purchase their properties, grants from the European Union, investment by the private sector and disposals towards the end of the HAT's life. Rigid disciplines are imposed on each HAT. The Financial Memorandum, drawn up by the DOE, has been reviewed and modified with the growing experience of HATs and the department itself. It is the basic document covering every aspect of each Trust's corporate activity. It covers the planning function, sources of finance and regulation of expenditure; it restricts delegated authority significantly in the initial stages of the HAT's life. The Trust's delegated powers can then be increased to a level which gives both board and executives an enhanced authority over planning and expenditure, usually after two satisfactory external audits and proof of competent management. The Financial Memorandum also confers a dual role on the chief executive. He/she is responsible with fellow directors to the chair and board; but is also the Chief Accounting Officer responsible to the namesake in the DOE. The responsibilities are to both the HAT and the department's Accounting Officer to ensure propriety, regularity and value for money in the HAT's expenditure. In this regime, the chief executive, in the role of Accounting Officer, has the authority and obligation to warn the chair or board in writing if it is considered the latter are embarking on a course of action which could be regarded as infringing financial propriety. If the board nonetheless decides to proceed, the chief executive must ask for the instruction in writing, comply with it but inform the DOE and the external auditor of what has occurred.

The 1988 Act vests the Trusts with certain obligations and powers similar to local authorities. A Trust may become the local planning authority for its designated area (an option not taken up so far by the new bodies, preferring, as they do, to work objectively and amicably with the local authority). It may give financial assistance in the form of grants or loans or purchase share capital in a company. It may acquire land within, adjacent to or outside its designated area to achieve its objectives. Waltham Forest and Tower Hamlets have both needed to exercise this power, the latter particularly through the purchase of one large site bisected by a disused railway track and owned by the Docklands Light Railway.

The whole planning process takes time and, in the interim, tenants are impatient to see an initial realisation of the policies for which they have voted. The area in which the HAT can make an immediate impact is that of housing management, whether contracted out or through an in-house organisation. The surveys of tenants' views mentioned earlier showed wide dissatisfaction with the way in which the majority of blocks or estates were managed. Many of them were basic: graffiti on buildings never removed, litter and poor refuse collection, dog mess, unsafe parking (often in underground garages under concrete podia) poor lighting in blocks or on walkways. Other complaints were design or crime related: inadequate cleaning of stairs and lifts, poor external maintenance of buildings, unreliability of lifts, vandalism to property, burglaries, thefts of and from vehicles, muggings and sexual or racial harassment. The list was endless: requests for repairs were managed inadequately whether plumbing, carpentry, glass, roofing or electrical; and above all in many instances records were inadequate and staff sometimes did not listen to their tenants.

It is early days for most HATs to have completed improvements to their own and their tenants' satisfaction. But two examples of radical progress are indicative. North Hull, with the involvement of its residents, has completed a Charter setting out standards of service which residents expect from the Trust covering all aspects of its performance including repairs, maintenance, improvements and what to do if things go wrong in the field of housing management. Waltham Forest's Tenant Satisfaction Survey in June 1994 showed progress made and targets still to be met. Since the Trust took over responsibility for the estates, 72% of tenants believed the housing service had improved, 18% believed it had stayed the same, 3% believed it had got worse and 7% had no opinion. Both North Hull and Waltham Forest have been awarded a Charter Mark under the Citizens Charter Scheme at their first attempt. The commitment of later HATs to a similar level of performance is no less. The Charter Mark assessors' judgements are based not only on the written instructions, systems and controls of these HATs, but equally on actual performance and the surveyed reaction of tenants.

Improving the social and economic infrastructure

The Trusts treat the need for improvements to the social conditions and general environment of the area with equal urgency. Social conditions are dependent not only on the quality of the housing but also on the economic health of the wider community. The majority of residents of working age want training, retraining and jobs. The major opportunity which all Trusts offer by virtue of the huge sums to be spent on redevelopment is through site jobs: bricklayers, carpenters, electricians, plumbers. Although HATs are not subject to legislation in the relevant Local Government Act on competition, they need to conform to EC law which forbids contractual clauses relating to the employment of local labour through the tender process; however, contractors have been persuaded to employ as many tenants as possible and limit the practice of bussing in skilled and semi-skilled workmen if tenants are available. Perhaps to their own surprise, they are finding that tenants are more motivated than outsiders in working on their own homes and perform no less well. The North Hull Trust has a Job Shop which achieved its first year target of finding 200 jobs for residents three months ahead of schedule, 77 of these residents being classified as long-term unemployed, out of work for a minimum of 6 months. The Shop is sponsored by the HAT based on a partnership between Hull City Council, Humberside County Council and the Employment Service. A new group in Hull including the four organisations mentioned, but also the Humberside TEC, Hull Chamber of Commerce and Shipping, Orchard Park and North Hull Enterprises Ltd, is now bidding for £7.5m of public and private sector funding destined to create 2,000 jobs and 300 full-time training places through a wide range of initiatives. Waltham Forest has achieved an equal number of jobs for tenants in large measure through the establishment of a Careers Advice and Placement Project which by September 1994 had registered 1,400 residents of the HAT estates seeking jobs or training. It has also set up two training centres, one at Trinity Park for computer and business skills run by the Waltham Forest Education service and the second the Langthorne Training Centre for construction skills, particularly bricklaying, carpentry and general trades, run by the construction manager Bovis. Both have been highly successful in placing trainees in permanent jobs. A further initiative to help train local firms to tender for supplies in the redevelopment and contribute towards the regeneration of the whole area is at an early stage. A similar move is being initiated in Hull which is making grants available to encourage local businesses to expand their skills and recruit local people. Many other initiatives are in various stages of development: child care schemes to enable single parents to train for employment; partnerships with local schools to address jointly the problem of drugs; training of tenants' groups to enable them to participate further in the decision making process at central and local level; and the setting up of business support groups attached to specific blocks or estates to bring support in kind from the private sector. Thus the third objective of the Trusts is being addressed, namely improvements to the social conditions and general environment of the area.

The fourth and last objective is the achievement of diversity in the ownership of the housing accommodation. This will only be realised if tenants can obtain decently paid employment which encourages them to move away from the safe haven of being council tenants with the protection that the latter enjoy. Only in this way can they truly exercise choice when the Trusts are wound up at the end of the redevelopment. In addition, it is the view of the Trusts that greater management of their housing by tenants must be encouraged whatever the future tenure; and the ability of tenants to decide their own future, particularly by choice of future landlord, will be based on their continuing empowerment. Training of members of the estate steering groups or tenants' associations is already leading to considerations of various forms of Tenant Management Organisations where tenants are in a majority on the board. In some cases this could lead to tenants taking over ownership of their properties, probably through the establishment of Community Based Housing Associations.

Summary: democracy and accountability

HATs have gone through several phases: the broaching of the scheme in the 1987 Consultation Document; the original selection of the areas proposed and then modified after the consultants' study; the negative reaction of the tenants and their local authorities; the Lords amendment allowing a ballot in each of the areas to be designated; the negative vote at Sunderland and Southwark; the growing recognition of the benefits and lengthy discussions between local authorities and the DOE, subsequently with the growing involvement of tenants and the shadow HAT; and finally the establishment of six HATs between 1991 & 1994 with work stretching into the next decade. The jury has not yet had the case proven for their success and will not even retire for some time yet, but it is possible to set out some of the arguments for their special role and to make an initial judgement on their achievements. Probably a final judgement will be possible only ten years after the HATs are wound up and it can be seen if they have left behind strong, self-sustaining communities.

Non Departmental Public Bodies or Quangos have been set up by both major parties when in power to achieve specific objectives in a limited time scale. They can be judged only on their results and not on abstract or a priori reasoning. The funding of social housing in a post-industrial Western society of low growth, low inflation and high expectations is no less of a problem in the two other leading European nations, France and Germany. There is a growing international concern that social housing must be supported if poorer groups are to be accommodated and urban conflicts avoided. In the UK, the role of local authorities is vital, but not sacrosanct in this area of provision. The problems not merely of social housing but of urban regeneration are growing and it is right that a number of routes should be investigated to see how money can be most effectively spent to provide decent housing while restoring the self-confidence of tenants and giving them the opportunity for training and jobs which will reduce or eliminate their dependence on the welfare state. The consultation period, the ballot and the involvement of the tenants in virtually every decision which affects their lives, allied to the strict controls on expenditure exercised by government, are initial testimony to the democracy and accountability of each of the Trusts. The concept of tenant participation is not unique; the Priority Estates Project set up in 1979 had two objectives: the involvement of tenants in decisions affecting them and localising the housing service to avoid the bureaucracy of town hall systems which impeded the response to the needs of the estates. The HATs are building on this work and that of other community initiatives and extending it to the whole field of urban regeneration.

What does a HAT bring which can not be provided by the local authority? It is a new body with new ideas and highly focused management. It involves the local authority, without being hampered by the complexity of the latter's problems. Its tenants play an ever greater role in its decision making. It has an open mind to involving other partners particularly local community organisations and private business. The presence of non-elected members of the board is criticised, but they balance the elected tenants and local councillors and bring experience in a range of functions much needed to guide the Trusts in how to achieve their stated objectives. Many of the non residents serve for altruistic reasons; they wish to contribute their skills and time for the public good and not for personal profit or with an eye for re-election. Above all, however, the HATs have instituted new structures and new systems. Former local authority tenants who live on HAT estates will never again accept a passive role in decisions affecting their own future — where the town hall alone disposes — whoever they choose as their future landlord. The growing number of visits from other tenants' organisations is an indication of the interest aroused by the HAT concept of partnership between all the players at national and local level. One of the most encouraging features of the HATs has been their ability to act as a catalyst, to break down barriers and help realise the full potential of all those living in the areas in which they operate. It is a logical development of other government initiatives and complements the initial work of the Single Regeneration Budget where local organisations join together to apply for government funding of their projects. Socio-economic problems are huge and growing. HATs represent an initiative which will contribute to successful long-term regeneration of specific local communities. It is on an assessment of their success by these communities themselves that they would wish to be judged.

The Accountability of Training and Enterprise Councils

BY ALISTAIR GRAHAM

chief ex. of Calderdale & Kirklees TEC.

TRAINING and Enterprise Councils (TECs) have come in for a substantial amount of criticism during the past year, not least because it is alleged that they are part of this government's policy of littering Britain with hundreds of new quangos which are being run by what the *Economist*, in an article in August 1994 called 'unelected quangocrats'. What needs to be explored is whether Training and Enterprise Councils are quangos like any other bodies that indisputably come within such a category of public body, whether the local authority model of accountability is appropriate for such bodies and, if not, what alternative model can be produced which will satisfy public concern and yet maintain the involvement of senior private sector figures in the effective running of TECs.

In its 1993/4 annual report the Audit Commission said that early indications suggested that the 'massive changes' taking place in the public sector, with devolution of responsibility to large numbers of service providers, were leading to better management and value for money. But Sir David Cooksey, the Commission's chairman, went on to say 'teething troubles were inevitable and change brought risks as well as potential benefits. Accountability could be blurred as responsibilities were reallocated.' He added, 'If full benefits are to be gained, we must ensure that effective mechanisms for accountability are put in place to underpin the process of change and to ensure the risks are minimised.'

The creation of TECs in 1989 represented a significant devolution of power to a local level and is one of the few examples of a government of any political persuasion devolving responsibility for the delivery of part of its economic objectives to such a level. This devolution arose because the attempt by central government to deliver a world-class workforce by the Manpower Services Commission and then the Training Agency was not seen to be successful as measured by organisations such as the National Institute for Social and Economic Research. Detailed studies carried out by the Institute throughout the 1980s on the level of skills and productivity of the British workforce compared to Britain's main economic competitors, showed serious deficiencies in both skills and productivity levels. What was remarkable about the decision to create TECs was that it placed senior private sector leaders in the frontline of creating thriving local economies sustained by skilled workforces. This means the issue of TEC accountability has to be seen in the context of the boldness of the experiment the government initiated in decentralising part of its economic machine.

What are TECs?

There are 82 TECs in England and Wales. In Scotland there are 22 Local Enterprise Companies (LECs) which are similar organisations but which also have a wider responsibility for physical as well as human resource development. TECs in England and Wales work within an operating agreement which is a standard contract between each TEC and the Secretaries of State for Employment and Environment. This is a legal contract, 119 pages long with 11 annexes. The reason why the Secretary of State for the Environment is also a signatory is because a number of the government programmes which are run by TECs are included in the Single Regeneration Budget (SRB), a recent development by the government bringing a wide range of government programmes together to achieve a more coherent approach to local economic development and regeneration issues. There are cynics around who say that it is a subtle device for ensuring further cuts in public expenditure. It has already meant that one of the national programmes currently run by TECs, the Business Start Up Scheme, ceases to be a national programme helping unemployed people to start their own businesses from April 1995. Although TECs can bid for SRB resources to continue to operate such programmes, given the limited money available, only a small number of bids are likely to be successful. In Scotland, Local Enterprise Companies receive their funds and are supervised through an intermediary body called Scottish Enterprise which in return is responsible to the Secretary of State for Scotland.

TECs (and LECs in Scotland) are independent private companies limited by guarantee/shares and therefore subject to company law. They spend primarily public funds which come mainly from the Department for Employment but also from other government departments, such as Environment, Trade and Industry and the Home Office. Many TECs and LECs attract money from the EU either from the European Social Fund or European Regional Development Funds. TECs in their operating agreement are defined as '... independent companies which have been set up as Training and Enterprise Councils for the purpose of providing training, supporting enterprise and undertaking other activities'. The agreement provides for a three-year corporate plan and a one year business plan to be produced by each TEC in accordance with guidance provided by the Secretary of State for Employment.

The Government's strategic guidance to TECs for producing their corporate plan for the period 1995–98 was published in May 1994 under the title 'TECs: Towards 2000'. It included a foreword by the Prime Minister and was signed by the six Cabinet ministers covering

Employment, Trade and Industry, Environment, Education, the Home Office and Transport. The introduction says that TECs have 'key local roles in the achievement of national competitiveness through: contributing to clear strategies and plans to help build robust, dynamic local economies; developing competitive businesses capable of taking on and beating global competitors; developing and encouraging a world class workforce with the skills needed for successful businesses.' The guidance goes on to stress the need for an integrated approach which is the rationale behind the establishment of integrated government offices for the regions and the bringing together of a variety of government initiatives to form a Single Regeneration Budget. The key paragraph of the introduction maintains that 'improving the competitiveness of the business and people is the central purpose of TECs. They are well placed to tackle issues at local level, particularly by helping to make local labour markets work flexibly, to raise the quality of business management, and by encouraging a climate where investment in people, technology, innovation and enterprise are seen as key to bottom line performance and where business is encouraged to think globally—act locally'. It is this key role of thinking globally and acting locally which makes the issue of local accountability of TECs so vital. Given their limited resources (on average a TEC has an annual budget of £20 million and falling year by year), it is not possible to make an impact locally with such limited funds unless each is working in close harmony with a wide range of local institutions, such as local authorities, Chambers of Commerce, Further Education Colleges and the local business community. In such a partnership approach, TEC plans should flow from a shared analysis of the position of the local economy and an agreed approach to defining and meeting local needs.

TECs can be summarised as follows: non-profit making private companies; holding a 'licence' to operate locally from the Department of Employment; contracted on an annual basis to provide a range of services including management and labour market information, for a number of government departments including Employment, Trade and Industry and Environment; governed by a board of fifteen or sixteen unpaid directors, two-thirds of whom must hold the office of chairman or chief executive of a company or be a senior operational manager, at a local level, of a company; the chair of the board is nominated by the board and approved by the Secretary of State for Employment; a significant proportion of funding is performance-related; they have freedom to spend surpluses on local projects in line with agreed Corporate and Business Plans and have freedom to attract/earn additional funds from public and private sectors. Most TECs act as strategic facilitators seeking to develop successful partnerships rather than engaging in direct delivery and are subject to extensive audit checks.

TECs, therefore, have to be accountable both to government, from which they derive their existence and funds, and to the local community which has a major stake in the success of their activities. Critics see them as just another example of unaccountable quangos which cannot, by their very nature, be part of the local community. It has to be accepted that, for the purposes of the current national debate, they have to be seen as 'quangos' as they primarily spend public funds and are perceived as such even if they have some characteristics unlike other quangos such as having Company Law status.

An example of this approach is the 'Accountability Index' produced by Chris Sheldon and John Stewart for the Association of London Authorities. This scores each type of London appointed quango against the key accountability characteristics of local authorities, namely: whether they are directly elected; whether they come within the remit of one of the public sector Ombudsmen; whether there is extensive statutorily-defined public access to policy and decision-making meetings; whether there is extensive statutorily-defined public access to information; whether members of the body are liable for surcharge; whether members of the body have a statutory requirement to declare any interests which may conflict with their duties; whether these are monitoring officers charged with a statutory duty to ensure probity and financial regularity. On such an index, TECs come out badly because the members of their boards are not directly elected and they do not operate within a statutory framework. However, the sort of accountability index does not get to the heart of accountability relevant to bodies such as TECs. No bodies dominated by private sector people are going to subject themselves to direct elections.

TECs are accountable and this accountability should be extended. There is a widespread recognition in TECs that there is a democratic deficit to be addressed and the TEC National Council which speaks on their behalf at a national level set up a national group to produce a framework for local accountability of which the author is a member. The purpose of such a framework is to define the parameters for corporate governance of TECs which, if observed, will ensure that they are willingly accepted within their community. The framework will draw upon the three fundamental principles of corporate governance as defined in the Report of Committee on the Financial Aspects of Corporate Governance (known as the Cadbury Report) published in December 1992 and the CIPFA discussion paper 'Corporate Governance in the Public Services' published in 1994. These are openness, integrity and accountability, with the last defined as 'the process whereby individuals are responsible for their actions. It is achieved by all parties having a clear understanding of their responsibilities and having clearly defined roles through a robust structure.'

Existing forms of accountability

There are currently a variety of forms of accountability through both Parliament and the provisions of the Companies Act. The arrangements for TECs to be accountable to Parliament via ministers are well defined and prescribed in the annual TEC Operating Agreement published by the Departments of Employment and Environment, heart of the contractual liability between TECs as private companies and government. The systems which provide central accountability and control to Parliament for the funds voted by them include: the annual Operating Agreement and its annexes on management information and reporting; the system of Financial Appraisal and Monitoring; the detailed performance measures of the new three-year licence agreement which comes into effect for those TECs granted a licence from April 1995; contract specification; the audit regimes of Departments, Treasury, National Audit Office, European Commission, private company auditors and the TEC's own internal auditors (which may be a contracted-out provision).

TECs do not suffer any democratic deficit through a lack of auditing of its financial regimes. It could rather be said that the multiple auditing arrangements are excessive in relation to their size of budget. The Operating Agreement contains a considerable amount of regulation and accountability in addition to financial matters. The 1994/95 Agreement requires TECs to publish an annual Labour Market Assessment and a summary of Corporate and Business Plans within three months from the beginning of the financial year. The full Corporate Plan has to be made available to the public during normal office hours. The provisions relating to Directors, Conflicts of Interest, Public Meetings and the publication of the Annual Report are worth reproducing in full as they represent the significant elements of accountability that are currently required of TECs.

'*Directors*
12.3 the TEC shall ensure that:
12.3.1 at least two-thirds of the Directors (including the Chairman of the board) must hold the office of chairman or chief executive of a company or top level operational manager at local level of a company or senior partner of a professional partnership within (in each case) the private sector;
12.3.2 the remaining Directors are chief executives or their equivalents from education, economic development, trade unions, voluntary organisations or the public sector. A managing director or chief executive of the TEC shall not be counted in either category;
12.3.3 a Director ceases to hold office as such within three months after ceasing to satisfy the eligibility requirements set out in this Clause unless the Secretary of State for Employment and the TEC agree that he may continue in office;
12.3.4 the Secretary of State for Employment is notified in advance of all appointments of Directors and is notified promptly of the resignation or removal of any Director. A Director shall join and remain on the

board of Directors as an individual and not as a representative of another company or organisation;

12.3.5 no Director shall (except where he holds office as chief executive of the TEC) draw a salary derived from payments made to the TEC by either of the Secretaries of State or receive any remuneration from a Subsidiary of the TEC;

12.3.6 in the case of the TEC Chairman the company of partnership referred to in Clause 12.3.1 shall be a company or partnership (as the case may be) of at least three years standing with either an annual turnover exceeding £5 million or 25 or more full time employees.

Conflicts of Interest

12.4 The TEC shall take all reasonable steps to limit any conflict of interest between its Directors and employees and any other person with whom the TEC has dealings and, in particular, the TEC shall ensure that:

12.4.1 Directors and employees of the TEC are under a general duty to declare to the board of Directors any direct or material interest which may at any time arise in respect of any contract or other matter to which the TEC is party or any contract which is under consideration by the TEC;

12.4.2 a register of the declared interests of Directors and employees of the TEC is maintained detailing the nature and extent of such an interest. The register shall be available for inspection by the Secretary of State for Employment at any reasonable time;

12.4.3 if there is any declared conflict of interest, the relevant Director or employee of the TEC shall not be involved in any decision in respect of such matter;

12.4.4 no contract will be made with, or funding given to, any person, organisation or company in respect of which a material interest has been declared, without prior approval of the Directors.

Public Meetings

12.5 As a means of communicating with the community within which the TEC operates, the TEC shall announce and hold a public meeting at least once in every year.

Annual Report

12.6 The TEC shall produce and publish an Annual Report and audited statement of accounts within four months of the End of the Year. The Annual Report shall be produced with due regard to Annex H which states:

H1.1 The TEC Annual Report shall contain an account of progress towards achieving:

H1.1.1 the TEC's strategic objectives as set out in the Corporate and Business Plans and which reflect the strategic priorities issued by the Secretary of State;

H1.1.2 the TEC's plans to bring together local partners to encourage local action towards the national targets for education and training.

H1.2 In order for the Report to provide the local community with a picture of the TEC's activity, the following specific topics shall be covered;

H1.2.1 an account of initiatives undertaken in support of the Single Regeneration Budget;

H1.2.2 particular European initiatives being undertaken, and any local initiatives involving EC funding;

H1.2.3 information on income generated from other sources and the uses to which it has been put;

H1.2.4 support for people with special training needs;

H1.2.5 achievements of equality of opportunity in training and enterprise programmes;

H1.2.6 a summary of the findings of evaluation of or research into its activities commissioned by the TEC.

H1.3 For each of the areas in paragraphs H1.2, the TEC shall include a mix of hard fact and description, to give a balanced picture of how successful the activity has been.

H2.1 the TEC shall give its Annual Report as wide a circulation as possible in the local community'

These provisions strongly reinforce the private sector leadership of TECs with the requirement that at least two-thirds of the directors (including the chairman of the board) must be senior level private sector people. This is the unique selling point of TECs and the dilemma in drafting any framework of local accountability is to keep this private sector leadership while ensuring TECs are seen to serve and listen to the local community they represent. *really?*

As private sector companies limited by guarantee, TECs are subject to the Companies Act. As a precondition for contracting with government, the Memorandum and Articles of Association must meet the approval of the Secretary of State so that he can ensure that acts committed within their jurisdiction conform with parliamentary authority. The Companies Act also sets statutory obligations for reporting, auditing and the conduct of directors. The Code of Practice on Open Government published by the Cabinet Office in April 1994 also applies to TECs.

It is worth referring in more detail to the introduction of a system of three year licences for TECs from April 1995 to see if they will strengthen accountability. Paragraph 3 of the Employment Department's document, 'The New Contract Framework', states, 'The new contract arrangements are designed to support, ensure and to demonstrate continuous improvement in TEC's performance, value for money and accountability. This relationship will bring benefits for government, TECs and customers.' It goes on to explain that, 'The new arrangements have similarities with the preferred supplier relationship common in industry. The key features will be the introduction of a 3 year licence, supported by individual annual service agreements for the activities for which the Government contracts with TECs.' TECs which meet the criteria will be awarded licences to operate from April 1995.

The key principles upon which the new contract arrangements are based are defined as: 'a strategic partnership based on trust and shared goals; a relationship which focuses on TECs' strategies and their impact on their local economies; a more stable relationship with government; authority for TECs, as separately established local companies, to operate in addressing the needs of their areas; a simpler process for contracting.' The document outlines twelve elements which support the key principles, of which one is the accountability of TECs locally, and to government through their contracts.

The benefits for licensed TECs are few and are said to be guaranteed funding for core administration costs, greater freedom in spending reserves, simpler contract and audit arrangements, opportunities to bid for government bursaries appropriate to TECs, and a shorter annual contract round. There are no guarantees about the level of funding of major government programmes over a three-year period which is the prize TECs would most value. It is widely believed that the Government highjacked the TECs ideas for a licensing system to convince the Treasury about their efficacy so as to justify their freedom to use public funds and use surpluses built up since their inception.

To qualify for a three-year licence, four criteria relating to the TECs Corporate Plans, indicators of the TECs strategic impact, programme performance and capability have been defined on a mixture of objective and subjective indicators. A TEC is assessed against these criteria by the staff of the Department of Employment's Regional Office who make a recommendation to a Regional Panel chaired by the Regional Director and will involve members of the TEC Assessors Committee, the department's Head Office and the Director, Employment and Training. Each TEC seeking a licence will make a case to the panel. The Assessors Committee advises ministers on the overall performance of individual TECs in England and on regional and national performance (including the degree to which TECs are fulfilling their broader remit to raise the skills base and to stimulate local economic growth) and the eligibility criteria for TEC directors and the composition and calibre of TEC boards. It is required to take an overview of all the recommendations before they go to the Secretary of State for Employment. There is no system for appeals. The three year TEC licensing system is potentially a powerful system for enhancing TECs accountability but in the early stages of development it is an internal system of assessment that only touches the local community through assessing the role of the TEC board members as part of the criteria against which TECs are judged for a licence.

Under the indicators relating to a TEC's capability, there is one indicator which specifically refers to its role in the community, 'What is the TEC's capability as respects; influencing its constituency?' (C1.5). On a scale of one to five, the TEC is judged by the following criteria. How much credibility does the TEC have?: match of board to local economy and businesses; representative of ethnic groups and women; directors' own organisations set an example; status and authority of staff; arrangements for communication with key local interests; what the constituency thinks of the TEC; response to corporate plan. What evidence is there that the TEC is effective at influencing: profile in the community; participation in partnerships and joint ventures; organisations upon which the TEC is represented; relations with and track records in influencing key players, for example FE colleges, local authorities and Chambers of Commerce; track record in putting strategies into action. The process has no provisions for consulting the community in any formal or public way as to whether in their judgement, the TEC warrants the granting of a three-year licence. Perhaps this will come in time.

So far we have seen that TECs have to operate within a complex system of centrally determined arrangements for accountability particularly geared to meet the needs of government's responsibility to Parliament for the use of public funds; to meet government's requirements for those functions it requires TECs to deliver and to agree its strategic plans. Companies Acts requirements and accountability to government for public money and the delivery of public programmes complement each other. They are both relevant to local accountability, but do not by themselves guarantee local acceptability. Neither the requirements of parliamentary accountability nor the Companies Acts prescriptions, are sufficient to demonstrate local accountability. As TECs are geographically defined and exist to serve their local communities, they must demonstrably meet their responsibilities to those communities. Which is why the TEC National Council is anxious to persuade them to sign up to a framework which encompasses the three principles of openness, integrity and local accountability.

A new TEC framework for local accountability

In drawing up the framework for local accountability, TECs see themselves accountable to the community in its area and specifically to employers in businesses of all sizes and in all sectors of the local economy and the self-employed, individual clients and customers, actual or potential, for all TEC sponsored or supported programmes. They recognise that two other constituencies play an essential part in the delivery of this accountability: partners in local government, the enterprise network, education, community and voluntary organisations, together with those sub-contractors who deliver TEC-supported programmes direct to customers.

If TECs are to develop a self-regulatory framework for local accountability successfully, it will need to be around a number of key themes:

clarity in the selection of Board members, with opportunities for the local community to put forward nominations; directors and staff seen to be acting without conflicts of interest; TEC fulfilling a duty to make information available, particularly about performance; information about financial operations to be made public; commitment to quality services; transparency and fair commercial dealing with subcontractors; partnerships characterised by trust and integrity; a robust complaints procedure. It is worth exploring each of these themes to see what problems there are in defining the specific arrangements TECs could credibly sign up to.

Clarity in the selection of board members, with opportunities for the local community to put forward nominations. TECs primarily draw upon the private sector leadership and business expertise to fulfil their main objectives. Boards may also include local authority Chief Executives, elected councillors, Directors of Education, headteachers, trade union officials and people drawn from the voluntary sector. Most will make serious attempts to include women and, where appropriate, representatives of the ethnic minority community. A number of TECs have membership schemes either separate from or in conjunction with the local Chamber of Commerce and there are now arrangements for TECs and Chambers of Commerce to merge where this is deemed to be appropriate. This may mean that the members help to determine the board membership at the Annual Meeting. The limitation of these arrangements is that membership will be drawn from a section of the business community and may not include all parts of the wider community served. A wide variety of selection processes exist and this will continue to be the case. What we need to see is the process used to select directors and the chairman being available in a public document and explained as the best route to achieving an effective board to carry out the TEC's mission, including the representativeness of the board to be demonstrated. Such a document also needs to describe the qualifications and experience which the board members bring to the role, the portfolio of special interests and responsibilities which each member has (where applicable), together with the pre-qualifications set by government in the Operating Agreement and the non-salaried status of directors (except chief executive) to be emphasised. The board should also discuss succession planning once a year, with directors appointments normally for three years but subject to renewal. A register of individuals interested in appointment could be maintained and for those TECs which have membership schemes, they would seek endorsement of recommendations for appointment of directors by the membership. In most TECs, induction training for directors takes place but this should be a compulsory requirement for new directors.

Directors and staff seen to be acting without conflicts of interest. It is clear in the current Operating Agreement for TECs that directors must act as individuals, rather than as representatives of an organisation or group, in the best interests of TEC customers, and that they must not use their position to further private interests. We need to strengthen this by ensuring all material interests are declared, recorded in board minutes and a register of interests is available for members of the public to examine. Directors need to withdraw from discussion of matters involving a direct personal material interest and must be able to demonstrate that conflict of interest has not occurred in board discussion of more general matters. Whilst hospitality is not an issue for TECs, it would help if there was a record of any hospitality and other expenses incurred or received by directors and senior executives available for inspection, and for a statement of the Conditions of Appointment of directors to be signed by newly appointed directors. The role of the chairman, directors and board and the relationship with the role of the chief executive should be documented and available. There would also be a requirement for the board not to enter into activities with political parties or organisations likely to bring the Secretary of State into disrepute, nor religious organisations unless they are not putting a religious viewpoint. Part of this provision is already covered in the existing Operating Agreement.

TECs have a duty to make information available, particularly about performance. It is vital that TECs set performance targets and measurements and communicate them widely. Statements of performance against these need to be published at standard, regular intervals and on a basis which makes comparison over time possible. Both self-assessment and appraisal by bodies independent of government and TECs should form part of this. Performance on the building of partnerships and on the profile and reputation of the TEC in the community to be included in any performance monitoring.

Information about financial operations to be made public. Full copies of accounts must be available to the public, including details of the contracts given and received. There will need to be some exceptions for reasons of commercial confidentiality but these should be carefully defined. Information on TEC costs, organisation, targets and results achieved should be published in the Annual Report and made public in the local community. Honest financial conduct is demonstrated through the processes laid down in the Operating Agreement and Licence and by the audit requirements of the Companies Act but it will be necessary to spell these out in any framework document.

Commitment to quality customer service. Any framework of local accountability must provide for the delivery of a quality service to its customers. Employers and individual clients should expect clear and accurate information and impartial advice on the choices available to them and the financial implications where relevant. It is also important for any framework to show how individual applications will be handled fairly and efficiently, with high quality training content, methodology and management. There should be provision for prompt payment of grants and financial support, where relevant, reliable and unbiased career and other counselling related to job choice, the right to be treated equally regardless of religion, gender or ethnic background and to have any learning difficulties or disabilities taken into account, and courteous and helpful personal service, on the telephone or face to face, by staff trained in good customer management.

Transparency and fair commercial dealings with subcontractors. This is another difficult area to cover in any framework because what subcontractors would want to see in a framework is far apart from what TECs would want to subscribe to. Many national employers and national training providers who were previously used to contracting with a government body, the Training Agency, have found it difficult to interface with 104 TECs and LECs. Pressure groups such as the Bridge Group of voluntary sector training providers have regularly published reports seeking an improved contractual relationship with TECs. In response to these pressures, TECs created a Forum of National Training Providers which is currently chaired by the author. Possible provisions for the framework dealing with subcontractors could ensure the following. Subcontractors who deliver most TEC supported programmes to end-users should subscribe to the standards of customer service, openness and complaints procedures established by the TEC. They have a right to be consulted on these. Subcontractors can expect to be consulted by TECs about their contracts and to expect contract terms which encourage the stability and improving performance that flows form a preferred supplier relationship, within the constraints of the TEC contract with government. Subcontractors should normally receive 60 days notice of the intention to terminate or not to renew a contract, except where a clear breach of the contract is involved. TECs should not impose on subcontractors unreasonable demands for additional information that are not required by the TEC's contract with government. The provision for 60 days notice to end a contract would be particularly controversial because TECs may not finalise their annual contract with the government until less than 60 days before their existing contract expires.

Partnerships characterised by trust and integrity. This would require TECs to publish and share data and analysis and to consult early with all relevant partners on all plans.

A robust complaints procedure. Within the TEC it would be necessary to institute a clear, accessible and well-publicised route for complaints, with a known point of contact. Complaints should be dealt with within a stated time period. Individuals should be kept informed of progress and granted a full and fair investigation. The confidence of the complainant should be respected and complainants should receive a comprehensive and understandable response and redress where appropriate and for complaints to be reviewed for lessons learnt and improvements to be made. Where the TEC cannot satisfy the complaint, or where the complainant is dissatisfied with the TECs response, the route of external moderation should be identified to the complainant and it might be possible to have a backstop provision whereby, if requested by a TEC, the TEC National Council would appoint an independent body to consider such complaints and make recommendations.

TECs are in a very different position to many other quangos because the board members are not paid and there are well developed systems of accountability even if the details of these are not well known. However, TECs are maturing organisations which need to demonstrate a more effective system of accountability to the local communities they serve. There is the will to lay down high standards of conduct and accountability and to ensure such standards are effectively monitored. As long as we have a voluntary system for improving the education and skills of the British workforce, we need to keep the private sector in the frontline of taking responsibility for achieving a world class competitive workforce. We must devise systems of accountability which maintain their commitment to this task while meeting public concern.

[handwritten note: If never says how the board members are appointed and by whom !!!!]

The Impact of Quangos and
New Government Agencies on Education

BY HELEN JOHNSON AND KATHRYN RILEY

THE institutions and functions of the British public sector have experienced a barrage of changes over the last decade or so. In a wider context, there would scarcely seem to be a public sector in the world (save the twilight zone of North Korea and its ilk) that has not been reformed and restructured. Degrees of loyalty to the public sector, its institutions and its social and economic roles differ. Sweden retains some belief in a model of governmental intervention and high taxation. In the UK, many of the institutions of the Welfare State have been dismantled, quasi-markets introduced and competitiveness emphasised. The context for this article is the evolving pattern of state involvement in one area of the public sector, education. It traces the origins of the relationship between central and local government for the organisation and delivery of education services. It examines how the long-established partnership between the two has become fractured and why, at the height of their powers and their bureaucratic form, local education authorities became regarded by some as being unsatisfactory. It suggests that the creation of quangos and new government agencies to fund, direct and monitor the performance of educational institutions which emanated from a central government critique of local government, has contributed to the depowering of Local Education Authorities. To highlight these issues, the article focuses on the Funding Agency for Schools and the new Integrated Regional Offices which are responsible for the administration of the Single Regeneration Budget.

Background

The growth of governmental involvement in the economic life of its citizens has evolved over time. Central government has moved from a position of reluctant acknowledgement of its role in the public life of its citizens to one of limited or neutral involvement, and finally to a position of direct or indirect intervention. To pinpoint when this intervention started is difficult. It is clear that the earliest and the most determined governmental involvement has been in the defence of the realm (and in collecting the taxes needed so to do). If really pressed, we could return to the Doomsday Book; the first government audit. But it is with the emergence of the nation state and capitalism that we can confidently say government both centrally and locally started to expand.

In the UK, the industrial revolution of the late 18th and early 19th centuries provided the impetus for government to smooth out the externalities of the market and to intervene in social matters. The development of the public sector as a vehicle for the implementation of the governmental social and economic policy is a relatively recent phenomenon. As late as 1890, total government expenditure comprised less than 10% of the gross national product and nearly 50% of this was spent on defence.

Until the 19th century, central government was reluctant to interfere in education which was deemed to be a largely voluntary activity carried out by private charitable bodies. It was not until 1833 that the government felt impelled to assist the work of the two main provider bodies, the non-conformist British and Foreign Schools Society, and the Anglican National Society, albeit in a modest way. In the same year (1833) that British slave owners were awarded £20 million compensation for the emancipation of their slaves, the two societies each received grants of £10,000. By 1857, the grant had risen to over £500,000 and a Department of Education was set up to administer this sum.

The 1870 Forster Education Act marked the beginnings of greater state involvement education. It brought about the creation of school boards, each with the power to raise rates and build schools where voluntary provision was inadequate. The Act was introduced in response to pressures for compulsory education from both the trade unions and employers and in the face of international competition. At its heart lay a strong economic imperative. W. E. Forster, in introducing the bill to the House of Commons, urged members to support it on the grounds that 'upon this speedy provision of education depends also our nation's power'.

Through the Balfour Education Act of 1902 and Fisher Act of 1918, central government began to stake its claim and to set the parameters for local government involvement in the organisation and delivery of education services. The former created a broad administrative base which placed board schools under borough or county councils (328 local education authorities took responsibility for the 2,568 school boards). The latter Act widened this provision to include ancillary services (such as medical inspection in nursery schools). It also formalised the relationship between central and local government, empowered the Board of Education to require local education authorities to submit schemes showing how they proposed to carry out their responsibilities, and enabled central government to exercise control over the activities it was grant-aiding.

The partnership between central and local government was consolidated by the 1944 Education Act. A Ministry of Education was established, with far wider powers than its predecessor (the Board of Education) and with the remit of ensuring that Local Education Authorities (LEAs) provided a varied and comprehensive educational service. Charged with this task, the LEA became one of the dominant institutions in educational policy-making and the provision of services for the next forty years or so; and although this period witnessed a number of battles between central and local government (on issues such as comprehensive education), local government retained its core role and responsibilities for education into the 1980s.

The election of a radical Conservative administration in 1979 marked the beginnings of dramatic changes. Many of the policies of the first Thatcher government (and subsequent administrations) represented a comprehensive critique of the public sector. That critique focused on the policy-making process, the dysfunctional behaviour of bureaucrats in their service of the public, the lack of genuine democratic control over elected members and officers, and, finally but certainly not least, on the prescriptions rather than the choices which public sector organisations offered to the public. Local authorities were accused of being producer—and professional-dominated, unwieldy, cumbersome bureaucracies which were incapable of responding to consumer demand.

Under the protection of two relatively benign Conservative Secretaries of State (Mark Carlisle and Keith Joseph), education escaped detailed structural reform until the mid-1980s. However, the seeds of the education reform agenda, which later manifested itself in the 1988 Education Reform Act, were set in that period and the 1988 Act was a visible and formal reflection of the currents which had begun to flow in other public service areas somewhat earlier. (In 1976 at Ruskin Colleges James Callaghan had criticised the failure of education to respond to technological and employer's needs.)

The 1988 Act contained strong decentralising trends through, for example, the introduction of devolved management to schools. It was also strongly centralising and created the framework for substantial direct state intervention (particularly through the introduction of the national curriculum and standard assessment tasks) and later (with the 1993 Act and the creation of the Office for Standards in Education, OFSTED) through inspection. The 1988 Act was a potent attack on what was seen as the paternalistic, controlling, self-interested activities of local education bureaucracies which were alleged to deny parents the schools of their choice or fail to respond to other legitimate demands.

The structural changes in all sectors of education since the 1988 Act have been dramatic. Central government has sought to establish educational institutions as separate units (sometimes separate and independent corporations) which in most respects must manage their own affairs, be accountable against some form of performance indicators, and compete against each other for customers. The structures, the funding and the form of service delivery have changed, or are changing, in response to the government agenda for a more business-like style, coupled with market responsiveness. The emphasis has been put very firmly on the customers and their right to choose.

Choice and accountability have become dominating themes, and organisational power has shifted away from local government bureaucracies to new bureaucracies (such as the various funding agencies for education) and new government units (such as the new regional arms of government). The development of quangos as arms-length agencies of government has created scope for indirect government intervention and influence in key policy areas and has been part of a power realignment strengthening central over local government.

Ministers are now responsible for over 42,000 appointments to public bodies: a thousand of which are renewed each year, only 24 of which have ever been advertised. Spending by quangos has risen over a four year period from £5 billion to nearly £47 billion. Ministers have argued that quangos are responsible through Parliament. William Waldegrave in a lecture in 1994 defined the role of quangos in the following terms: 'The key point is not whether those who run our public services are elected but whether they are producer responsive or consumer responsive. Services are not necessarily made to respond to the public by giving our citizens a democratic voice, and a distant and diffuse one at that in their running; but by giving them choices, or by instituting mechanisms for publicly approved standards, and for redress when they are not attained.' An elegant rebuttal of the need for any democracy—locally, or centrally.

Within education, as many other areas of the public service, quangos are now major players. Through them, the tentacles of central government now reach into increasingly complex arenas. Training and employment issues have come under the aegis of Training and Enterprise Councils; the Higher Education and Further Education Funding Councils have taken responsibility for the allocation of grants, student numbers and the establishment of quality criteria in further and higher education; the Teacher Training Agency assumes new responsibilities for teacher education and research; OFSTED supervises inspection; the School Curriculum and Assessment Agency has responsibility for the national curriculum and assessment strategy; Education Associations wait in the side-lines to take over 'failing' schools; and the Funding Agency for Schools manages the distribution of grants to grant-maintained schools and shares responsibility (with LEAs) for planning school places.

The particular focus of this article is on two of the 'new kids on the block', the Funding Agencies for Schools and the Integrated Regional Offices of central government whose responsibilities include the new urban funding regime, the Single Regeneration Budget.

The Funding Agency for Schools
It would not be an exaggeration to say that the policy for grant-maintained schools and linked issues such as the Common Funding

Formula (CFF) remain some of the most controversial in education today. To write about the Funding Agency for Schools (FAS) by focusing on its structure and operations may to some observers seem like posing the question, 'and apart from that, Mrs Lincoln, what did you think of the play?' Tight battle lines have been drawn around the general issue of unelected quangos, the selection and remuneration of quango board members, the accountability and the policies as they have been charged to implement. But the FAS itself, unlike some of the new agencies, has not drawn the heavy fire of public criticism about how it operates.

The FAS first opened its doors in York in April 1994. There is no modern precedent to it as a public body in the field of education and it is therefore unsurprising that a number of questions are emerging about how it implements policy, especially in terms of how it can exist and cooperate with LEAs, and vice versa. This is of particular interest given that the FAS and LEAs already share functions, such as planning, or perform similar functions in parallel, certainly for a period of time. The exact time-scale for such development becomes increasingly difficult to predict as the trend for opting for grant-maintained status has slowed down significantly. (In the six months from December 1993 to May 1994 there were 182 ballots in schools about opting out, with 58% voting yes; between December 1992 and May 1993 there were 393 ballots, 79% voting yes.)

The legislative framework. The Funding Agency for Schools (England) was set up under the terms of The Education Act 1993 (section 3). It consists of 10 to 15 members who are appointed by the Secretary of State for Education. Thirteen board members had been appointed by the Secretary of State by September 1994. The one local government figure is Edward Lister, leader of the Conservative Wandsworth council which has given high-profile support to government policies. Sir Christopher Benson, who chairs the FAS, is also chairman of Sun Alliance which has given £280,000 to Conservative Party funds over a six-year period. (*Observer*, 29.5.94).

According to the schedule of the Act, board members are to have expertise in: primary and secondary education; voluntary aided or grant maintained-schools; industry, commerce, finance, the professions; and/or special education needs. The board meets monthly and each member has regional responsibilities to establish links with elected members. Five committees have been set up for finance, planning, audit, remuneration and new schools.

Section 4 of the Act gives the Secretary of State power to set up a schools funding council for Wales which is to comprise of 8 to 12 members, again appointed by the Secretary of State. Its members are expected to have similar experiences and capacities as those outlined above. As yet, it has not been set up and the Secretary of State for Wales is to carry out the appropriate functions until there are enough grant-maintained schools to justify the setting up of the Schools Funding Council which differs in ways that are as yet unclear from the FAS.

Under the terms of the Act, the FAS is a Non-Departmental Public Body, accountable to Parliament through the Secretary of State for Education. The board and chief executive (as the Accounting Officer) are directly responsible to the Public Accounts Committee, the Select Committee on Education and the National Audit Office. Under section 10, the Audit Commission can carry out studies at the request of FAS in order to improve the economy, efficiency and effectiveness of its own management, or that of a grant-maintained school (the governing body of which may also request a study).

Responsibilities and structure. The functions of the Funding Agency for Schools for the provision of school places are determined by the number of grant-maintained schools in a LEA. Its degree of responsibility changes on a sliding scale, as the number of pupils in grant-maintained schools in a LEA area goes up. The White Paper 'Choice and Diversity' (1992) identified responsibilities under five broad headings:

Information. The FAS has to supply information to the Secretary of State as required, to LEAs, and vice versa.

Calculation and payment of grants. This includes the Annual Maintenance Grant (which is calculated by the FAS and paid to each grant-maintained school governing body) and the Capital Grant (which is decided on the basis of criteria set by the Secretary of State and is calculated through a mixture of formula based allocation and allocations made as a result of the bidding process).

Financial monitoring. The FAS has a duty to monitor the spending of grant-maintained schools to ensure that grants are used for the purposes for which they are paid. It is also required to carry out value for money studies (VFM), on either the economy, efficiency and effectiveness with which the governing body of a school has used grants, or how the economy, efficiency and effectiveness in the management or operation of the school might be improved.

Provision of school places. The FAS is also responsible for the provision of sufficient school places in certain areas.

Minor Functions. The Secretary of State may transfer other minor functions to the FAS in the future, including functions in respect of the governance of schools; making and receiving payments to and from the City Technology Colleges; payment of Section 11 grants to LEAs; and the power to determine proposals for change published by grant-maintained schools.

The Funding Agency as an operation unit was set up following the recommendations of a Department for Education working party. It operates in part out of a pleasant but not palatial office building on the side of the river Ouse in York. The York base houses the board secretariat and the planning division and is within ten minutes walking distance of York railway station and a range of inter-city services which include a two-hour service to London. There is another office in Darlington which is responsible for the calculation and payment of capital grants and personnel matters. The Agency is about to open a London office in Centre Point for board meetings.

The Agency's basic structure is hierarchical but the FAS view is that its culture is not in danger of becoming bureaucratic; the speed of change mitigates against bureaucratic mind-set and does not allow for the concomitant dysfunctional behaviour to develop. According to senior FAS officers, since staff morale is high and the work is carried out in teams, the organisational culture does in fact have the attributes of a flatter structure. Staff have been recruited from the Department for Education and other ministries, the Further Education Funding Council, LEAs and a range of private sector backgrounds.

As well as its central duties, the Agency has a regional dimension and new regional teams are being set up to service its functions in respect of revenue and capital grant, and in some areas planning. There are currently eight teams: North, Midlands, Essex, East, North London, South London, South, Kent. Those with planning responsibilities are empowered to request relevant demographic and other information from local authorities. The teams are currently 'home based' but the FAS has the power to set up regional offices, subject to approval by the Secretary of State. Staff spend about 50% of their time in their regions and the other half in York. The FAS has no presence in areas without grant-maintained schools, such as Cornwall.

The philosophy of the FAS. The Chief Executive of the FAS, Michael Collier, has made unequivocal public statements about what he regards as its current role and its likely evolution. He sees the Agency as 'an integral part of the grant maintained movement' but carrying out its activities as a partner with the LEAs, rather than competitor. His perception is that although the functions are laid down by statute, there is scope for a wider interpretation of its role, which goes beyond the implementation of policy made elsewhere—payment of grants and projections about school places—to create policy. This is seen as a gradual process, perhaps implicitly made through 'steering by funding' and through the building up of case law precedent which will guide the use of administrative discretion by its officials.

Echoing the themes in 'Choice and Diversity', Michael Collier has suggested that the Agency's prime objective 'is to preserve the new environment which allows the self governing schools to become autonomous, to be creative, to flourish and have the freedom to meet parents and pupils needs more effectively and be more accountable to them whilst assisting the Secretary of State to fulfil his or her accountability to Parliament'. He has described FAS as being on the 'fulcrum of this balancing out between freedom and national accountability.' (*Exchange Monthly*, July 1994).

Others take a different view of the FAS and the issue of accountability.

Roy Pryke, Director of Education for Kent, writing in *Education* (July 1994) has described his concerns in the following terms: 'It will not be long before we see LEAs presenting proposals about the future development of schools in a locality to committees which meet in public and which are widely reported in local papers, whilst the FAS meets secretly in York (or London) discussing the same issues.'

As might be expected from someone with an impeccable CIPFA (Chartered Institute of Public Finance and Accountancy) background, Michael Collier has also identified the significance of financial control as a significant element in the FAS philosophy. In his view, the desire to allow grant-maintained schools to have autonomy must be balanced against the development of proper accountability in the use of public money. This is no hypothetical concern; the National Audit Office, in its report 'Value for Money at Grant-Maintained Schools,' found poor target setting and identification of priorities, coupled with short-term financial planning in many of the 70 schools examined in visits by its officers in the period October 1993 to February 1994.

The Chief Executive is also concerned with the issue of educational quality. Although he regards the prime players in this area as being The School Curriculum and Assessment Agency (SCAA) and the Office for Standards in Education (OFSTED) he feels that the FAS cannot totally ignore this issue. What the Agency does in exercising its main responsibilities 'must be supported to the creation of an environment which encourages an improvement in standards'. This is especially relevant in terms of VFM and school place planning.

The Local Education Authority perspective. The nature of the relationship between LEA officers and FAS has been a matter for personal interpretation and individual experience, although in some instances influenced by the political stance of elected members to the grant-maintained sector. By and large, pragmatism has taken over and good or workable professional relationships forged in an attempt to get the job done. Looking more closely at those relationships, the education finance officers interviewed had had little or no contact with the FAS regional team leaders in their area. On the face of it, there would seem to be no obvious reason for them so to do. However, the LEA planning officer did meet with the regional team leaders on a fairly regular basis and in some geographical areas initial teething problems (if not entirely resolved) had improved. This is perhaps a reflection of the amount of time and importance which the FAS has given to establishing effective contacts with operational managers within the LEA and of the professional commitment of those officers. FAS Board members do not appear, however, to have actively pursued similar relationships with elected members.

The relationship between the education finance officer and the FAS has clearly been structured by the timetable in which they were expected to supply information and to prepare the budget calculation for the grant-maintained schools in their areas. There was great variation between LEAs on the time spent on FAS issues, as the amount of work depended on the number of grant-maintained schools within the areas. One officer thought that on a rule of thumb basis he spent two to three days a week on grant-maintained schools and Common Funding Formula business, another that she spent two to three days overall in a period of nine months or so. The Department for Education's role in the new framework was regarded by LEA officers as being somewhat mysterious and this was compounded by the feeling that any correspondence between the LEA and the Department or the FAS, seemed to be automatically photocopied to the other.

Some LEA officers were amused about being questioned about the cost of the time spent by them on the FAS. One thought with a degree of levity that it should be invoiced for their time. Others were not so amused and felt strongly that the FAS was 'buying information for free', not only the information it required (as stipulated in section 21 of the Education Act 1993) but the expertise of education professionals. (Few if any of the FAS officers at operational level are qualified accountants, and in the area of planning FAS regional team leaders seem to have varying degrees of expertise.) In the view of the LEA, its expertise was not limited to that of individual officers but was essentially 'the synergy of the LEA and the entire local authority'.

The FAS story: the next instalment. In attempting to find out how a relationship is developing, it is sensible to talk to both parties, as in this small study. However, there have been difficulties in defining what and who is involved in the particular interface. Even within one organisation, views differed according to the task to be completed, the organisational work context and the personal and professional opinion of those directly or indirectly involved. There has also been the inevitable difficulty of finding out what is happening behind the official view for public consumption. When talking to individuals, there were instances when the words of a woman of more recent historical significance than Mrs Lincoln would come to mind: 'Well they would say that wouldn't they.' However, what certainly emerged from all parties was that the tasks were being tackled with unfailing professionalism and, in some instances, remarkable good humour.

But a number of questions have emerged from this initial insight into the development and operation of the Funding Agency. One central question is whether it is flying solo or simply managing with a little (or perhaps considerable) help from its 'friends', some sharing the same perspective and some pressed into that task. The indirect costs to LEAs of supplying information and expertise to the FAS can be considerable and, undoubtedly, its development has depended on the historic and contemporary data supplied by LEAs. One may speculate whether it could function if an operational divorce from the LEAs occurred.

The development of the FAS also raises a number of other questions about accountability and decision making. There has been a lack of publicity about the decision-making processes; but given the technicalities and the frequency of contact between officials from LEAs, the Agency, and the Department for Education, it would now appear that those officers are the only ones who know or understand the budgeting and planning process for the grant-maintained sector. If this is so, then is it another instance of the continuing depoliticisation of decision making? The FAS is quite clearly developing a philosophy of its own through the exercise of administrative discretion. What are the implications of this for public accountability?

Integrated Regional Offices and the Single Regeneration Budget

April 1994 also saw the birth of the new integrated regional offices (IROs) for England. The creation of the ten offices which are headed by senior civil servants (who act as regional directors for the Departments of Employment, Environment, Transport, and Trade and Industry) potentially represents a massive reform of Whitehall. The Department for Education and the Home Office are occasional 'bit' players in this shifting drama of changing power relations and new funding arrangements.

The new regional directors are civil service high-flyers who, on past record, are likely to relish new challenges. Robin Young, for example, who has become 'Mr London', comes from the Department of Environment where he set the agenda for compulsory competitive tendering. Marianne Neville-Rolfe, who now heads the North-West office, is a former head of the Civil Service College, where she created a new management agenda.

The arrival of the IROs on the scene was greeted with cautious welcome by Labour and metropolitan authorities; few could object to a strategy designed to reduce duplication and overlap between a plethora of funding regimes and aimed at creating a more integrated approach. Twenty existing funding regimes were to be subsumed into the new £1.4b Single Regeneration Budget (SRB) pot which would be administered through the regional offices.

A range of factors and influences had combined to bring about the new integrated regional office strategy; not least of these had been Michael Heseltine's particular interest in urban regeneration. In London, pressure from the private sector was certainly instrumental in forcing the government to recognise that the voice of London had become dissipated since the abolition of the Greater London Council and the Inner London Education Authority. The collapse of a number of London ventures, such as the Olympic bid, and the perceived insularity of many London boroughs has also provided further evidence of the need for change.

The creation of the new IROs is also part of the post Maastricht shift designed to strengthen regions; a move which has created sceptics in a number of camps. Whitehall sceptics have raised concerns about parochialism, local government sceptics about the ever-spreading tentacles of central government. Both have acknowledged, however, that the new regional arrangements could increase the opportunity for urban areas to bid successfully for European Union money.

The Single Regeneration Budgets complex but brief bidding process took place during the summer of 1994. Through it, local authorities were required to bid across borough or city boundaries, with a range of other institutions and agencies from both the voluntary and the private sector—an activity which was both challenging and time-consuming. As one Director of Education, described it: 'I've got all my staff running around like headless chickens. But whether I'll get any money remains to be seen.' The result of the process—an allocation of £100m—will be announced early in 1995. Undoubtedly, there will be more losers than winners—a likely ratio of 4:1. In the case of London, 169 bids were submitted, 25 of which were short-listed for the Environment Secretary. In total, 469 short-listed bids, from the ten offices, totalling £375m, were submitted.

Implications of the new funding regime. A number of issues are emerging in relation to the Single Regeneration Budget and the Integrated Regional Offices. This article focuses on just three. The first relates to a general theme of the article: the trend towards increased rule-setting by central government and the creation of new bureaucracies—in this case a new regional arm of government—to sustain those new rules.

This trend has significant implications for local government, as local authorities increasingly become excluded from critical decisions about the allocation of resources which will define the scope and nature of the local landscape. Local government finds itself in the role of petitioner in a complex game, the rules of which are decided elsewhere. From the point of view of the local citizen, issues about who makes decisions and how those decisions are made in a locality become increasingly obscured.

The jury is still out on the second issue: the impact of the Single Regeneration Budget on education. On the one hand, it has provided the opportunity for education to be tackled in the broader context of other urban issues, such as housing and employment. One senior local authority officer described this shift in the following terms: 'The challenge of the SRB is that instead of being based around individual programmes, like section 11, or literacy, all sorts of issues are being thrown up for us about school effectiveness strategies which incorporate much wider issues. It raises issues for us, for example, about the needs of those 20% of young people who are not reached in the inner city.' On the other hand, there are real concerns about how far education will be a loser in this wider framework. The Single Regeneration Budget has no defined educational categories, no clear ways of ensuring that the education elements of a broadly based funding proposals are spelt out. The Department for Education's cursory involvement in the bidding process has added to education's vulnerability.

The impact of the Home Office decision to place section 11 funding (which was specifically designed to meet the needs of ethnic minorities) into the SRB melting pot is deeply significant for education. Urban authorities must contend with a vastly reduced section 11 as part of the generic pool, and the irony is that rural authorities can still apply to the Home Office for section 11 funding. Similarly, the Department's decision to place in the 'pot' money allocated to GEST 19, Raising Standard in the Inner City (which has been used in the past to focus on specific projects, for example literacy) creates other tensions. Past funding which had specifically been directed towards education has now become part of a wider funding regime which appears to favour large-scale urban regeneration projects at the expense of bids with a social content, such as language projects for non-English speakers. (Because of pressure, a further £15m was added in late 1994 for section 11.)

The third relates to the nature of the bidding process itself. From a school perspective, it has been difficult to be a player in a time-consuming and complicated bidding process which requires an under-standing of how networks operate, how complex decisions are made which involve a range of parties and which ultimately may offer little. One headteacher, who had been a successful 'bidder' in the past from a range of urban funds, described the challenges in the following terms: 'If I look at other heads in (the LEA), many of them don't network. It very much depends on their perception of leadership of their organisation. Too many heads still see their life as being within the school. There are direct financial gains to be made from networking and there is also the opportunity to develop thinking, but there's also the dilemma of how much time to spend on it when there is so much else to do.'

Concluding thoughts

This article began by dipping into the history, scope and nature of local and central government intervention in education, and in particular the partnership between the two. It argued that the reformulation of roles and relationships in the last decade has resulted in the creation of a complex range of organisational patterns which seriously challenge that partnership. It suggested that the central government agenda has been to reduce the power of Local Education Authorities and locate aspects of important decision-making outside the local authority area. The examples of the Funding Agency and the Integrated Regional Office illustrate this point.

The analysis has highlighted a number of points and we emphasise just two in this conclusion. Firstly, many aspects of decision making have been wrested from the local democratic arena and transferred into the realm of interpretation by an officer core at the FAS (responsible to a non-elected board and the Public Accounts Committee) or a civil service core at the Integrated Regional Office (responsible through complex Whitehall and parliamentary procedures). In making this point, we are not questioning either the integrity or the commitment of those officers but highlighting the democratic deficit and the risks inherent in a decision-making process which takes decisions at a distance from those concerned.

Secondly, a consequence of the shift from a system of local government to one of local governance has been that the decision-making process has become increasingly complex and responsibility for decisions diffuse. Those who wish to participate have to commit resources and energy, even though, as the sanguine headteacher quoted earlier, reflected, 'there is so much else to do in education'.

This article is underpinned by work supported by the ESRC and the Local Gevernment Management Board. The FAS analysis draws on interviews with members of senior management and regional teams and with LEA officers. The IROs analysis draws on a project, The New Management, Citizenship and Institutional change in Local Governance, by Professor Kathryn Riley and Keiran Walsh and Drs Vivien Lowndes and Jackie Woodham.

Accountability in the National Health Service

BY PHILIP HUNT

TWO key factors are driving the current interest in public involvement in the National Health Service. First the 1991 reforms gave District Health Authorities (DHAs) a clear responsibility for the health of their populations and underpinned this by allocating funding for hospital and community health services on a per capita basis. Before the reforms they were preoccupied with managing the hospitals and other units in their district; today, their focus is on meeting the health needs of the local population. Second, regardless of the way in which the service is managed, patients preferences, scientific and technological advances and the emphasis on quality of service are transforming the face of health care. A report published last year by the National Association of Health Authorities and Trusts suggested that not only were we moving to a primary care-led health service but that by the end of the century a pattern of secondary services would have emerged of a small number of high-technology centres complemented by community hospitals.

If an inherently conservative public is not to prevent the NHS from making the most of these advances, effective ways have to be found to bring the public into discussions about how the service might respond to them. Legitimacy for radical change in a much-loved public service has to be won. Early in 1994 Dr Brian Mawhinney, then Minister for Health, asked every DHA in the country how it was seeking out the views of its residents. 'I want to ensure', he explained, 'that consultation with your local community is and remains at the heart of your DHA's purchasing agenda. I expect your DHA to be involved in a regular high-profile dialogue with your local population, to find out people's views about health services, and to take account of these views in your purchasing plans and contracting decisions.' And there is the rub. While advances in health care point to fewer, more intensively used hospitals, local communities do not want to see themselves as local communities without a hospital in their backyard. The result is an intense national and local debate about health care which has stimulated the interest of some local councils which see the potential for town hall control of health purchasing.

This interest by local government in taking on health has coincided with the hotting up of the debate about the relevance of our current governmental institutions, and more specifically the role of quangos and criticism of them for their lack of local accountability. Given the size of the NHS and the wide-ranging nature of its services to the whole of the population, it is not surprising that NHS authorities and trusts have come under the microscope. There are, of course, many facets to the notion of accountability in the NHS, including the accountability of doctors to patients, of NHS Trusts to health authorities and GP fundholders through the contracting process, and of ministers to Parliament for the overall performance of the NHS. But undoubtedly it is the relationship between the NHS and its local population, together with the sensitivity and acceptability of the decisions made by NHS authorities and Trusts which has caught public and political attention.

This is not the first time that there has been a debate about accountability arrangements in the NHS, but it is probably the most serious and potentially influential debate since the discussions which led to its formation in 1948. Before the introduction of the NHS many hospitals and a number of other health services were provided by local authorities. The 1944 White Paper, *A National Health Service*, pointed out that: 'In a long series of public health acts and similar measures, Parliament has placed the prime responsibility for providing the health service on local, rather than central authority.' However, the 1929 Local Government Act was permissive and many local authorities had failed to develop acute hospitals. When details of the new NHS were being discussed within the Attlee post-war Labour government, there was a division between Herbert Morrison, who wanted the NHS to be made part of local government, and Aneurin Bevan, who countered with what he saw as its weakness, the enormous variation in services and the doctors' opposition to being under local government. Bevan argued that an NHS under local government would be a less ambitious, second class service. The Bevanite view prevailed and the NHS was established as a national service. A minister was made answerable to Parliament, with local bodies appointed as his or her agents to run hospital and contractor services. Bevan hoped that by the selection of the right people to serve on boards and committees, substantial executive powers could be devolved to them. Indeed, an early circular issued by the Ministry of Health to Regional Hospital Boards informed them that they were agents of the minister but that they should feel a sense of independent responsibility.

The issue of whether local government should control the NHS has been revisited many times since that original decision. As early as the Guillebaud Committee Report of 1956 on the cost of the NHS, a reservation by Sir John Maude said: 'The system in some respects appears to combine the disadvantages of centralised administration with the disadvantages of local government.' This remained a minority position, however, and the Committee came down against the transfer of the NHS to local government. It pointed out that hospital planning demands regional organisation and that joint boards would have to be established for that purpose.

The first NHS reorganisation Green Paper in 1968, which started the process leading to the reforms of 1974, proposed an integration of health services under appointed area boards but it did not rule out that these could be committees of the new type of local authority likely to be recommended by the Royal Commission on Local Government, chaired by Redcliffe Maud, which was sitting concurrently. Although the Wilson government (1964–1970) toyed with the idea of placing the NHS within local government, it rejected this option. The key reasons given were the view of the health professions that only a service run by special authorities with professional representation would assure clinical freedom and that the financial resources of local authorities were not sufficient for them to take it over. The 1970 Green Paper concluded that Area Health Authorities must be established serving the same areas as those local authorities providing personal social services. It was intended that one-third of the members of the Area Health Authorities would be appointed by local authorities. The Heath government which actually piloted the resultant NHS reorganisation of 1974 through Parliament took the same view, but reduced to a quarter the number of members of the Area Health Authorities to be appointed by the corresponding local authorities.

This was not the end of the debate. The incoming Labour government of 1974 increased local authority representation on health authorities from a quarter to a third, whilst the relationship between the NHS and local authorities was reconsidered by the Royal Commission on the NHS which reported in 1979. The Commission was much taken with the need for the closest possible collaboration between the NHS and local government because of their overlapping responsibilities. It discussed the option of transferring the NHS to local government but, in the end, decided that although a transfer had many attractions and was in some ways a logical development from the present structure, it could not recommend it. It felt that a further reorganisation of such major dimensions should be avoided, at least in the short term. It is worth noting that the Commission also rejected a transfer of personal social services into the NHS, as had been put forward by the Royal College of Nursing and the relevant union, NUPE, and has been argued by various groups since them. It stated, such a move in itself would not produce the integrated planning of the full range of health and local authority services. Whilst it would shift the dividing line between the NHS and local government, the dividing line would still remain, particularly in relation to housing and education. It also felt that whilst the NHS depends heavily on personal social services, it probably generated well under half the caseload of social workers, the rest coming from their other responsibilities.

Despite this consistent rejection of local authority control, it is notable that from its inception, the NHS encountered criticisms of the effectiveness of the boards of health authorities and their predecessor organisations. Two reasons suggest themselves. First, that the characteristic of the NHS in its first forty years was one of a very clear professional dominance which left little room for decision making by lay people. Second, there was ambiguity about the role of health authorities. With their mixture of local authority, professional and lay members and with the requirement to implement the policies of central government, it is not surprising that they often found it difficult to develop the necessary corporate ethos to ensure that they were effective bodies. This was focused upon by the 1989 White Paper, *Working for Patients*, which led on to the current reforms and which proposed radical changes in the composition of NHS authorities. It said: 'At district level, the arrangements for appointing members reflect a long standing lack of clarity about the role of health authorities. At present, they are neither truly representative nor management bodies. The government believed that authorities based on this confusion of roles would not be equipped to handle the complex managerial and contactual issues that the new system demands and that if health authorities are to discharge their new responsibilities in a business-like way, they need to be smaller and to bring together executive and non-executive members to provide a single focus for effective decision-making.' The same principles were adopted in relation to NHS Trusts and Family Health Services Authorities although there were some differences in regard to the number and make up of executive and non-executive directors.

From an NHS point of view, the new boards have proved their worth. The bringing together of a small number of executives and non-executives has allowed for more challenging and realistic discussions and greater corporate cohesion. They are in a position to set the strategic direction of their organisation, set the way they do business and ensure that financial targets are achieved within the context of their accountability—whether direct or via the regional health authorities—to the Secretary of State. What they have not avoided is criticism for their lack of local accountability.

This criticism has undoubtedly been fuelled by John Stewart's and others writing on quangos which point to a growing range of responsibilities which have been removed from local authorities to non-elected agencies and organisations, in addition to an increasing intervention by central government over local government finance. He points, as examples, to the boards of health authorities and NHS Trusts, Training and Enterprise Councils, the board of governors of grant-maintained schools, the governing bodies of Colleges of Further Education and Housing Action Trusts, and argues that a new magistracy is being established in the sense that a non-elected elite is assuming responsibility for a large part of local governance. There is no sense he argues in which those appointed can be regarded as locally accountable, and what accountability there is within the system will increasingly rest on central government. Critics believe that unless new forms of accountability are developed, a burden is being put upon the accountability of ministers that is probably beyond their capacity to accept. They urge a revitalisation and revaluation of local government, and by implication to include the NHS within it.

This line has received support within the NHS by the Institute of Health Services Management (IHSM) president, David Knowles. In his incoming presidential speech in June 1993, he argues the case for local government taking over the purchasing role of health authorities in order to exercise local choice concerning the rationing of locally available resources. He considers that unelected health authorities, even linked as they are to a democratically elected central government, do not constitute a sufficient level of legitimacy, maintaining that 'Whatever the perceived frailties of local authorities, they are at least legitimate.' He points to the replacement of the old style health authorities, with members directly nominated by local authorities, by the smaller, more managerially-focused bodies have shifted accountability and legitimacy away from the community. One reason often given why local authorities should not be directly involved in the NHS is that they do not have the necessary competence to manage the provision of health services. But Knowles argues that with the purchaser/provider split and health authorities' new focus on commissioning, this ceases to be an issue. He considers that 'Despite much commitment and good intention, the lack of democractic legitimacy makes the current tension between purchaser and provider lacking in impetus to reshape services — away from acute care to integrated care, for example.'

A powerful case can be made but it is important that it is fully tested before NHS authorities are rushed into the eager arms of their counterpart local authorities. A plethora of mechanisms is already available to ensure that the NHS is accountable.

The Secretary of State for Health is accountable to Parliament for the running of the NHS. Health authorities and NHS Trusts are, in effect, her agents and this is underpinned by the Secretary of State's appointment of chairmen of District Health Authorities and Family Health Services Authorities; the chairman and a proportion of the non-executive directors of NHS Trusts, and the chairmen and non-executive members of Regional Health Authorities. The accountability of the Secretary of State to Parliament means that MPs can ask parliamentary questions about every aspect of the running of the NHS and, indeed, hundreds of such questions are asked each year. In addition, frequent debates are held to discuss NHS issues at which Health Ministers respond on behalf of the government. At regular intervals, bills relating to the NHS are introduced, subject to the rigours of parliamentary scrutiny, before becoming law. Ministers frequently have to defend their decisions both in Parliament and in the media.

Parliamentary accountability is reinforced by the work of the Select Committee on Health and the Public Accounts Committee of the House of Commons. The former regularly invites evidence from organisations and individuals on aspects of policy and management in the NHS, and witnesses, including ministers, can be asked to give oral evidence. Its reports have been influential in developing and changing health service policy. The latter is responsible for reviewing the way the NHS spends the money voted to it by Parliament. As Accounting Officer, the chief executive of the NHS Executive is regularly called to give evidence and answer questions about aspects of NHS spending, and where appropriate, NHS chairmen and officers can also be called alongside the chief executive.

The Public Accounts Committee is supported by the National Audit Office which regularly publishes reports about aspects of running the NHS. As part of her announcement to abolish Regional Health Authorities, the Secretary of State indicated her intention to increase the accountability of health authorities and trusts by looking at the feasibility of making their chief executives the Accounting Officers for the resources under their control. The Audit Commission audits local government and NHS spending below department and NHS Executive level, and examines value for money in the use of resources. Like the National Audit Office, the Audit Commission publishes frequent reports about the NHS.

There are various mechanisms in place to ensure that the NHS delivers on the policies laid down by ministers. Extensive systems of review and the development of corporate contracts from the NHS Executive to Regional and then to District and Family Health Services Authorities; and the oversight of NHS Trusts by the NHS Executive, are all designed to ensure that the activities of authorities and Trusts are consistent with ministerial priorities. The new arrangements for regional offices of the NHS Executive are aimed at consolidating this process.

The Patient's Charter sets clear and specific performance standards on which the NHS is expected to deliver. These include guarantees on waiting times for admission to treatments and the right to have detailed information about quality standards and maximunm waiting times.

Community Health Councils exist to represent the public interest in the NHS. Their members are drawn from voluntary organisations, local authorities and the local community. To support them in their role, the Councils have the following rights: relevant information from NHS authorities; access to certain NHS premises; consultation on substantial developments or variations in services; observers at meetings of DHAs and FHSAs. Each Community Health Council also has a duty to publish an annual report.

Health authorities and Family Health Services Authorities are required to hold their meetings in public. Trusts are not but many do, and they are required to hold an annual meeting in public and to publish an annual report.

The separation of the purchaser (or commissioner) and the provider roles within the NHS enables purchasers to exert pressure on providers through contracts and treatment protocols. In addition, there are extensive arrangements laid down by the Department of Health for dealing with individual complaints which have to be followed by NHS authorities and trusts. Complaints can also be made to the health service commissioner.

NHS trusts are also subject to various inspections by the appropriate Royal Colleges and considerable progress is being made in the development of clinical audit. Audit programmes by institutions like the King's Fund are another of the mechanisms being used to review the performance of trusts.

All this suggests that even allowing for the devolution of considerable responsibility to NHS authorities and Trusts they are still subject to central control and direction, and therefore proper accountability is being exercised, at least to the centre. But is this sufficient? And would local government control of the NHS purchasing function add value to the current arrangements? Knowles certainly thinks so. He argues that it would make for local legitimisation of potentially difficult purchasing decisions and it should ensure that responsiveness of the NHS to local priorities would increase. A particular gain would be the potential for greater cooperation across health and personal social services, leading both to a clarification of respective responsibilities and to joint purchasing approaches which should promote more responsive and better integrated services. A further advantage claimed would be the potential for building health alliances between the NHS and all the other parts of local government, including transport, planning and housing, which can have a positive impact upon improving the health of the local population.

What this overlooks, however, is that local government's bid to take over health care purchasing would threaten one of the fundamental features of the NHS which has overwhelming public support: whether you live in Newcastle or Newquay, Birmingham or Brighton, you have a right to expect a similar standard of service for similar needs. The NHS is a national service. There is absolutely no sign of the public wanting a Surrey, a Shropshire or a Southwark health service. And any alternative arrangement which saw local government acting merely as an administrative agent for the Department of Health would be inconsistent with the main advantage claimed by proponents of a town hall role in health purchasing — local democratic accountability. The local ballot box is not an appropriate mechanism for holding an administrative agent to account.

It is also difficult to see how local democratic accountability could be secured unless at least some of the resources required for the NHS were raised locally. Yet funding largely through general taxation and national insurance contributions underlines the national nature of the service. Accountability and funding cannot be separated. To do so either leads to the purse-holder calling the tune or to the risk of irresponsible local management and frustration at both national and local levels.

In many services, the NHS transcends district boundaries — tertiary referrals and regional specialties are an example. The likely reduction in the number of district general hospitals in the future, with a trend towards more regional specialty hospitals and a much more developed primary care service, means that a strategic overview is required over and above the local level. How is this to be dealt with in the context of local democratisation? The option of regional goverment is one obvious answer, but this brings with it many questions about the relationship and potential conflict between a democratically elected regional tier and a democratically elected local tier, vying with central government for control of the NHS.

What also can not be overlooked is the role of GPs, and specifically GP fundholders. The numbers and range of influence of GP fundholders is growing and the recent review of fundholding, initiated by Dr Mawhinney as Minister for Health, will extend that influence even further. How would this fit into a pattern of local government control of NHS purchasing? Would there continue to be a significant purchasing role for transfer to local government? Even if there were, in all likelihood GPs would refuse to be in contract to local authorities. This would mean the continuation of centrally appointed Family Health Services Authority-type bodies, dealing with GPs and making coordination of health purchasing extremely difficult.

And it is not just GPs. Perhaps one of the most significant advances being made in the NHS is the effort to ensure that doctors are accountable for the effectiveness of their clinical performance. The purchaser/provider split has built in the pressure and leverage for questioning the performance of doctors in a way which has never been seen before. How would local authorities perform in this regard? How would they stand up to the shroud-waving doctors who use the media quite mercilessly to defend their own particular empire.

The separation of responsibility between health authority purchasers and NHS Trust providers has been one of the most significant changes arising from the reforms. What would happen to providers if local authorities took over as health purchasers? Those on the radical right would no doubt see this as a heaven-sent opportunity to privatise NHS hospitals or, at the very least, put them outside the NHS into the 'not for profit' charitable sector. This would, however, dilute the very notion of the NHS and be very unpopular with the public.

If providers were to be brought under the direct control of the local authority, there would be a clear risk that the role and responsibilities of purchasers and providers would become increasingly blurred and that the local authority's responsibility for the provider units could become their dominant concern, as was the case with District Health Authorities before 1991. Even if local authorities acted as 'enablers' and the local authority/provider unit relationship was kept on an 'arms-length' basis, it would be extremely difficult to prevent the former becoming over-involved in provider issues. Given the intense public interest in hospitals, and the nature of the electoral and political process in local government, the focus on the overall health needs of the population might be very difficult to sustain. Perhaps more importantly, given the cross-district boundary nature of the NHS, there would be very difficult issues to tackle in relation to the funding of provider units and relationships with other local authorities. If provider units were the direct responsibility of the local authority, the incentive to see as many patients as possible referred to its own units would be overwhelming.

Arguing for the status quo does not mean that there are no ways of improving the currect system of appointments by ensuring that the boards of NHS authorities and Trusts have a high calibre non-executive membership which is also credible with the local community. Indeed, drawing on current examples of good practice it should be possible to establish an effective framework which embraces the following key elements; attracts more people to put their names forward for consideration for appointment; shows greater balance in the people appointed to embrace different skills, experience, attitudes and background; makes transparent the process of appointing chairmen and non-executives with short-listed persons interviewed by an appointments panel. All chairmen and non-executives should be regularly appraised and these appraisals should be taken into account when their current term of office comes to an end. All should sign up to induction training and after appointment to commit themselves to a regular programme of further training and development.

The pace of scientific and technological change is leading to such far-reaching changes in healthcare that the legitimacy of any system of governance would, in all likelihood, be called into question. The present system is by no means perfect. It does, however, support a national health service. It has led to a growing commitment to listening to patients and the public and to involving them in decisions about how services should be developed. Backed up by a more rigorous approach to the appointment of chairmen and members of the boards of NHS authorities and Trusts, ensuring that they come from a wide cross-section of the community, there is every reason to hope that the NHS can continue to be effectively accountable at a national level to Parliament but equally sensitive to the needs of the local communities it is there to serve.

Quangos: Questions of Democratic Accountability

BY STUART WEIR

THE phenomenal proliferation of executive bodies over the past fifteen years in the United Kingdom is perhaps best illustrated by the bare statistic that there is now an executive quango for every ten thousand people in the country. I am using the term quango not as shorthand for Non-Departmental Public Bodies (NDPBs), the government's usage, but to describe all executive bodies which have been created, or pressed into service, to perform public functions or deliver public services, and which receive public funds to do so. As in the Democratic Audit report, *Ego Trip*, on which this article is based, I describe all these bodies as 'EGOs', or 'extra government organisations'.

Government figures for such bodies are unreliable, but the current estimate of the size of executive quangoland stands at 5,573 executive bodies, or EGOs, in the United Kingdom. If advisory bodies, tribunals and Next Steps Agencies are included, the quango count rises to nearly 7,000 bodies in 1992–93. In that year, EGOs spent £46.6 billion— nearly a third of total central government expenditure.

In this article, my main purpose is to scrutinise the mechanisms of democratic accountability for EGOs. Government ministers routinely claim that such bodies are part of a 'democratic gain' and provide a surer form of accountability for public services than that afforded by elected local authorities and local ballot. Both traditional and 'new' forms of accountability are examined with this claim in mind. I cut through the confusions in government categories and figures by concentrating on the accountability of all explicitly executive bodies of a semi-autonomous nature which effectively act as agencies for central government and carry out government policies. I exclude 'executive agencies', which do not have their own boards and are still officially regarded as part of their original departments. Also excluded are the NHS Management Executive and its regional outposts, although they are a significant part of the hierarchy of health bodies and, at the lower end of the scale, fund-holding GPs. I do count the eight Northern Ireland executive bodies, including the powerful NI Housing Executive, which the government still excludes, with no apparent sense of irony, on the historic grounds that they 'fulfil functions carried out by local government in Great Britain'.[1]

The most significant departure from official categories that I make is to include over 4,500 bodies which operate at local level under appointed or self-appointing committees of people, now popularly

1: Extra Government Organisations				
	National	Regional	Local	Totals
Executive NDPs	261	66	31	358
NHS Bodies	18	289	322	629
Non-recognised EGOs	164		4,422	4,586
Totals	443	355	4,775	5,573

known as the 'new magistracy'.[2] These bodies are excluded from government figures because they may be private companies, like the Training and Enterprise Councils (TECs), or voluntary and charitable bodies, like registered Housing Associations. Others, like the new further education and sixth form college corporations, and grant-maintained schools are undeniably public bodies. The only explanation for the government's failure to acknowledge parentage of such bodies is either to keep the quango count down or just carelessness. The fact is that all these local bodies have been created or pressed into HM Government's service to perform public functions and deliver public services. They are almost wholly funded by government and act under the direction of ministers and their departments and major executive bodies under government control, like the Housing Corporation or the Funding Agency for Schools. They are responsible for social housing, schools, further education, training for employment, hospitals and health care— public services of great importance to people at local level, some of which until recently were mainly the preserve of elected local authorities.

As Table 1 shows, there are 5,573 'extra governmental' organisations, or EGOs, in the United Kingdom. Of these, there are 44 at national level; 355 at regional level; and 4,775 at local level. The great mass of these—4,586—are bodies which are not recognised by government in its own figures for quangos—they are thus classified as 'non-recognised' bodies. The full breakdown is as follows:

Recognised executive NDPBs	350
'Non-recognised' NI NDPBs	8
NHS bodies	629
'Non-recognised' bodies:	
Grant-maintained schools	1,025
City Technology Colleges	15
Further Education Corporations	557
Higher Education Corporations	164
Registered housing associations	2,668
Training and Enterprise Councils	82
Local Enterprise Companies	23
Police Authorities	52
Total	5,573.

In 1992–93, the last year for which reliable figures are available, Britain's non-elected executive bodies (EGOs) were responsible for

£46.65 billion of public expenditure.[3] This represents a 24% rise in real terms over the £35.20 billion spend (at constant 1992–93 prices) in 1978–79, when the Conservatives took power, pledged to reduce their numbers and cost. This £46.65 billion spend (£48.16 billion in today's terms) represents nearly a third—30%—of total central government public expenditure, a more useful measure than the widely-used estimate of a fifth of public expenditure. It dwarfs the £12 billion expenditure that the government owned up to—the official figure for expenditure on all recognised NDPBs.

The size of this expenditure on public goods is not in itself a cause for reproach; few would quarrel with increases in expenditure on health services or social housing. The point is that the bodies spending this huge tranche of public money are under the control of an appointed and self-appointing magistracy in a multiplicity of bodies. In 1993, this magistracy amounted to between 57,000 and 63,000 people (see Table 2).

2. EGOs, the New Local Magistracy and Elected Councillors

	Exec. NDPs	NHS Bodies	Non-Rec. EGOs	Total	Cllrs	Local Magistry
England	234	557	3,981	4,772	20,852	51,148–55,953
Scotland	47	23	304	374	1,977	3,324– 3,843
Wales	23	33	158	214	1,682	1,707– 1,967
Northern Ireland	54	16	91	161	582	1,117– 1,357
Total	358	529	4,534	5,521	25,093	57,296–63,120

The case for 'auxiliary precautions'

The vast expansion in the activities of government itself, as well as this huge explosion of unelected and largely invisible activity in its shadow, requires what the great democrat, James Madison, one of the three authors of *The Federalist Papers* and later a US President, recommended as early as 1788 in Paper 51 with a clarity rare in history. 'In framing a government which is to be administered by men over men the great difficulty lies in this: you must first enable the government to control the governed: and in the next place oblige it to control itself. A dependence on the people is, no doubt, the primary control on government: but experience has taught mankind the necessity of auxiliary precautions.'

Britain's tradition of 'strong' government leaves no room for doubt about its ability to 'control the governed'. What is more in doubt is the reality of the people's 'primary control' of government—that is, the electoral system and its results: and secondly, the presence of adequate 'auxiliary precautions' to reinforce electoral control of government and quasi-governmental activity. The first principle of democracy is that of 'primary control' over the processes of decision-making in government. In a large and complex society, the public can only exercise this control indirectly, by electing others to take decisions on its behalf. This does not exclude the possibility of 'direct control' by citizens over collective decisions where it is practicable, for example in very localised meetings, in jury service or through a local referendum. But for the most part, popular control over decision-making in a representative democracy means control over the decision-makers. The second principle is that of political equality: that people should be equal in the exercise of popular control. In Bentham's famous phrase, 'everyone should count for one, and none for more than one'.[4]

Since 1979, Conservative governments have introduced mechanisms which are designed to improve 'auxiliary' accountability in government. The departmental select committees, introduced in 1979, have increased Parliament's powers of scrutiny. In 1982, the government established the Audit Commission which has since won respect for its systematic resolve to make local authority and health services more effective as well as cost-efficient. In 1983, the National Audit Act strengthened the relationship between the Comptroller and Auditor General, head of the National Audit Office, and the Public Accounts Committee. The PAC also benefits from its close partnership with the Treasury. 'We made a rod for our own backs, but I am proud of that', the Minister for Public Services said in the Commons (24.2.94).

The Citizen's Charter initiative, the creation of separate Executive Agencies and the limited Open Government programme seek between them to improve public services, to make the processes by which they are organised and delivered more open, and to introduce 'new forms of accountability'. But this new accountability and openness depend in all sections of central government on the government's own discretion, not on enforceable rights. The government has also made local government subject to a remarkable regime of scrutiny, openness and disclosure since 1979 through the Local Government (Access to Information) Act 1985 and other legislation. It has not, however, applied the same rules to government-appointed and self-appointing public bodies, even those which provide essential public services.

William Waldegrave, the former minister in charge of 'reinvented government', explained how the new forms of accountability which have been introduced reinforce the old. In reply to complaints of a 'democratic deficit' in the new arrangements, he claimed in July 1993 that the government had in fact created a 'democratic gain' in the management of public services. 'We have not in any way altered or undermined the basic structure of public service accountability to Parliament and hence to individual citizens. But we have made it useable. We have strengthened these formal lines of accountability by making our public services directly accountable to their customers.'[5]

Public services, he argued, are there to serve: 'It is the output, the end product, not the internal whys and wherefores, that are of crucial concern.' For 'internal whys and wherefores', read the democratic processes of local government.

Much of what Waldegrave said is true: so far as it goes. Too often the voice of citizens in local government has been 'distant and diffuse'. As opinion surveys have demonstrated, local authorities frequently seem remote and out of touch to local residents, and fail to involve local people in their decisions.[6] It is an extreme reaction to conclude from this, however, that central government should without public consultation deliberately by-pass local government and create non-elected bodies to provide public services instead. Reformed local government could provide not simply the discipline of electoral power over the framing and delivery of local public services but known and accessible points of contact for users and countless opportunities for more direct forms of participation and involvement in their provision.

The government also presents us with a false dichotomy. Public services can—and should—be both democratically controlled and 'consumer-responsive'. The government's insistence on standards of service, courtesy and information raises recipients from the status of being, at worst, the mere object of administrative procedure to that of a consumer, empowered to complain and seek redress. But consumers are a poor and passive shadow of the self-confident citizens of a mature democracy, entitled to choose who runs their services, to participate and be consulted in the way they are run, and to know what decisions are being taken in their name. Nor is it proper for the provision of public services to be determined between national government and those who supply or receive them. At stake is a larger public interest which can only be satisfactorily determined by a public wider than that involved in the contract between providers and users implicit in Waldegrave's view.

The role of EGOs in 'reinvented' government

No EGOs are elected by the general public. The only bodies which exhibit the least element of 'primary control' are grant-maintained schools, where parents and teachers elect a minority of representatives to the governing bodies. EGOs are in essence the government's creatures, to be created or abolished as ministers see fit. Ministers determine their exact status and functions and refuse to divulge the considerations which lie behind their decisions. Ministers and their officials appoint the vast majority of chairpersons and board members. It has also become common for ministers to give instructions to the chairs of national NDPBs about their policy goals in letters of appointment which are rarely made public. Ministers agree corporate strategies with the boards, set performance indicators for their activities and strictly control the finances available to them. The similarities with the regime for departmental Executive Agencies, which remain an official part of the civil service, are striking. Sir Robin Butler, the Cabinet Secretary, has stated that the delegation of responsibility—'using providers in all sectors of the community'—is of central importance to the 'reinvention of government' in Britain.[7] His description has a comforting pluralist ring to it, but the reality is that only managerial tasks are delegated, and to a greatly circumscribed set of 'providers'. The overall strategy is that ministers and senior civil servants in Whitehall (and its satellites in Belfast, Cardiff and Edinburgh) set out the direction of policies and allocate resources from the centre, and delegate responsibility for delivery through Executive Agencies, executive NDPBs and local authorities. Butler did not specifically mention any of the host of local bodies which I describe as 'non-recognised' EGOs, and drew attention merely to 'the greater use of the private sector'.

Yet EGOs are integral to 'reinvented government'. They form new hierarchies of 'providers of public services', with the large EGOs, like the Housing Corporation, comfortably astride hosts of lesser EGOs at local level. These 'providers', being unelected and near invisible, have no claim to belong 'in all sectors of the community'; indeed, all the available evidence suggests that they are confined to very few sections of the community as a matter of public policy. The government's radical changes in the way public services are provided has, in fact, involved a vast extension of the powers of central government and their non-elected national agencies. There are no countervailing elected authorities at regional level and the independent decision-making powers of elected local government have been severely reduced. Butler's 'delegation' is a poor substitute for devolution, or subsidiarity, involving as it does the deliberate curtailment of representative government at the local level and the transfer of functions and services to non-elected EGOs. In 1992–93, these local bodies spent over £35.02 billion of public money (£35.23 billion at today's prices), delivering services of vital importance to the public. This spend is just over half that of elected local authorities (£69 billion in 1992–93).

Ministers in Britain notoriously possess wide-ranging discretionary powers. The creation of the new host of EGOs has greatly strengthened the range and diversity of ministers' effective powers by providing executive agents to put government directives into action and enabling them to retain a measure of control over the interpretation of their own statutes. Ministers have increasingly taken powers in statutes and through delegated, and largely unscrutinised, legislation—statutory instruments and Orders in Council—to direct the activities of EGOs, local authorities and other subordinate bodies in the minutest detail. This includes the systematic use of 'Henry VIII' clauses empowering ministers 'in very wide terms indeed'[8] and enabling them to issue statutory instruments to change parliamentary legislation or, in the octopus language of the Local Government Finance Act 1988, to: 'make such supplementary, incidental, consequential or transitional provisions as appear to him to be necessary or expedient for the general purpose or any other particular purpose of the Act.' These powers are often taken in legislation which is controversial in itself. No comprehensive list of their accretion exists, but in a single act — the Educational Reform Act 1988 — Jack Straw MP estimated that the Education Secretary took '415 new powers of central control' — a figure which was not challenged by the minister (Commons, 18.7.88). It is the existence of the new corpus of EGOs, along with local authorities, which makes the adoption and use of powers on this scale possible.

Members of the new magistracy continually assert their independence of government in media interviews. This is assumed to be a public good, though the exercise of independent powers by unelected bodies would subvert basic principles of democracy. The reality, however, is that EGOs possess scarcely any independent room for manoeuvre. They have specifically been created, or adapted, to act as dependent agencies within parameters of policy and resources set by government.

For example, the Housing Corporation was originally set up to promote the voluntary housing movement. But as it has become the main channel for public investment in housing, David Edmonds, a former chief executive, recently observed, 'Its role is perhaps too important for the Department of the Environment fully to respect the original statutory functions.' In evidence to the Select Committee on the Environment, the Corporation said that it saw its role as an executive, carrying out government policy. Senior officials, according to Edmonds, have used the phrase, 'We are a government agency'; board members 'have often queried their role when all main decisions are taken by ministers, civil servants and Corporation staff'; and 'the DOE and its regional structure duplicates and double-checks much of the Corporation's work' (*Guardian*, 10.9.93). Active members of Housing Association boards complain about the absence of consultation downwards to them; as one recently wrote, 'take it or leave it' is the implicit attitude (*Guardian*, 21.1.94).

Consider also the TECs, which as private companies run by local businessmen would at first sight seem to possess independence from government. In fact, their operating framework is dictated by the government's priorities and they work within sets of parameters laid down by contractual obligations and enforced by intrusive departmental regulations and financial incentives and penalties. In the absence of independent sources of funds they are driven by the invisible hand of government — by cash and contracts, not by their directors. It is a system within which, according to one private-sector chair, 'civil servants remain the puppet master and TECs become mere puppets in all practical terms'.[9] TECs were set the task of developing a strategic vision for local economies and employment markets, but the government soon obliged them to concentrate on make-work schemes for unemployed workers during the recession. One observer commented, they 'find themselves in nominal control of privatised arms of the civil service, delivering unpopular and underfunded schemes for the unemployed'.[10]. A survey and editorial in the *Financial Times* (10.5.93) concluded that

TECs were 'being paid huge sums of money to do a task they do not much rate, while being denied freedom and funds to get on with the things their leaders think are most important'.

The accountability of EGOs

Here I note the mechanisms of scrutiny and control over EGOs, including the Ombudsman's writ and public audit by the National Audit Office (NAO) or Audit Commission (AC). I also look at the relevance of the government's chief new measure to strengthen accountability — the Citizen's Charter. Table 3 summarises the position. Broadly, it shows that the coverage of the two main instruments is fitful and inconsistent. All NHS bodies are subject to full public audit (by the Audit Commission) and to partial supervision by the Health Service Ombudsman (clinical matters, including scrutiny by Family Health Service Authorities of complaints against doctors and dentists, are excluded). The National Audit Office has responsibility for full audit of only just over half (53%) of executive NDPBs and the Ombudsman's writ runs in only a third of them. Of the non-recognised EGOs, only the 1,025 grant-maintained schools are subject to full audit by the National Audit Office. No non-recognised EGO falls under the jurisdiction of the Ombudsman. Thus, local residents who wish to complain about maladministration in council-run state schools or public housing may complain to the Local Government Ombudsman. But they have no rights to investigation or redress through the Ombudsman in cases of maladministration by Housing Associations (2,668), grant-maintained schools (1,025), Colleges of Further Education (557), universities (164), Training and Enterprise Councils and their Scottish equivalents (105). Though the Ombudsman does not cover Housing Associations in general, tenants of homes owned by Scottish Homes or the Northern Ireland Housing Executive may forward complaints for investigation. The Housing Corporation and Scottish Homes have also set up internal 'ombudsman' services for Housing Association tenants. Overall, the arbitrary and patchy nature of the Ombudsman's jurisdiction over public bodies strengthens the case for a thorough recasting of the classification of all such bodies, with clear criteria for all categories which take into account the need for effective accountability.

3. Scrutiny of EGOs by the Ombudsman and Public Audit

		Ombudsman		Public Audit	
(358)	Executive NDPs	124	(35%)	191	(53%)
(629)	NHS Bodies	629	(100%)	629	(100%)
(4434)	Other EGOs	0		1,025	(22%)
(5521)	Total	753	(14%)	1,845	(33%)

The Citizen's Charter seeks to improve public services to established standards; to make services responsive to consumers' demands through information, complaints procedures, independent adjudicators and the like; and to provide redress in certain cases where standards of service are not met—all within a 'value-for-money' framework. So far, 38 Charters have been published, of which 17 may be described as 'generic' and apply either nationally or in England or London; 20 are Northern Irish, Scottish or Welsh equivalents and one is specific to Northern Ireland. The 17 generic Charters cover executive bodies in three major service areas within which EGOs are active: education (grant-maintained schools, further education and sixth form colleges, and universities); health (health authorities and NHS Trusts); and public housing (Housing Action Trusts and Housing Associations). Housing Associations fall outside the Charter remit, but the Tenant's Guarantee, overseen by the Housing Corporation and its Scottish and Welsh equivalents, is designed to play a similar role. The effect is to bring 629 NHS bodies and all but 105 of non-recognised EGOs under generic Charters.

The position of executive NDPBs is less clear-cut. All public bodies and public servants are supposed to adopt the Charter's principles, even if the generic Charters do not apply directly to them and neither they nor their sponsoring departments have published Charters of their own. Departmental replies to parliamentary questions reveal a somewhat slow and haphazard approach to applying Charter principles to executive quangos. The Lord Chancellor's Department regards the Legal Aid Board as being 'subject to the Charter'. Seven departments 'encourage' their executive NDPBs to adopt Charter principles; three state flatly that Charter principles 'apply', the Department of the Environment 'requires' that they apply, and the Department of Social Security's Occupational Pensions Board is said to be 'committed' to them: at Employment, 'Charter provisions are agreed where appropriate'; the Foreign Office says its NDPBs are 'subject to' the Charter and the Welsh Office 'expects' all bodies to adopt it. It does not seem a systematic approach.[11]

This is not the place for a detailed critique of the Citizen's Charter. However, a series of parliamentary questions by Hugh Bayley MP, seems to have established that progress has been slow and patchy; out of 89 specific opening commitments, the government had met 31 by March 1994, and completely failed to meet 32 (*Guardian*, 9.3.94). A detailed *Financial Times* analysis of the generic Charters also concluded that they were so far 'selling the citizen short' (14.3.94). The rights of service users are largely procedural. They are given access to information but not a substantial role in designing or improving public services; they receive, for example, a right to change doctors without giving a reason, but not the right to prompt and appropriate treatment. The basic problem of the inequality of status between service agencies and consumers is not addressed, other than through the so far patchy and inadequate device of standards. There are vague provisions for 'consultation', but in practice citizens are not collectively involved in setting overall standards or allocating resources. Instead, they are restricted to the role of the consumer, with rights to react to poor service after the event, but with no more than a distant role in planning services in advance.

Plainly, the ultimate responsibility for major decisions on resources — both in terms of money and legal powers — must rest with a government responsible to Parliament. But the host of EGOs and the terms of accountability introduced by the Citizen's Charter and other mechanisms shut out the participation of customers as citizens, of organised citizen's groups and of the wider community alike. Market research surveys are used in place of consultation, but individual people questioned by interviewers have no right to frame or challenge the questions, no opportunity to discuss what is involved, no means of knowing how their replies have been interpreted. The reinvention of government reinforces an already over-centralised system with no democratic input at regional level, and a reduced input at local level.

British government remains one of the most secretive and closed systems in the democratic world. Thus, it is hardly surprising that the conduct and activities of public bodies of all kinds, including EGOs, are scarcely more open. Table 4 summarises the figures for three sets of mechanisms designed to create open government. As it shows, only 124 bodies operate the open government code. Public rights of access to papers and meetings vary; none are obliged to release policy papers to the public; only 289 health authorities, and six bodies in Northern Ireland, admit the public to board meetings; just over a third allow the people to inspect the minutes of meetings; and just under half maintain a public register of members' interests. Under half (42%) are required to publish annual reports, but 90% must publish annual accounts. Finally, only 421 bodies, mostly NHS trusts, are required to hold a public meeting at least once a year. These provisions mean that the host of local EGOs are far less open to local residents than local government. Local authorities are obliged to keep a public register of members' interests; all authority meetings are open to the public; and there are public rights of access to agendas, minutes and background papers for all council meetings. Further, local authorities are obliged to publish locally both auditors' criticism and sets of performance indicators on housing, refuse collection, schools, etc. They must also consider an auditors' public interest report at a meeting open to the public and press, and make the report publicly available. There is no such requirement on any executive body, national or local, not even those which provide the same services (housing, schools, etc) as local authorities, to publish either auditors' findings or performance indicators. From 1995, the Audit Commission will publish local authority performance figures nationally. There exists no uniform requirement to publish similar information for any EGOs (where performance indicators are largely for purposes of internal control).

4. EGOs and Open Government

	Exec. NDPs 358		NHS Bodies 629		Unrec. EGOs 4,534		Total 5,521	
Number subject to Open Government Code of Practice	124	(35%)	0		0		124	(2%)
Number which public right to								
inspect register of members' interests,	6	(2%)	0		2,668	(59%)	2,674	(49%)
attend board/committee meetings,	6	(2%)	289	(46%)	0		255	(5%)
inspect minutes of meetings,	5	(1%)	289	(46%)	1,701	(38%)	1,985	(38%)
see policy papers/meetings documents	0		0		0		0	
Number of EGOs which are required to								
publish annual accounts,	191	(53%)	248	(39%)	4,534	(100%)	4,973	(90%)
publish annual reports,	201	(56%)	248	(39%)	1,566	(41%)	2,315	(42%)
hold public meetings	2	(0.5%)	314	(50%)	105	(2%)	412	(7%)

The United Kingdom is almost unique among modern democracies in denying political expression through elected institutions at the regional level. This omission is especially notable because of the presence of two nations within the body politic—Scotland and Wales have a history, a socio-industrial identity and political culture of their own. Instead, the Scottish and Welsh Secretaries administer the two nations through the Scottish and Welsh Offices, departments of state which are to be regarded as part of Whitehall. In Northern Ireland, which did have its own assembly at Stormont until the 'troubles' forced its abolition in the 1970s, a Secretary of State and the Northern Ireland Office rule.

The Department of City and Regional Planning at the University of Wales has published an analysis of the 'governance question' in Wales.[12] The analysis is confined to the relationship between the Welsh Office and recognised NDPBs and NHS bodies, which doubled in number from 40 in 1979 to 80 in 1991. Executive NDPBs are established within a clear policy context; they frame their corporate plans in accordance with current policy, and these plans are submitted annually to the Welsh Office in draft form for approval. The Welsh Secretary appoints most chairpersons and members and meets the former regularly; his department holds regular meetings with their chief executives and finance officers. This is a highly secretive process, and will remain so under the government's Open Government code. Many quangos do not publish their corporate plans because they may contain 'commercially sensitive information'. The Commons Welsh Affairs Committee took odds with this position, arguing: 'We do not accept that the requirement for confidentiality is sufficient justification for publishing no information on future proposals and activities. In the absence of published political and operational guidelines ... the responsibility falls more heavily on NDPBs to explain how they propose to spend the public money by which they are financed.'[13] Party-political patronage is freely exercised in Wales. The Welsh study delineates a systematic network of interlocking appointees, who have ties with the Conservative Party, at the heads of key EGOs, stating that the Welsh Office and its quango network constitutes a formidable system of power, influence and patronage, which is controlled by a minority political party ('minority' in Welsh terms, of course). The Scottish Office and Northern Ireland Office both operate similarly through networks of executive and advisory bodies — Scotland has 374 EGOs and Northern Ireland 161.

At local level, the idea of the 'new magistracy' is well-established. But the new magistracy does not only sit locally. The boards of major high-spending national authorities — such as the Housing Corporation and its Scottish and Welsh partners, and funding agencies for schools and further education — sit at the apex of non-elected hierarchies of power which take and see through decisions of great importance for local communities. For example, the housing hierarchy in England consists of the Corporation, nine regional offices and 2,300 registered Housing Associations. This hierarchy exercises substantial powers over the provision of social housing in local areas and decides how virtually all the government's investment in public rented homes (£1.8 billion in 1993–94), as well as substantial private finance, should be allocated. There are similar hierarchies in health (under the departmental NHS Management Executive and Regional Health Authorities); further education (under the Further Education Funding Council); schools (Funding Agency for Schools); housing in Scotland and Wales (Scottish Homes; Housing for Wales); and training and enterprise in England and Wales (the department's Training and Enterprise Directorate), and in Scotland (Scottish Enterprise and Highland and Island Enterprise). In a comparatively brief period, these unelected hierarchies have acquired spending responsibilities which begin to rival the overall expenditure of the United Kingdom's local authorities. In 1992–93 the total EGO share of public spending on local services came to about £35 billion — some 50% of the total £69 billion spend by local government in the same year.

There is a single, highly significant difference in the issues of accountability for these hierarchies of national and local bodies and solely national bodies. At both levels, similar questions of democratic scrutiny and openness, financial control and probity arise. But it is also axiomatic for the British state that accountability for both lies ultimately at national level — through ministerial responsibility to Parliament. It is appropriate that national bodies with national responsibilities should be made accountable at a national level — even though, in principle, mere ministerial responsibility is not sufficient even at that level. There is a need for a regime of accountability entirely separate from ministers. But local communities can not rely only on arrangements at national level. It is entirely inappropriate that the direction such bodies receive is solely from ministers, departments and national appointed agencies. Bodies discharging local functions should be made accountable at local level — what the former Citizen's Charter minister, Robert Jackson MP, calls 'low accountability'.

Local government in Britain is being overwhelmingly replaced by an unequal and confused dyarchy, made up of two forms of local adminis-tration—the new system of agencies run by the unaccountable new magistracy and the much-weakened and dismembered system of elected local authorities. Both are increasingly subject to central control. Not only are Madison's 'auxiliary precautions' absent or inadequate, but the 'primary control' of local election has been made nearly powerless. As thoughtful Conservatives like Robert Jackson are already warning, there is a need for a 'certain Tory statecraft' of the kind that Lord Salisbury showed when he created the elected county councils—in place of the 'old magistracy'—to run the new state services in the nineteenth century. This statecraft held that there were advantages for the state in a wide diffusion of responsibility, so that the workings of the national government were not clogged up with detailed problems of local administration, and so that a wide cross-section of people were involved and indeed implicated in the processes of local government (Commons, 24.2.94).

The courts are the natural place to look to as the major alternative to government and parliamentary oversight. But as no two statutes establishing agencies (where they exist) are the same, the means of legal redress vary accordingly. The absence of general legislation regulating the status and structure of quasi-public bodies is fairly common throughout western Europe. But some do provide legal regimes by way of articles in their constitutions or special laws, thus making their activities subject to a full judicial process. In the UK, the individual acts establishing NDPBs and other public bodies rarely prescribe legal regimes establishing mechanisms of accountability or requiring them to involve the public. A significant number of local EGOs do not legally belong in the public domain at all. For example, TECs are governed by company law and Housing Associations by charity law—neither of which has much relevance to their activities as public bodies providing public services. The courts therefore normally have no statutory or constitutional criteria by which they can review the activities of most EGOs—and certainly few provisions for public consultation, disclosure, redress, etc. The inherent common-law jurisdiction does provide for judicial intervention, but largely only on formal issues arising out of the form of decisions of executive bodies, not their substance. Judicial review is confined to fairly narrow grounds, such as illegality, 'irrationality' and procedural propriety. The judiciary, until recently, has been reluctant to trespass upon the political dominion of govern-ment. And plainly, it would be undesirable for it to intervene in the political realm. What has happened recently is that it has felt obliged to fill the vacuum caused by the absence of a developed system of public law and to some extent to provide a degree of restraint of an unbalanced political regime. The growth of judicial review has been the result but has occurred selectively in areas of administrative action without the guidance of a code of law developed through the democratic process.

If appointed boards are not made accountable through the variety of old and new mechanisms, then the question has to be asked: where does democratic accountability for the myriad policies and decisions they make actually lie? The only answer is through ministers to Parliament. It is an answer that is profoundly unsatisfactory for a variety of reasons, the chief of which is that Britain is governed through Parliament, not by it. It is almost universally acknowledged that far from being 'accountable' to a modern Parliament, the government's party majority in the Commons, the whipping system and patronage normally make Parliament the creature of the government. The traditional doctrine of ministerial responsibility has long since become a political myth. If it stands for anything, it is not government's responsibility to but its assertion of independence from Parliament. Equally the principle that ministers are responsible for every act of their civil servants has decayed over time. Ministers no longer accept political responsibility for the bad judgement or major mistakes of their officials, while the officials themselves are protected from scrutiny by the continuing fiction that they have no identity other than through their ministers. Moreover, as senior officials are responsible to ministers alone, they give evidence to Parliament on ministers' terms. They are forbidden under the Osmotherly rules from discussing policy options or decisions and from commenting on 'questions in the field of political controversy'. The entire bureaucratic structure, including public bodies of all kinds, is almost entirely detached from democratic control by the secrecy of the system.

The primary instruments of parliamentary scrutiny are the Public Accounts Committee and departmental select committees, entitled to examine the expenditure, administration and policy of the 'associated public bodies' of the departments concerned which, in practice, does include EGOs. It is probably too strong to talk of 'the pathetic inadequacy' of the attempts by select committees to hold government to account, as Hugo Young does (*Guardian*, 5.4.94), but their powers, resources and influence are very limited, especially by comparison with similar committees in some other Western democracies. The Osmotherly rules restrict their ability to inquire into the critical policy-making areas of government, which provide the direction for all EGOs. In any event, select committees, with all the calls upon their attention, can be only one means of making such bodies accountable. There are too many bodies, and too much is going on, for Parliament to provide effective oversight, even with more powerful committees and a more universal Ombudsman service. The answer lies as much outside Parliament as inside — with standing machinery and dedicated agencies for examining government institutions across the board (as, for example, in Sweden, Australia and the USA) and with a broader system of public law.[14]

The government's solution to the de facto weaknesses of the discredited system of ministerial responsibility has been internal to the administrative system—framework agreements, performance indicators, Charters, targets and audit. The purpose is to replace notional responsibility at ministerial level with managerial responsibility. But the government's managerial reforms apply weakly and unevenly, and especially so to EGOs. Even if the reforms eventually improve the managerial performance and responsiveness of all such bodies, there will remain a major accountability gap. The government presents the public with a false choice between, on the one hand, effective performance and responsive services and, on the other, democratic accountability. Both are required, but at the moment neither at national nor local level are there effective mechanisms for making the policies and decisions of EGOs democratically accountable. 'Reinvented' government, in effect, leaves accountability standing at best on one leg only. It does nothing to introduce real accountability for policies and decisions, which remain in the fictional realm of ministerial responsibility to Parliament. EGOs are, in effect, accountable solely to ministers and their departments. Ministerial responsibility works to block effective parliamentary scrutiny and control of the policies and decisions of ministers and senior officials.

So far as the public accountablility of EGOs and other public bodies are concerned, it fails in two other important ways too—the first a matter of principle, the second practical. First, it is a deceit to suggest that a general vote—'a distant and diffuse one at that' (to quote Waldegrave again)—every four or five years can give government ministers and their officials the democratic authority to decide highly specific issues in all significant public services in every part of the country; and it is absurd to suggest that a national Parliament is the proper arena for making government accountable for this local universe of decision-making. Secondly, even if the public found such a highly centralised system of accountability desirable, it is anyway a practical impossibility. The seven major departments of state, and the host of agencies and advisory bodies attached to them, constitute a vast and complex range of responsibilities that ministers simply can not begin to oversee. Not since the Crichel Down Affair in 1954 have ministers of either party shown an inclination to accept responsibility for the mistakes of their own departments. But the logic of the government's reforms, the disabling of local government and proliferation of EGOs is to make ministers virtually the single ultimate point of responsibility for the billions of spending and policy decisions of a host of EGOs, 94 Executive Agencies and 439 local authorities. A very modern ideology has produced a practical nonsense.

Conclusions

In area after area of public life, elected government is being replaced by appointive government. Those who are elected count for ever less (unless they happen to be MPs appointed as ministers); those who are appointed count for ever more. This hastily erected apparatus of appointive government lacks the essential democratic underpinnings of scrutiny, openness and accountability, but is now responsible for nearly a third of central government spending. Appointees now run some 6,700 bodies of all kinds at national and local level, though it is at local level that the growth has been greatest. This apparatus intensifies over-centralised big government in the United Kingdom, enables ministers to grasp more detailed control over the implementation of their policies, and encourages executive patronage. The absence of electoral arrange-ments and an effective countervailing apparatus of independent accountability is a matter of profound constitutional significance.

The replacement of the elective principle, especially at local level, has been possible only because of the absence of fundamental constitutional safeguards. The unasked-for revolution which has taken place—and the sweeping partisan deployment of patronage power which has accom-panied it—are direct consequences of an unregulated political system in which government has wide discretionary powers at its disposal and is insufficiently constrained by constitutional checks and balances. The conventions of the unwritten constitution are unable to restrain govern-ment, to protect civil liberties and a pluralist public life, or even to ensure competent legislation and 'good government'. The phenomenal growth of rule by appointed EGOs lays bare the damaging consequences of the two fundamental canons of British government: parliamentary sovereignty and ministerial responsibility. Far from creating a demo-cratic framework of parliamentary and public accountability, these doctrines raise the executive above the judiciary and Parliament and institutionalise its independence from their scrutiny. The spread of EGOs is a sympton of a systemic disease. The body politic itself has to be cured if they are to be brought under democratic control.

This article draws heavily upon *EGO-TRIP: Extra-governmental organisations in the UK and their accountability*, Democratic Audit Paper No 2, University of Essex/Charter 88 Trust, 1994. Edited by W. Hall and S. Weir, it was the work of Antony Barker, Howard Davis, Norman Lewis, John Stewart, Stuart Weir and Anthony Wright MP.

(Source of tables in the text of this article: Simplified from *EGO-TRIP*)

1   *Cabinet Office, Public Bodies, 1993,* HMSO, 1994. All figures are based on the 1993 report, except where otherwise stated.
2   The phrase, popularised by John Stewart, was coined by Bob Morris, the former education officer of the Association of Metropolitan Authorities.
3   For detailed figures, see Table 2, *EGO-TRIP* (1994).
4   For a fuller discussion, see D. Beetham, *Auditing Democracy in Britain,* University of Essex/Charter 88 Trust, 1993.
5   W. Waldegrave, speech to the Public Finance Foundation, July 1993.

6   P. J. Dunleavy and S. Weir, 'Democracy in doubt', *Local Government Chronicle*, 29 April 1994.
7   Sir R. Butler, 'Reinventing British Government', Aston University McLaren Lecture, 1993.
8   *Making the Law*, Report of the Commission on the Legislative Process, Hansard Society, 1993.
9   The leader of LETEC in the House of Commons, 1991, cited in M. Boddy, 'The restructuring of labour markets', in M. Campbell and R. Duffy, *Local Labour Markets*, (Longman, 1992)
10 M. Emmerich and M. Peck, *Reforming the TECs,* Centre for Local Economic Strategies, Manchester, 1989.
11 Parliamentary Questions lodged by Anthony Wright MP, 1993.
12 K. Morgan and E. Roberts, *The Democratic Deficit: A Guide to Quangoland,* University of Wales, Cardiff, 1993.
13 *The Work of the Welsh Office*, Welsh Affairs Committee, 1993, cited in Morgan and Roberts.
14 See *EGO-TRIP* for a more detailed discussion of alternative arrangements.

'Snouts in the Trough': the Politics of Quangos

BY TONY STOTT

SPEAKING in the House of Commons debate in 1978 (1 August), Michael McGuire, Labour MP for Ince, said 'I get the impression that what really hurts the Conservative Party is the fact that some of our lads have their snouts in the gravy train, whereas at one time it was entirely the lads of the Conservatives.' This quotation from a Labour MP defending the actions of a Labour Government seventeen years ago highlights what many politicians and the media still see as the central feature of the debate about quangos. With accusations of sleaze in public life hitting the headlines in 1994, the issue is now about how many Conservatives are getting their 'snouts in the quango trough'. Concern over the activities of quangos and non-elected bodies began to re-emerge in political, media and academic circles in late 1992. Since then quangos have acquired increased political visibility.

The purpose of this article is to examine the political conflicts both in the late 1970s and since 1992 about the use of quangos and non-elected bodies by government. There are many parallels between the latest bout of interest in quangos and the manner in which similar worries about them surfaced in the late 1970s. The whole question of quangos and their use has largely become a political game. This game of musical chairs has involved a barrage of claims and counter claims about the political bias of appointments, the abuses of patronage and financial irregularites and mismanagement. In opposition, parties attack quangos and non-elected bodies and when in government use them as instruments for carrying out their policies. The game has directed the debate away from the more fundamental constitutional issues about the role of quangos and their relationships to elected bodies.

The article is divided into three broad sections. The first section briefly examines quangos as an issue on the political agenda and focuses on the role, nature and context of the issue. The second section examines how the issue developed between 1977 and 1980, while the final section will examine the political conflict that has developed over quangos and patronage since 1992.

Quangos as a political agenda issue

Quangos and patronage have not been regular high profile issues on the political agenda. Non-elected bodies were in existence long before the term was coined and popularised during the 1970s. Despite the fact that non-elected bodies have been a continuing feature of the administrative structure in Britain, it was only in the periods between 1977 and 1980 and since 1992 that they have secured real political visibility, even notoriety. However, even in these periods, when quangos and ministerial patronage were the subject of political conflict and media coverage, they have not been the most significant or most central matter commanding the attention of either politicians or the media. At best, they have been only secondary issues. Non-elected bodies have been created and used regularly by both Conservative and Labour governments in turn as instruments for carrying out their policies. If concerns about quangos and patronage surface so rarely, it is important to consider what was so special about these two periods to create such interest as to push the issues on to the political agenda.

Non-elected bodies have been created for a variety of different administrative, managerial, policy and political reasons. The process of creating them has been a piecemeal one. New bodies or types of bodies have been established as new needs and policy demands dictated. In the 1970s these were mainly national, whereas in latter part of the 1980s and into the 1990s the major growth area has been at the local level. The end result is a heterogeneous pattern of bodies which vary greatly in size and character, in their relationships to central government departments, Parliament or local government, and in the extent to which they are democratically accountable. What has emerged, as Hood has argued, is 'a largely unrationalised development in that it is something born of expediency and pragmatism rather than of conscious philosophy or strategy'.[1] The result of this pragmatism is the lack of a coherent constitutional framework governing the creation and opera- tion of these bodies and lack of a clear exposition of the political case for the use of non-elected bodies. Quangos are easy targets for political attack. There was no agreed definition of the term. In addition, there was a general absence of public information about numbers and appointments and no framework for their operation.

In this constitutional vacuum, and in political contexts both in the late 1970s and early 1990s when governments were electorally unpopu- lar and appeared to be in decline, issues of quangos and patronage could be exploited for wider political objectives. In many ways, their importance on the political agenda stemmed from their value as another means of harrying the government of the day. They generated some politically useful campaigning and headline-catching stories, providing another stick with which to beat an unpopular government. Thus a number of imperatives from the wider party-political game helped to drive them forward onto the political agenda. In the 1970s attacks on quangos and patronage fitted in with the political mood that the public sector and trade unions were out of control. In the 1990s these attacks tended to substantiate a feeling that there had been a decline in standards and financial propriety in public life. Thus the political context clearly shaped the way in which quangos and patronage were handled on the political agenda.

The continued use of non-elected bodies raises constitutional issues. These are related to the suitability and effectiveness of the existing mechanisms for ensuring accountability for their activities. They also relate to the accountability of the government for their use as instruments of public policy. Given the general lack of publicly available information, this raises questions about how the appointments process and the activities of quangos can be made more open and accountable. In particular, there are questions about whether they should be accountable to ministers, directly to Parliament, or to elected local authorities. These issues have been raised both directly and indirectly, particularly by academics and others on the fringes of the party-political game.[2] Although constitutional concerns were never far below the surface, they tended to become submerged under more pressing political imperatives.

Political opportunism was a major motivating force in driving the quango and patronage issues on to the agenda. Considerations of political advantage and strategy were important factors in determining the definition and presentation of the relevant issues. It was in the interest of the opposition rather than the government to bring the issue forward. The dynamics of party conflict meant that quangos and patronage issues came on to the agenda with a negative image, and the debate was defined in terms of a 'discussion' of what was wrong with quangos and other non-elected bodies rather than their value as instruments of government. Party-political issues about who had a share of the patronage or who had 'their snouts in the trough' were given priority over debating solutions to the underlying constitutional issues.

Quangos on the political agenda 1977–1980

In the late 1960s and early 1970s, academics became interested in examining the role of those organisations that were not governmental bodies but which had some public functions and which were used by government to deliver parts of its policy. In this context, the term quango, meaning 'quasi-non-governmental organisation', was used. Hogwood notes that, by the late 1970s, as interest in quangos moved from academic circles to the political arena, the coverage of the term changed. From bodies that had only indirect links to government, they now came to include all bodies to which government made public appointments other than of civil servants.[3] The original, more specific and narrower meaning of the term had been broadened into 'quasi-autonomous national government organisations' as the term became popularised by the press and politicians. But to add to the confusion, it was also used to mean 'quasi-autonomous non-governmental organisation' as well. As a result, it became a loose and elastic term. It has remained vague ever since, thereby providing different political actors an opportunity to play a political numbers game.

During the second half of the 1970s concern about an increase in the numbers of non-elected bodies and in the extent of ministerial patronage steadily grew in political circles, especially among MPs. Initially, the Labour MP Maurice Edelman drew attention to the growing range of appointments made by ministers. Before his death in 1975, both through questions to ministers in the House of Commons and through articles in the press, he pursued the issue of patronage and ministerial appointments. In articles with titles such as 'The Patronage Explosion' (*New Statesman*, 11.7.75), 'How the new system of patronage in government scatters the confetti of privilege' and 'Time to stop the public appointments merry-go-round' (*The Times*, 14/15.10.75), he argued that the growth of government intervention had enlarged the area of patronage available to ministers. He felt that there was 'bland acceptance of the manifold abuses of the new patronage system, primarily because it has grown up as an outcrop of wider and worthwhile purposes.' He called for more searching public scrutiny to contain this 'patronage explosion' and suggested replacing the system of jobs within the gift of ministers by a Public Service Commission 'which would set standards and rules for public service appointments'. He also wanted a Select Committee on Public Appointments which would be required to endorse appointments for posts with salaries over £30,000.

After Edelman's death, it was the Conservative MP Philip Holland who vigorously pursued the issue through a stream of questions designed to elicit a broad range of information about the existence, operation and membership of so-called quangos. Holland, who gained a reputation as a quango hunter, did much through his questions and pamphlets, such as *The Quango Explosion*, which was written with Michael Fallon and published by the Conservative Political Centre in August 1978, and *Quango Quango Quango*, published early the next year by the Adam Smith Institute, to raise quangos as a matter of political concern and to push the issue up the political agenda. Other Conservatives also helped to publicise the issue. For instance, Geoffrey Johnson Smith sought to promote a private members bill which would have limited the power of governments to appoint people to quangos, required Parliament to confirm the appointment of all chairmen and the government to publish an annual register of jobs and who filled them. The issue was also raised by a leading Conservative peer, Baroness Young, in the House of Lords in November 1978 when she initiated a debate on the growing importance of quangos. In effect, Holland's persistent efforts, together with those of some other Conservative MPs and peers, had stimulated a political campaign.

The campaign fitted well into the themes of the Conservative opposition as it attacked the Labour government in late 1970s. The central thrust was directed at economic issues and the need to revitalise the economy. This was to be achieved by creating a favourable climate that rewarded enterprise, initiative and innovation through tax cuts, curbs on the power of the trade unions and the elimination of waste in government bureaucracy. In its 1979 manifesto the Conservative Party argued that by enlarging the role of the state and diminishing the role of the individual, the Labour government had crippled enterprise. By heaping privilege without responsibility on the trade unions, Labour had also given a minority of extremists the power to abuse individual liberties. While quangos were not directly mentioned, it was suggested that 'the reduction of waste, bureaucracy and over-government will also yield substantial savings'. According to the Conservatives, Parliament's traditional role had 'suffered badly from the growth of government over the last quarter of a century', and they intended to restore the supremacy of Parliament and 'make it effective in its job of controlling the Executive'.

Thus the main attack on quangos formed part of the new right's attack on the corporate state. Criticising quangos, and particularly the appointments held by leading trade unionists, fitted well into an attack on the increasing power of the state. Quangos and the associated questions of patronage were not the central or most important areas of the opposition's attack, but what Philip Holland achieved in concentrating on them was to open up a small but useful front in the political war. The impression created of ministers abusing their position and using public appointments for partisan political ends helped to provide justification for Conservative proposals for curbing the power of the state and of the trade unions. The attack clearly implied that quangos needed to be curbed. Therefore, with the approach of a general election, the issue was pushed forward in 1978 and 1979 as another weapon with which to harry and undermine an unpopular Labour government.

Media coverage helped to reinforce their negative image resulting from the activities of hostile politicians. The press highlighted the patronage dimensions and the rather sinister nature of their growing power. A number of stories with headlines like 'How quango rewards the good and the great' (*The Observer*, 2.5.76), 'Quango, the name for Whitehall's latest gravy train' (*Daily Telegraph*, 8.9.76), 'Ministers "have 10,000 jobs for the boys"', and '"Jobs for the boys" a growth industry' (*Daily Telegraph*, 18/26.5.78), suggested a growing network of uncontrolled patronage. The feeling that there was 'something not above board' about these developments was enhanced by the media emphasising the secrecy and lack of public information about the numbers and costs of quangos and appointments to them. Stories about ministers packing quangos with Labour Party supporters and removing Conservatives from their positions helped to created an impression of political abuse of power.

The political campaign and the media coverage tended to create an image of quangos as something disreputable. In many ways, the debate was ill-informed. Anne Davies suggested that 'the impression has been generated that quangos are a bad thing'.[4] The debate did not focus on the reasons for them or their value as instruments of government. The Davies Report was one of the few contributions to systematically address the constitutional issues of how to control and make these bodies accountable. Lord Peart, replying for the Government in the Lords debate in 1978 (15 November) initiated by the Conservative peer Baroness Young, argued that the criticism of public bodies had distracted attention from the advantages they can bring. There was, in his view, a need to redress the balance, as there were 'perfectly good and respectable reasons for creating organisations which operate at arm's length from Ministers, with some degree of independence in day to day management'. It was difficult to mount a strong case for quangos when the government was on the defensive on the issue and when some of its own supporters in Parliament also had concerns about the growth in the scale of patronage and about the lack of openness and accountability relating to the operation of many of these bodies. It may also have been difficult for the Conservatives to focus on specific constitutional issues because, as Michael McGuire (the Labour MP quoted at the beginning of this article) suggested, the Conservative Party's opposition to quangos was based solely upon its exclusion from the spoils of office rather than on deep constitutional principles.[5] Perhaps Nevil Johnson was right when he argued that 'the anti-state attitude smacks just a bit of political opportunism and of the desire to make capital out of a popular hostility to bureaucracy which it is always easy to stir up'.[6]

An examination of the Conservative case against quangos suggests that their interest was really political rather than constitutional. They exploited the lack of a clear definition of the term quango and, with some success, imposed their definition on the public debate. In his pamphlet, *Quango Quango Quango*, published in early 1979, Philip Holland claimed to have identified 3,068, which involved 9,633 paid and 30,890 unpaid appointments. To arrive at this figure, he had used a very wide definition of the term to mean 'official bodies to which a government minister appoints members other than civil servants.' As a piece of political publicity, the pamphlet listed these organisations on a long pull out sheet which in its different sections covered executive, advisory, state industry, judicial and academic quangos. While it may have been effective politics, doubts must be raised as to how useful this classification was when major public schools such as Harrow and Rugby featured in the list.

Compared with the more limited definitions and numbers emanating from official Civil Service Department sources, Holland's approach helped the Conservatives to argue that there had been a 'quango explosion' and that power was passing into the hands of unelected and largely unrepresentative public bodies which effectively acted as executive agencies of government. This explosion of non-elected bodies constituted an important element of a growing corporate state. In a speech in the House of Commons during the 1978 summer adjournment debate (1 August), which coincided with the publication the pamphlet, *The Quango Explosion*, Holland argued that 'a great constitutional change is taking place to concentrate power in the hands of the Executive and its nominees' and that there was a 'rapid spread of bureaucracy by the proliferation of unelected, unrepresentative bodies beyond the reach of Parliament and in many instances not accountable to anyone for the expenditure of large and growing sums of public money'. In the Lords debate in November 1978, Baroness Young similarly expressed the fear that the establishment of quangos as a way of government was being forced on the public. The government was handing over power to the executive in a secretive way. In effect, ministers and the bureaucracy were out of control. In the *Financial Times* (1.8.78), Holland was quoted as saying: 'Quangos are the outriders of the corporate state. Through these unelected unrepresentative bodies, ministers are exercising control out of reach of Parliament. Inexorably, the frontiers of bureaucracy are being advanced by a calculated extension and abuse of political patronage.'

In support of this argument, much was made of the fact that 42 new major national and powerful quangos had been created by the Labour government since 1974. In Holland's view, it was not just the sheer scale of patronage exercised by ministers that caused public disquiet but the politically biased way in which appointments were made. These served to reinforce the corporatist trends in British society to which the Conservatives were opposed. In *The Quango Explosion*, Holland and Fallon argued that 'the principal beneficiaries of this largesse have been senior trade union leaders'. Through answers to his parliamentary questions, Holland claimed to have discovered the extensive number of appointments held by individual trade union leaders. Much was made of the thirteen appointments held by Jack Jones, who retired as the General Secretary of the Transport and General Workers Union in 1978. Multiple appointments were common. According to *The Quango Explosion*, 'Labour ministers have also succumbed to the temptation of making unashamedly political appointments'. These included replacing Area Health Authority chairmen 'with Labour Party members, officials or known supporters' and replacing Conservatives on the National Gas Consumers Council 'with either union officials or members of left-wing pressure groups, (see also *Daily Telegraph*, 27.6.78 and *The Guardian*, 20.6.78).

In *The Quango Explosion*, Holland and Fallon suggested that 'tackling the mushrooming empire of public bodies must be a high priority for the next Conservative government.' A review of all bodies was needed to trim and slim their number, size and costs. Those no longer needed should be abolished and all remaining ones should be subject to automatic dissolution after every five years unless renewed by Parliament. All bodies receiving more than half their income from public funds should be made directly and openly accountable to Parliament.

To avoid the abuse of the appointments system, they wanted the process of nomination to be more open by making ministers more accountable to Parliament for each nomination, advertisements for full-time paid appointments and a limit on the number of paid public appointments held by a single individual.

Political appointments should cease. They went on to argue: 'We reject the view that if these bodies are to exist, then a future Conservative government should replace known Socialists with known Conservatives where possible. The new quangos now act as powerful executive agencies: they patrol and extend the frontiers of the state. It should be no part of our task to recruit Conservatives for Labour's frontier force.' Clearly, they were suggesting that the new government should not stoop to the high level of patronage abuse that was a feature of the Labour government. This point was emphasised in *Quango Quango Quango* when Holland concluded that 'the replacement of leftist academics, trade union leaders and ex-Labour councillors who dominate the key quango appointments by Conservative supporters is no answer, either, to the alienation of public scrutiny and control which has taken place. The malady calls for surgery rather than analgesics.' This view may now seem either rather naive or ironic in view of what happened since the Conservatives regained power in May 1979.

The result of this activity was that Mrs Thatcher's government was under pressure to take action. The issue remained on the agenda as Holland and others pressed for the new government to cut down the number of quangos and ministerial appointments as well as cutting their expenditure. In the summer of 1979, the new Prime Minister urged her ministers and the departments to review and abolish unnecessary quangos. In September the Department of the Environment, under Mr Heseltine, produced a list of 57 organisations to be wound up. At the same time, the Prime Minister asked Leo Pliatsky, the former Permanent Secretary to the Department of Trade, to examine the issue and to make recommendations about which bodies could be wound up. In his 1980 report, he used a narrower and more precise definition for what he called Non Departmental Public Bodies (NDPBs) rather than quangos. He identified three types of bodies: executive, advisory and tribunal systems, and recommended winding up 30 of the 489 executive bodies and 211 of the 1,561 advisory bodies, with a saving of £11.6 million.[7]

Hood, reviewing government action on quangos in their first year in office, suggested that this exercise was largely one in cosmetic surgery 'to achieve impressive-seeming reductions in numbers by eliminating or amalgamating egregious and marginal quangos'.[8] In its editorial comment, *The Guardian* (17.1.80) suggested that it had only been a 'light cull' and the reason for this was that the government was finding them more useful than its campaign in opposition might have suggested. The government did nothing about reforming the appointment and patronage process. The pressures of office had caught up with it. Quangos then began to lose political visibility. The new government found that it was difficult to take significant action on the issue and that, like its predecessors, it needed to create new non-elected public bodies.

Quangos on the political agenda since 1992

The latest bout of concern over the development of quangos began to surface publicly towards the end of 1992. John Stewart argued that a 'new magistracy' was 'assuming responsibility for a large part of local governance.' The new, non-elected elite, which was largely unknown and unaccountable locally, was to be found among the boards of the health authorities and hospital Trusts, Training and Enterprise Councils, Housing Action Trusts, and the governors of grant maintained schools and Colleges of Further Education.[9] This involved elected representatives being replaced by what Stewart called 'a burgeoning army of the selected'. At the same time, the House of Commons Public Accounts Committee was becoming concerned about the financial mismanagement of non-elected bodies, particularly the Welsh Development Agency.

Throughout 1993 and 1994 interest in quangos, as an issue on the political agenda, grew steadily, reflected in the number of parliamentary questions asked by MPs and in the regularity of stories and 'in-depth' articles in the press. Opposition parties recognised that they could use publicity about patronage abuse and financial mismanagement to pursue wider political agendas about sleaze in government. Although quangos themselves were not the central political issue, they became the subject of some sharp exchanges between the major parties as the opposition sought to press home its attacks on an unpopular government. Compared with the 1970s, the government was much more willing to counter what it considered to be the scandal-mongering stance of opposition parties and to defend what it saw as an attack on its policies to reform the public sector.

The main attack on quangos in the 1990s came from the left and centre of the political spectrum. Labour and the Liberal Democrats attacked the growth in the number of unelected bodies, the political bias and conflicts of interest in appointments, the inefficiency shown by some, and their lack of accountability. This formed part of an assault on the ever-widening 'contract state' and the 'marketisation' of the public sector. Criticism of conflicts of interests and the apparent pursuit of financial self-interest by various individuals, together with concerns about mismanagement in unelected bodies, contributed to wider perceptions of a decline in the standards of public and political life. Sleaze became a matter that increasingly commanded the attention of politicians and the media.

Faced with a paucity of public information about the numbers and types of bodies in existence and about the backgrounds of those appointed to them, a number of Labour MPs, including Peter Kilfoyle, George Howarth and Tony Wright, using the techniques pioneered by Philip Holland in the 1970s, set about trying to gain a fuller picture of the situation through questions to ministers. In May 1993, Tony Wright argued that 'we badly need a reliable map of the patronage state and I have been trying recently (with the aid of written questions) to start to put one together.'[10] This search for information was given a higher political profile when Jack Straw, the shadow Environment Secretary, launched a 'quango watch' campaign, backed by Labour councils, to monitor the activities of unelected bodies. He wanted local authorities to set up registers of quangos, naming the people serving on them together with their qualifications and party affiliations.

'Quango watch' may have been, as *The Times* described it, a 'routine political stunt' but establishing the existence of a Conservative patronage network provided good ammunition for political campaigning. George Howarth claimed to have discovered extensive links between appointments to unelected bodies and corporate donations to the Conservative Party. He had examined a hundred quangos and found that 157 individuals appointed to them had ties to firms which had donated money to Tory party funds. There was now an 'unelected state' which was 'stuffed with men and women who are intimately connected with the finances of the Tory party'. He claimed that this unhealthy relationship between certain business interests and patronage by the Conservative Party was a symptom of sleaze in government. Indeed, he went as far as to say 'that sleaze, quangos and the Tory party have now become a de facto part of the British constitution'.[11] The connections involving quango appointments, business and the Conservative Party provided fertile ground for good campaigning stories about 'Tory placemen' having their 'snouts in the trough'. This approach also fitted in well with Labour's efforts to make the financing of the Conservative Party a political issue and enabled it to imply that positions on quangos were the reward for financial contributions to the Conservative Party.

Labour's campaign highlighted the way in which the Conservative government operated an extensive and growing patronage network. In her first speech as Shadow Health Secretary in October 1994, Margaret Beckett, accused the government of packing the boards of Trust hospitals with its supporters. She said that a study of the expertise and backgrounds of those appointed show that 'they are overwhelmingly representative of Conservative interests' and that 'only a tiny percentage have medical expertise, or expertise in the national health service'. Sixty-six of the Trusts were chaired either by a Conservative or someone from a firm that contributed to the Conservative Party. The boards also included retired or defeated Conservative MPs and MEPs as well as the spouses of Conservative MPs, often without their particular qualifications or experience for membership being made clear (Commons, 25.10.94). Douglas Henderson, shadow Local Government Minister, suggested that people appointed to local quangos would soon outnumber elected local councillors. 'From schools to hospitals, from economic development to farming—the voice of the elected councillor is being replaced by the voice of the non-elected Tory worthy' (*Municipal Journal*, 20.8.94).

Labour was using the concerns about quangos as part of a wider effort to paint the Conservative Party in government as the party of patronage and sleaze, and it claimed that the government's policies were leading to a decline in public standards and opening the potential for corruption. An example of this approach was seen in the Commons debate on unelected state bodies, initiated by Labour in February 1994 (24 February). Michael Meacher, the shadow Citizen's Charter spokesman, strongly attacked the government's use of patronage, which was 'playing a bigger underhand role in British society than at any time since the days of Lloyd George' and, as a result, 'a private, unconstitutional and undemocratic power structure based on patronage and money' was replacing Britain's constitutional and democratic system. Meacher claimed that 'the general message is clear: the more one serves the Tory party's interests and preferably contributes to its coffers, the more likely one is to get an honour, a key position in the new magistracy and favourable access to contracts.' He concluded: 'The Opposition believe that democracy and openness should prevail—not patronage, sleaze or secrecy.' Jack Straw, shadow Environment Secretary, questioned the Conservatives' fitness to govern. 'This is a government which is finding it impossible to distinguish between private and party gain on the one hand, and the public interest on the other.' (*Financial Times*, 5.2.94) The linkage of quangos to the wider questions of sleaze and conflicts of interests was also made by the new Labour leader, Tony Blair, during the payment for parliamentary questions affair in October 1994. He proposed that the Prime Minister should publish a list of all members of quangos, their payments, perks and any position with any political party and should ban ministers who privatised a company from joining its board (Commons, 20.10.94).

Scandals relating to the affairs of a number of quangos served to heighten their political and media visibilty. In the view of the House of Commons Public Accounts Committee, lax financial controls in the Welsh Development Agency and the Wessex and West Midlands Health Authorites had led to inadequate stewardship of public money. In the light of these and other cases, the committee was becoming increasingly worried about the standards of financial management in both quangos and central government departments. A special report published in January 1994 dramatised these concerns by suggesting that 'these failings represent a departure from standards of public conduct which have mainly been established during the past 140 years.'[12] Despite these failings, the committee felt that the government's programme for promoting economy and efficiency in the public sector did not conflict

with a proper and honest handling of public money. The political effect
of this report from a highly respected all-party parliamentary committee
was to provide more ammunition for politicians and the media, who
saw these failings as the result of the government's policy for reforming
the public sector.

As Wilson's article shows, given the concentration of Labour MPs in
Wales, the government was particularly vulnerable to political attack
over its use of quangos in Wales. A target for criticism was the number
of individuals with direct and indirect links to the Conservative Party
who were appointed to senior positions in Welsh quangos. Controversy
surrounded the reappointment of Beata Brookes, chairman of the
Conservative Party in Wales and a former MEP, as chairman of the
Welsh Consumer Council. Controversy also surrounded the former
chairman of the Monte Carlo Conservatives Abroad Association, David
Rowe-Beddoe, who in 1993 had been appointed to reorganise the Welsh
Development Agency. With a series of irregularites revealed in connection with the Welsh Development Agency, the Development Board for
Rural Wales, and the Health Promotion Authority for Wales, Welsh
quangos appeared to be out of control.[13]

In general, the press was hostile to what it saw as the government's
abuse of power in creating a vast network of unelected bodies to which
they systematically appointed its friends. Stories abounded of Conservative appointments. For instance, *The Observer* with articles entitled
'Tories put friends in high places' (4.7.93), 'Tory peers pile aboard the
quango gravy train' (6.2.94) and 'Exposed: Scale of Tory cash link to
quango jobs' (6.11.94) sought to show that 'political patronage is
rampaging throughout John Major's Administration as government
allies and Conservative Party donors amass key posts in Britain's
burgeoning quangocracy.' The *Financial Times* (14.1.93) concluded its
survey of appointments to quangos by saying that 'if there is a new elite
running Britain's public services, it appears the best qualifications to
join are to be a businessman with Conservative leanings'.

The press also emphasised the 'explosion' in the numbers of quangos.
The Guardian, in a survey entitled 'The Quango Explosion' (19.11.93),
predicted that, as a result of the government's reforms of the public
sector, by 1996 there would be over 7,700 quangos spending £54
billion. Commenting on the Democratic Audit 1994 report, *'Ego Trip:
Extra-governmental Organisations in the UK and their Accountability'*,
the *Independent on Sunday* (22.5.94) noted that there was now one
quango for every 10,000 people, while the 73,000 quangocrats outnum-
bered elected local councillors by three to one. Press stories also
connected quangos to sleaze and mismanagement in government.

The place of quangos on the political agenda was reinforced during
the summer and autumn of 1994 by the 'money for questions' affair
and related scandals. Two Conservative MPs, Graham Riddick and
David Tredinnick, were alleged to have received payment for asking

questions in the House of Commons. As a result of further allegations about a failure to declare payments in the Register of Members' Interests, two other MPs, Tim Smith and Neil Hamilton, resigned as junior ministers. A Cabinet minister, Jonathan Aitken, was at the centre of a row about the payment of a bill at the Ritz Hotel in Paris. These cases brought to a head the issue of standards and propriety in public life and the connections between financial interests and politicians. While these events were not directly related to quangos, they gave added weight to allegations of sleaze relating to the whole area of patronage. This enabled those who wanted changes in the procedures for quango appointments to put forward demands to the Nolan Committee, appointed by the Prime Minister in autumn 1994 to investigate standards in public life.

Since 1992 the political contest surrounding quangos revolved around three areas: numbers, patronage and accountability. As Hogwood's article shows the term quango itself is vested with political significance. Central to this contest was a numbers game involving varied political and policy stakes. The Conservatives did not want to be seen to have increased the number of quangos. They had come into office in 1979 with a pledge to reduce their numbers. The government therefore relied on the very narrow definition of non-departmental public bodies (NDPBs) as established in the Pliatzky review in 1979. This enabled William Waldegrave, then Cabinet minister in charge of public services, to claim, during the Commons debate on unelected state bodies in 1994 (24 February), that the government had cut the number of NDPBs from 2,167 in 1979 to 1,389.

To attack the growth of the patronage state, the opposition needed to demonstrate an explosion in the number of unelected bodies. It did not accept the government's narrow definition which excluded the new non-elected bodies that Stewart saw as constituting the basis for the 'new magistracy'. The Democratic Audit report, which provided information on a wide range of local and national bodies, argued that the groups constituting the new magistracy were now an important element in the world of non-elected bodies. For the government, however, the imperative was to have a definition accepted that would have kept the number of recognised quangos as low as possible. Waldegrave therefore argued that *The Guardian*'s prediction of 7,700 quangos by 1996 was based upon a 'rather bogus definition of quangos' which included each individual hospital Trust and organisations such as the TEC's and Local Enterprise Companies that were in the private sector. In his view, the Labour Party were being dishonest in complaining about large numbers of quangos as 17 new quangos were mentioned in Labour's 1992 election manifesto (Commons, 24.2.94). Far from cutting the number, Labour's policies were likely to increase them. As the government and opposition had different political stakes in the issue, there was not much ground for agreement.

The second area around which this political contest revolved was patronage. Opposition parties sought to make political capital from highlighting the unrelenting way in which Conservative ministers had used their powers systematically to exclude non-Conservatives from the network of unelected bodies. The political imperative for the opposition in making quangos a political issue was to demonstrate as much misuse of patronage as possible. The Labour Party's activities in pursuing patronage issues irritated ministers. There was a feeling in Conservative circles that Labour was playing party-political games and was essentially scandal mongering. Given Labour's own record in making public appointments, Conservatives felt that its approach was hypocritical. With the press also attempting to play up the growth of patronage and the sleaze factor, the government saw itself on the defensive in the face of an onslaught of stories about its use of appointments.

In response to this attack, the government attempted to undermine the credibility of the Labour Party's claims by pointing out the way in which the last Labour government appointed its friends, such as leading trade unionists, to key posts. For example, William Waldegrave and David Davis, Parliamentary Secretary in the Office of Public Service and Science, in their speeches in the Commons debate on unelected state bodies (24.2.94), emphasised the close links between the trade unions and the last Labour government. Waldegrave listed the numerous posts held by Jack Jones and recalled that the 39 members of the TUC Council held 180 state appointments. In addition, Labour's Health Minister had sacked 32 chairmen of health authorities who were suspected of Conservative sympathies and replaced them with Labour placemen.

According to John Major, prominent figures in the Labour Party currently hold quango positions. During Prime Minister's questions (25.10.94), armed with a long list, he began to read out their names, including those of Bill Morris, the current general secretary of Transport and General Workers Union, and Jack Jones, one of Morris's predecessors, Lord Plant, an academic who chaired Labour's committee on electoral reform, and Lord Barnett, a former Labour Cabinet minister. The Prime Minister cited a Labour Party document as evidence of 'the sleazy way in which the Labour Party deals with non-departmental bodies.' This document had suggested Labour Party members use their positions on non-elected bodies as a platform for campaigning.

John Major also attacked the Labour Party report, *Quangos and the Conservatives*, published in October 1994, as containing 'fatuous nonsense' when it tried to suggest that General Sir Peter de la Billière, the British Commander in the Gulf War, and the Duke of Kent were appointed to quangos because of donations they made to the Conservative Party. Responding to a BBC programme which suggested that 24 spouses of Conservative MPs and peers and 33 unsuccessful parliamentary candidates had been given quango jobs, Jeremy Hanley, chairman of the Conservative Party, accused Labour and the media of conducting a quango witchhunt. He said that it was pure chauvinism to suggest that Lady Howe, Mary Archer, Lady Taylor, or any of the others mentioned in the programme were appointed simply because of their husbands. They were all well qualified and experienced people in their own right and were appointed on merit. Nonetheless, the government recognised that the whole question of patronage and appointments needed review. In answering questions put to him by Tony Blair (Commons, 20.10.94), the Prime Minister revealed that in May 1994 he had established an independent working party to examine the system of appointments as well as asking the Chancellor of the Duchy of Lancaster to review appointments to all public bodies. This was taken a small step further by the inclusion of non-elected public bodies within the area to be examined by the Nolan Committee on Standards in Public Life.

The third area around which the political contest developed was the issue of accountability and whether the growth of non-elected bodies had created a democratic deficit or a democratic gain. Despite the fact that this raised important constitutional matters, issues of accountability were not debated in detail but seemed to take second place to scoring party-political points. However, different notions of accountability — political versus consumer accountability — began to emerge. It became apparent that the government and opposition parties gave priority to different notions of accountability.

The government's critics argued that the large-scale transfer of power from elected to non-elected bodies was creating a democratic deficit. The severance of the direct link to elected representatives at the local level had resulted in a loss of channels for public accountability. Stewart argued that in no sense could the 'new magistracy' be seen as locally accountable. This was because its membership was largely unknown locally and the organisations were not required to hold open meetings, give access to information or subject themselves to local scrutiny. He rejected the idea that the line of accountability could run effectively through ministers and argued that 'Ministers do not resign these days even when things go wrong in departments they directly control let alone in quangos.' In his view ministers were too remote from the local level and therefore 'people need to able to go to local representatives they can hire and fire'.

Stewart's writing was influential in the development of the views held by opposition politicians on the question of accountability. They stressed the importance of accountability through political institutions and argued that a 'democratic deficit' had resulted from the undermining of local democratic institutions. Marjorie Mowlam, who was the shadow minister for Citizen's Rights, argued that the government was playing games with local democracy. 'Ministers talk the language of citizen's rights, of empowering and enabling people to make choices for themselves in their local communities. In reality, the government has dictated from Westminster a far-reaching programme of legislation which is undermining public participation and public accountability. Local democracy, close to the provision of services, is where accountability ought to work.'[14]

Ministers rejected the argument that the growth of quangos had undermined accountability. Favouring a more consumer-oriented approach, they argued that there had in fact been a democratic gain. Accountability had been strengthened by making clear who was responsible for the service, and by establishing standards of service for the customer and by making services responsive to their customers. Citizens had been given the power of the consumer over public services and they now had more opportunities to complain and secure redress. Alongside these developments, accountability through ministers to Parliament remained. Responding to the arguments put forward by Stewart, Waldegrave argued that the government's critics had failed to understand how accountability had been strengthened by the management reforms introduced into the public sector. His case rested on a view that the democratic voice through the ballot box was not necessarily the best way of securing efficient, accountable and responsive public services. The key point was 'not whether those who run our public services are elected, but whether they are producer-responsive or consumer-responsive.'[15]

A consumer oriented notion of accountability was seen by Ministers as vital to the development of new forms of accountability. However, Lord Skidelsky, a supporter of these reforms, expressed reservations in the Lords (19.1.94) about the progress being made when he suggested that the government had 'begun to dismantle the democratic model by appointing non-elected managers without properly designing alternative means of accountability'. As the conflicting parties to this debate gave priority to different notions of accountability, political and consumer accountability became seen as being mutually exclusive rather than complementary.

Since 1992, quangos have acquired a disreputable image as a result of the negative way in which opposition politicians and the press used them as a weapon for discrediting the government. The prediction by Liberal Democrat MP, Robert Maclennan, that the discussion would concentrate on appointments which would 'serve to distract the attention from the wider constitutional questions' had been borne out by the way in which the issue had developed since 1992.[16] The Labour Party mounted a political campaign against the Conservatives rather than focusing on a constitutional debate about non-elected bodies. This issue has been dominated by party-political considerations rather than constitutional needs. In that respect, at least, there was not much difference with the late 1970s when quangos also acquired notoriety.

Conclusion

At different times quangos have come onto the political agenda because this served the interests of party politicians. The politics of quangos has been dominated by an adversarial party political game in which all sides have attempted to achieve short-term party advantage. Political imperatives arising from the adversarial nature of British party politics have dictated how the parties have pursued the issue. The political game requires opposition attacks on government so that parties in opposition campaign against governmental use of non-elected bodies, while themselves using them when in office. The view of both the Conservative and Labour Parties at any particular time depended on whether they were in government or opposition. However, they could not successfully exploit quangos as an issue unless there were some grounds for public concern about the way in which the government of the day was using or abusing them. For the point scoring to seem credible, there had to be some real issues underlying the political game.

Both in the late 1970s and since 1992, there were real concerns about the way power appeared to be shifting to non-elected bodies. Questions of accountability were never far below the surface. However, the focus upon party political manifestations, such as the political bias in the composition of these bodies, served to conceal the more fundamental constitutional issues. Despite their stance when in opposition, both major parties have found organisations of this type useful instruments of government. The developments of the last twenty years suggest that non-elected bodies will remain a significant feature of the administative structure in Britain. Highlighting and attacking the number of Conservative or Labour supporters on these bodies makes good copy and is good party-political campaigning tactics. It is naive to think that governments of whatever political colour will not want to place people sympathetic to their views and policies in organisations that are responsible for the delivery of government policies.

It is perhaps therefore not in the interest of either major party fundamentally to change a system that serves them well when in office. Despite all the fuss that was made about quangos by the Conservatives in opposition in the late 1970s, in office they only undertook some essentially cosmetic measures to curb the growth of non-elected bodies. Given the Labour Party's current attack on patronage and political bias, there must be doubts as to how far it would make any significant change in the system if it returned to government. The whole debate so far has neglected the fundamental constitutional issue of how appointments by any party in government should be controlled and scrutinised, and how these bodies should be made more accountable and opened up to public scrutiny. With the present government's reforms of the public sector resulting in decentralisation and fragmentation of the organisations responsible for service delivery, it is vitally important that new patterns and forms of public accountability be developed. The adversarial party-political nature of the campaign against quangos has not been conducive to allowing a detailed debate about these new forms of accountability to emerge. A cynical public, however, might be forgiven for thinking that the politics of quangos is really about which lads have their 'snouts in the trough'.

1   C. Hood, 'Governmental bodies and government growth', in A Barker (ed.), *Quangos in Britain* (Macmillan, 1982), p. 51.
2   See e.g. A. Davies, What's Wrong with Quangos? (The Outer Circle Policy Unit, 1979) and S. Weir and W. Hall (eds), *EGO TRIP: Extra-governmental organisations in the United Kingdom and their accountability*, Democratic Audit Report (Charter 88 Trust, 1994).
3   B. Hogwood, 'Much Exaggerated: Death and Survival in British Quangos', Political Studies Association Annual Conference, 1993.
4   A. Davies, What's wrong with Quangos? (The Outer Circle Policy Unit, 1979) p. i.
5   C. Hood, 'Axe person, Spare that Quango . . .', in C. Hood and M. Wright, *Big Government in Hard Times* (Martin Robertson, 1981), p. 107.
6   N. Johnson, 'Quangos and the Stucture of British Government', *Public Administration*, Winter 1979, p. 381.
7   Report on Non-Departmental Public Bodies, Cmnd, 7797, HMSO, 1980.
8   C. Hood, *op cit.*, p. 109.
9   J. Stewart, 'The Rebuilding of Public Accountability', European Policy Forum Conference, 1992.
10 T. Wright, 'Government by appointment', *The House Magazine*, 17 May 1993, p. 14.
11 G. Howarth, *Quangos and Political Donations to the Tory Party*, Knowsley North Constituency Labour Party, September 1993, and *Quangos and the Conservatives*, Labour Party, October 1994.
12 Committee of Public Accounts, *The Proper Conduct of Public Business*, 8th Report, Session 1993–94, HMSO, 1994.
13 K. Morgan and E. Roberts, *The Democratic Deficit: A Guide to Quangoland* (Department of City and Regional Planning, University of Wales, Cardiff, 1993).
14 M. Mowlam, 'Rescuing the community', *The House Magazine*, 17 May 1993, p. 10.
15 W. Waldegrave, 'The Reality of Reform and Accountability in Today's Public Service', Public Finance Foundation/BDO Consulting Public Service Lecture, July 1993.
16 R. Maclennan, 'Jobs for the boys', *The House Magazine*, 17 May 1993, p. 12.

Quangos and Democratic Government

BY PAUL HIRST

ASSESSMENTS of how democratic a country is concentrate on the degree to which government is accountable to the people and the effectiveness of the means of ensuring accountability. For a government to be properly accountable its decisions and actions must be transparent, and the people and their representatives must have ready remedies with which to sanction poor governmental performance. Quangos must thus be, almost by definition, a matter of concern for anyone committed to democratic accountability, for they place public money and government functions in the hands of unelected persons whose links to the elected bodies that supervise government are tenuous at best. For this reason quangos have been an issue of public concern in Britain since roughly the mid-1970s. This concern has two peaks, the late 1970s when it was expressed by the right, and the early 1990s, when it came from the liberal left.

In the 1970s it was Conservatives who saw such quasi-state bodies as the Manpower Services Commission as a symptom of a rapidly developing corporatist state and thus a danger to the power of elected governments and the sovereignty of Parliament.[1] Conservatives feared that such quasi-autonomous bodies made both public policy and public expenditure difficult to direct and control from the centre.

Despite promising to cut back the tentacles of the quango state, the Conservatives have done nothing of the kind. They have curtailed the role of corporatist representation and abolished some organisations (like the National Economic Development Office, NEDO) but have greatly expanded the scale and role of quangos. Thus in the early 1990s concern was voiced about the enormous growth in government through unelected bodies. The issue now was not the power of organised social interests as against elected representatives but of new market-oriented and managerially-run institutions that substituted consumer responsiveness and bureaucratic hierarchy for political accountability. It is the Conservatives who have created a new and much larger quango state on the back of the one they strove to curtail in 1979. The key issues are the sheer number of such unelected governmental bodies, the scope and scale of the public functions they perform, the high proportion of public expenditure that they administer, and the unrepresentativeness and political bias of their personnel.

John Stewart focused this concern in his telling phrase the 'New Magistracy', raising the spectre of an unelected quangocracy ruling the country like the old Justices of the Peace.[2] He charts the shift from a prevailing conception of public accountability being realised through political mechanisms, such as elected local governments, to the very different and much weaker conception of accountability through the market satisfaction of consumers and through contract compliance, an accountability in the hands of accountants. Likewise, the Democratic Audit of the United Kingdom, in its survey of quangos, *Ego-Trip*, has catalogued the vast scale of extra-governmental bodies (EGOs) performing public functions and has outlined the constitutionally ambiguous position of these institutions in terms of accountability to Parliament.[3]

The public discussion of quangos thus focuses on the issue of 'accountability', and specifically accountability to elected bodies and through them to the people. The danger in the rhetoric of the growth of 'unaccountable' government is that we tend to fall back on existing forms of political accountability as if they were unproblematic. There is now a serious issue about the degree to which representative institutions can render government in general accountable and not just quangos. The issue at stake is not merely whether the policies of the Conservatives since 1979 have led to deviation from the norm of accountable and representative government, but whether there is a viable status quo ante to which we can return. We must extend the question of accountability beyond quangos and question the current effectiveness of traditional mechanisms of accountability. The growth of quangos is just one, unimaginative and undemocratic, solution to a general crisis of representative government and to a specific crisis of government in Britain.

The main themes of this article are as follows:
1. That the core institutions that ensure representative government originated in the eighteenth century and were developed in the nineteenth, whereas since the beginning of this century the scale and scope of state functions and public administration has expanded beyond the capacity of such institutions for competent supervision.
2. That Britain has suffered particularly from this general problem; because of its unwritten constitution, the obsession with preserving parliamentary sovereignty and the growing concentration of power in the executive, the UK has found it difficult to create a stable and well-defined relationship between central and subsidiary governmental powers and also between the state and the public institutions of the wider society.[4]
3. That the solutions to the general problem of accountability and its specifically sharp form in the UK require that the traditional institutions of representative democracy be supplemented by new institutions that give greater powers to citizens and that redraw the boundaries between public authority and civil society.

The limits of representative democracy

Quangos must thus be placed in a wider framework if the problems of accountability they pose are to be fully understood. The crisis created by the growth of quangos should lead us to reconsider the foundations of our democracy and renew them. The basic institutions of modern representative government are now quite old, they have been with us since the 1780s. Democratic franchises were gradually added to these institutions and in most countries fully democratic electorates were only created well into the twentieth century. These representative institutions, and specifically the supervision of the executive by the legislature, were designed for small governments with a limited range of activities and, outside of the armed forces, a small number of personnel. Thus these institutions superintended what were in effect 'nightwatchman' states and substantially self-regulating societies. The relationship between government and Parliament was intimate and could rely primarily on informal knowledge, and the role of legislation was limited, with bills relatively few in number and simple in content.

Modern omnicompetent public service states and the large official bureaucracies that go with them were superimposed on these institutions of representative government. The combination of eighteenth century constitutionalism, nineteenth century liberalism, and modern big government and mass democracy worked well enough for most of this century, only beginning to pull apart quite recently. The reason for this relative harmony between very different types of institution is that most of the new public services were collectivist. They were uniform in administration and universal in provision, with the result that they could be administered through stable bureaucratic hierarchies and fixed rules.[5] These were relatively straightforward to supervise. Moreover, the common people (who formed the democratic publics of the new collectivist and industrial states) were happy enough to be protected from common contingencies, like sickness or unemployment, or offered standard basic services, like elementary education or public housing. Democracy could appear to be a matter of voters choosing between parties in terms of their promises with regard to such services.

The state's ability to protect citizens from the vagaries of the market and yet not exercise excessive administrative discretion helped to maintain the arm's length relationship between governors and governed necessary to a liberal society. It also simplified the task of democratic supervision. Keynesian macro-economic management in the UK preserved both the autonomy of private property and the structures of liberal government. A small elite of civil servants controlled the level of economic activity through relatively traditional policy mechanisms and under the overall policy supervision of ministers. Moreover, to the extent that government dealt directly with industry, it was assisted by the fact that employment and output were highly concentrated in a small number of mainly nationally owned firms.

These saving features of the relationship between big government and liberal democratic accountability have diminished rapidly and radically, especially since the early 1970s. In Western industrial states the great post-war boom promoted a growth in public spending and the range of public services. The public sector rapidly outgrew the old collectivist security state, leading to a system of such complexity that it is difficult to control by traditional mechanisms of political accountability. Moreover, modern publics have become more demanding, better educated and less deferential. Their attitude to public services has changed from one of gratitude to a consumer consciousness. They demand higher quality and also more diverse services of greater complexity. Whereas they were once satisfied with elementary education and payment of the doctor's bill, the majority are coming to expect things like higher education or organ transplants as a right. They demand legal and administrative protection from a far wider and more differentiated range of contingencies, particularly in the environmental field. As the expectations of the majority have risen, so the willingness of a core constituency of the successful to accept and to pay for the old basic collectivist services had declined. Those old simple standard services succeeded in their own terms, they enabled people to escape poverty and insecurity. But as they did so, the needs and attitudes of the majority of recipients of the services changed; they created a demand for a more complex and differentiated public service state.

The majority of the population are no longer the struggling unskilled manual workers and their families that they were at the beginning of the century. Yet as a large part of the population has become more prosperous, more demanding in its expectations of what it will pay the government to provide, massive constraints have been placed on public expenditure and service provision in the UK by successive economic crises and mass unemployment. Thus economic stresses have produced renewed demand for basic welfare services at the same time as the demand for enhanced services has risen. This has made administration more complex, has placed constraints on public expenditure, and has made it difficult to determine the main direction of policy — providing basic services like income support and social housing that sustain the poor or providing differentiated high quality services for those who are prosperous enough to protect themselves against basic contingencies.

Secondly, from the 1973 oil price crisis onwards, the economies of almost all the advanced industrial countries have changed in ways that have made economic governance by the national state much more difficult. These economies have internationalised even further, being severely constrained by the outcomes of international financial markets and also facing intensified foreign competition in trade and manufacturing. They have also become more diverse and complex internally, generating features such as the following that made government regulation more problematic. Technological change has accelerated to a point where a centrally directed 'industrial policy' that attempts to manage change and 'pick winners' has become all but impossible. The population of firms has differentiated in size, structure and management style: large firms no longer enjoy an inherent competitive advantage (as the examples of US Steel and IBM show). The result is that governments have to deal with a much more complex business sector and, in particular, have to pay attention to the conditions that enable small and medium-sized enterprises to prosper. Divisions of labour have changed out of all recognition and labour markets have differentiated, making the working population less homogenous and creating new problems for training policy, labour market policy and workers rights. Centralised corporatist structures based on large firms and stable industrial labour forces have lost some of their salience, thus weakening cooperative economic governance between industry, labour and the state.[6]

The upshot of all these international and internal changes is that modern economies cannot be directly and quickly changed in their performance by the macro-economic policies of the medium-sized nation states.[7] Such economies are less 'national', so that governments have less control of the economy and so the success or failure of their policies is more difficult to judge and hold to account. The two most effective methods of economic regulation, Keynesian demand management and economic coordination through the cooperation and bargaining of the central organised economic interests, are no longer readily available. Instead, if governments are to intervene they require more complex and localised knowledge. If they are to promote successful economic performance they need to be able to tailor policies toward difficult areas like industrial training, collective services for manufacturing and local investment.

Many countries have been aided in coping with these problems of changing mechanisms of economic regulation by having effective regional governments that have the local knowledge to aid industry and also well-structured industrial districts that can provide collective services to industry through public-private cooperation.[8] They have also benefited from extended dialogue between the organised interests at local level and thus the possibility of wider cooperation that can survive the demise of highly centralised corporatist bargaining. In general, the scope for top-down bureaucratic control, whether public or private, is now much less. Most large bureaucracies lack the high-quality local knowledge and the responsiveness for effective responses to a complex and rapidly changing economic environment.

The UK, lacking regional governments, having allowed its industrial districts to decline into insignificance, and having set its face against dialogue and cooperation between management and labour because it smacks of 'corporatism', has found itself ill-placed to cope with the new demands for public intervention in the economy.[9] It has continued to pursue centralised and highly ambitious macro-economic policies — behaving as if the only thing obsolete in the post-Keynesian era is Keynes himself. Where it has tried to deliver services to industry it has done so in top-down forms through quangos like Urban Development Corporations or Training and Enterprise Councils that do not really involve the full range of local interests or give them a say in policy. This combination of macro-economic ruthlessness in Whitehall and unde-mocratic quangoism in the regions is a major contributing factor to the failure of UK manufacturing and the poor performance of the British economy.[10]

Thirdly, in the Anglo-Saxon states in particular but the tendency is observable throughout the advanced world, publics have become more tax averse. This is partly because the participation of the majority of the population in direct taxation is a relatively recent phenomenon but also because they have competing demands for the private provision of enhanced services. Low growth has constrained citizens and govern-ments alike. In the USA, for example, real incomes for the bulk of the employed population are stagnant or have fallen since the 1970s. In this context governments find it difficult to avoid constraints by generating additional public funding out of growth. States also now enjoy less autonomy in fiscal policy in an internationalised and highly competitive world economy.

The result has been that demands for high-quality responsive public services that are necessarily expensive have rocketed and yet govern-ments have faced severe constraints on their ability to pay for these services either out of the consumers' own pockets or by borrowing. The result has been to put immense pressures on the public sector, both in the simple form of expenditure cuts and in the more demanding form of needing to deliver high-quality cost-effective services. In the past, basic services were sufficient and/or additions could be paid for out of an expanding budget. Now the pressures towards quality and efficiency demand responses that traditional bureaucracies and the old forms of accountability that went with them find difficult to provide. Public sectors throughout the advanced world have faced a period of intense turbulence and have sought new models of funding, organisation and service delivery.

The result of these changes has been to put a strain on the relationship between government and accountability. Government has become com-plex and increasingly diverse. Far from being stable it has been involved in a continuous process of experiment to cope with the demands and constraints under which it operates. The scale and scope of legislation has grown. Societies are anything but self-regulating, nor can they rely on big bureaucracies (public and private) efficiently to manage their own internal affairs. Citizens' demands for protection against risks have grown. Societies have become less uniform and less easy to regulate by general rules. The result has been an explosion of legislation against multiple and changing contingencies, forcing frequent changes in rules and a proliferation in their provisions. Legislatures throughout the advanced world have become virtual law factories, churning out rules and sanctioning powers of administrative regulation at a rate that makes detailed scrutiny almost impossible.

These are problems that are common to almost all advanced countries. The tasks of government have become more difficult, the satisfaction of citizens with government has become less as the expectations they have placed upon it have become greater, and the capacity of representative institutions to supervise administration, always threatened by the rise of big government, has diminished to the point of crisis. Legislators and elected officials are marooned at the centre of states that have finally grown beyond the capacity of nineteenth century representative democratic institutions to supervise.

If this problem has become general and acute in the last twenty years, it is at its sharpest in the UK. The reason is that Britain has had an underdeveloped version of the liberal democratic constitutional state; it has long put pragmatics and policy at the heart of democratic politics rather than a formal architecture of constitutionally ordered political institutions. Indeed, the very features that have made British government effective in the past and enabled it to make rapid decisions, that is the concentration of power in Whitehall and parliamentary sovereignty, are now liabilities when more decentralised, open and responsive forms of power have become necessary.[11] The defining features of the British system of government—an unwritten constitution, the absence of codified and entrenched citizens' rights, the dominance of the executive over the legislative through prime-ministerial power and the disciplines of the party system, the loose doctrine of ministerial responsibility and the relative underdevelopment of a system of administrative law—mean that the UK's mechanisms for the supervision and restraint of government are very much at the mercy of government.[12]

The massive growth of quangos can be seen as a response to the general problems of government outlined above within the context of the British system of highly centralised power and attenuated accountability. Undoubtedly, the extensive use of quangos owes much to the Conservatives' mistrust of local government and to the belief that government can be reinvigorated by private-sector practices and personnel. It is also true that English local government was ill-adapted to take on and manage the new tasks of government and also that many British institutions like the nationalised industries and the NHS were in a state of advanced bureaucratic sclerosis. However, the extent to which the quango model has been used exceeds explanations based on either ideology or previous administrative failure. Quangos have penetrated not only into every area of government, but their influence extends throughout the wider society and to an extensive range of non-state institutions. One of the reasons for this spread of quangos is that not only were the institutions of central and local government ill-adapted to the changing environment in which they had to operate, but that the relationship between the state and the wider society in Britain had become extremely problematic by the time Mrs Thatcher came to power.

Democracy and civil society

Quangos have not only come to undertake functions hitherto directly performed by central and local government, they have also intruded into the state's relation to the wider society and have come to exercise governance functions in relation to public bodies, voluntary associations and private firms. The growth of the quango state has significantly transformed the relation of government to public (but non-state bodies) like the universities and to private bodies of some consequence to public policy (like housing associations).

Every society has a political constitution that defines and limits the power of the state, but it also has what we may call a 'social constitution', that is a complex of laws, practices and procedures that defines the ways in which the political institutions and the wider society interact. This social constitution is more diffuse and less formal, but it is none the less real. Its effective working is crucial to the health of democracy in the wider sense, as government balanced by an open and pluralistic society. The relation of the state and those activities that it regulates is normally thought of in terms of the concept of 'civil society'. Civil society is frequently thought of as a private sphere composed of individuals and their associations, as a spontaneous order that should be independent of the state in a democratic country. The problem with this traditional liberal view of civil society is that, in emphasising the independence of society from government, it tends to ignore the fact that many of the components of this wider society are not spontaneous. Rather, 'civil society' is made up of institutions, associations and corporate bodies whose powers are defined and regulated by the state. Modern industrial societies do not just include the state and private individuals, they are also made up of many large and complex organisations such as professional bodies, broadcasting networks, major charities, trade unions. How the state defines the powers of action and the forms of internal governance of such associations and organisations, the degree to which it intervenes to affect their workings, is central to the workings of democracy.

The issue here is that a democratic state must ensure that such organisations do not violate the rights and interests of its citizens, but also that such organisations enjoy an appropriate measure of decision-making autonomy and self-government. Many of the institutions can be regarded either as private or as non-state but public agencies of governance of an area of activity; they are of political consequence in the widest sense. This is especially true if they are in receipt of public funds and/or perform roles the government has delegated to such agencies. Thus citizens can expect that charities receiving public money for public purposes are accountable and regulated, or that self-regulating organised markets like the Stock Exchange deal fairly with the public. The issue is how this is done, whether government is too intrusive or too lax in its regulation.

I would contend that Britain's social constitution is now as problematic in its workings as is its unwritten political constitution. A good part of the reason is that government is either excessively interventionist, for example in the way government departments and quangos control charities in receipt of public funds, thus bureaucratising the voluntary sector, or excessively non-interventionist, for example allowing too lax a self-regulation in the financial services sector. The use of quangos in relation to the non-state sector has grown considerably, but it has neither increased democratic, as opposed to managerial, accountability, nor has it directly empowered citizens in their dealings with such bodies and associations. The general tendency of government, with significant exceptions in the financial and business sectors, is to increase its direct and indirect control over such bodies, whilst failing to protect and enhance forms of democratic self-governance within such bodies.

Until the early 1960s in Britain, the general response across the political spectrum would have been that the relationship between the state and the wider society—the social constitution—was reasonably satisfactory. The social constitution at that time had three main features: control by an Establishment; self-regulation and voluntarism; an arms' length relationship between government and the major public but non-state bodies. These features were seen to have several advantages: they minimised the need for formal regulation; they ensured, through the common presence of like-minded personnel, a measure of consistency in the way the different institutions behaved; and they achieved a balance between public funding and the autonomy of public but non-state institutions.[13]

The interlocking elites of the Establishment meant that central government, big business, the media, the universities, the Anglican Church, and so on, shared common perceptions and followed broadly similar unwritten codes of conduct. Self-regulation and voluntarism allowed major social activities to be governed with minimal state intervention. Thus limited companies were regarded as little republics of their shareholders, investors being protected by their rights under company law to participate in company governance. The Stock Exchange was in essence like a club, its rules being made and policed by its members. Trade unions were purely voluntary bodies but were given the privilege of certain legal immunities from damages arising from trade disputes. Institutions like the BBC, the Arts Council and the University Grants Commission made it possible for the state to fund activities like the arts or higher education whilst leaving it to the appointed members of such bodies to make decisions about policy and the distribution of resources without overt intervention by ministers or civil servants.

Why did this very particular and extremely British pattern of informal social governance develop? The main reason is the nature of Britain's central political institutions as they evolved from the eighteenth century onwards. Britain, unlike many continental states, did not bring the majority of its major social institutions within the public realm or subject private activities to close legal and administrative regulation. This has less to do with Britain's ancient traditions of liberty than with the limited scope for such developments within the unwritten constitution. Because of the legislative sovereignty of Parliament, because of the considerable discretionary power of the executive centralised in Whitehall, and because the unwritten constitution excluded the entrenchment of rights and powers, it was almost impossible to create a system of constitutionally-ordered lesser authorities and public but non-state bodies. Except for the dominant core political institutions, all other bodies, public and private, had to be constitutionally makeshift and to exist at the central states' fiat.[14]

Hence the attractions of the voluntary, the quasi-private and the informal governance of social affairs. Self-regulation was a way to escape from inclusion within the state or from legal regulation without constitutional protection. The unions, for example, preferred to be voluntary bodies rather than accept a system of positive labour law that would be subject to the changing whims of a sovereign Parliament. What they wanted from Parliament was legal immunities, not active regulation.

Lastly, many British institutions developed before large-scale industrial and social organisation became the norm. In a world of local and face to face commercial and social relations, informality made good sense. Lloyds grew out of a coffee house and provincial stock markets from the private and informal meetings of traders. Voluntarism was attractive in this period because the alternative had been the privileged monopoly corporations established by Act of Parliament, favouring the few and excluding the mass of traders.

These facts underlay and helped to sustain the notion of the continuity and exceptionalism of British social institutions. Like the unwritten constitution, they were a uniquely British inheritance. Until very recently the traditions of voluntarism and self-regulation were seen as assets, as part of a viable and distinctly British way of doing things. However, by the 1960s questions were beginning to be raised about aspects of this relatively stable pattern of social governance. In particular many politicians and commentators, Conservative and Labour, thought that the unions needed more formal legal regulation. But in the main politicians and informed opinion remained happy with the informality and self-regulation characteristic of the social constitution, much as they did with the major political institutions and the unwritten constitution.

The same could hardly be said today. The unwritten Constitution survived so well because its practices and conventions compensated for the fact that Britain's formal political institutions were obsolete by international standards. The gradual collapse of shared understandings among politicians that began to be a serious problem in the mid-1970s undermined the supports for the existing settlement. Mrs Thatcher's tendency in office to treat the unwritten constitution as if it were written, stretching the limits of convention to party political advantage where practices were not explicitly prohibited, gravely damaged the old system.[15]

The social constitutional worked well enough for similar reasons but it too began to come under pressure at about the same time. It worked and had some definite advantages, provided four conditions were met. First, that governments accepted the practice of voluntarily limiting their intervention in the affairs of public but non-state bodies like the BBC. Ministers generally recognised the need for bipartisan appointments to governing bodies and the need to let institutions make policy, refraining from imposing explicit agendas or extending central government control.

Second, this system was tolerable when private self-regulating institutions controlled activities that were primarily the concern of their own members, where those members were willing to bear the risks involved, and where others who were affected were prepared to defer to such informal governance. The London Stock Exchange developed as a self-regulating body, for example, at a time when private investors were the norm. But by the 1970s the main investors were financial institutions trading in order to generate financial assets for members of the public who had taken out insurance policies or pension plans. Informality would seem an inadequate protection for such indirect and unrepresented stakeholders.

Third, informality made sense when the elites were small and their members shared a common background and, in the main, abided by the unwritten rules. The Establishment was overwhelmingly public school and Oxbridge educated, and to a considerable degree our elites still are. What put paid to such cohesion was internationalisation, for example the entry of foreign banks and institutions into UK financial markets on a large scale, and also domestic social mobility, producing less a change in personnel at the top than a lessening of the willingness of those below them to practice deference and trust.

Fourth, social governance through informality worked when tacit and essentially local knowledge was adequate to ensure members' effective participation and when insiders' perceptions were an effective check on adherence to informal codes by the majority of those involved.

Britain could not remain the clubby self-enclosed society its elites had shaped and simultaneously remain an effective competitor in dynamic internationalised markets and accommodate the modest measure of social mobility created by the post-1945 welfare state, in particular its broadening of access to education. Informality could only survive on the basis of parochialism and exclusivity. However, the wider world was less inclined to accept the amateur and private government of institutions like major financial markets, nor would the new educated middle class continue to defer to the Establishment forever.[16]

In the later 1960s and the 1970s economic and social turbulence shook many established institutions to their foundations. Conservative and Labour governments tried to modernise Britain but without changing the fundamentals of its social constitution. This is a major reason why they failed. Both major parties experimented with corporatism. Labour, in particular, tried to reform economic governance with quasi-state bodies like the Industrial Reorganisation Commission and the Manpower Services Commission. The result was an incoherent compromise. Britain became corporatist enough for organised labour and the representatives of big business to have tremendous influence. It did not become corporatist enough to ensure genuine and ongoing cooperation between the major organised economic interests. It was, therefore, unable to achieve effective economic regulation through coordination of action between industry, labour and the state. Both individual firms and unions clung to voluntarism and self-regulation. Employers' organisations and the TUC were unable to enforce collective discipline on their members or make sure that top-level bargains would stick, as was the case in countries like Germany or Sweden.[17]

Governments of both political colours remained committed to Westminster executive discretion and exclusive party rule, refusing to concede a sufficient degree of joint and collaborative control over economic policy to the social interests or to obtain the cooperation of non-ruling parties. Mrs Thatcher's victory in 1979, after the disastrous collapse of government-union collaboration in the Winter of Discontent, and her conviction that the corporatist state needed to be demolished ended any remaining chance that Britain would evolve in a continental Social or Christian Democratic direction.

Mrs Thatcher's government was also committed to the thoroughgoing internationalisation of British financial markets and to ending the rule of a cosy bipartisan Establishment. In theory, therefore, the Conservatives ought to have reformed Britain's social institutions on a coherent neo-liberal programme. Yet she, no less than Wilson or Heath, failed to modernise Britain's institutions of social governance. The Conservative governments of the 1980s failed to remodel the public but non-state and the major private organisations in a coherent and democratic way. A market-based but well-regulated, transparent and meritocratic neo-liberal system remained a matter of rhetoric.

Three tendencies have prevailed in Conservative policy in reshaping the social constitution since 1979. The first is to centralise power and to subject to active government intervention public bodies like the Arts Council, the BBC and the universities that had been perceived internationally as the success stories of the arm's length approach. Moreover, the government extended its influence over and active management of voluntary bodies and charities, using the lever of public funds. Bodies like Housing Associations and Citizen's Advice Bureaux were forced to managerialise themselves and to accept Whitehall imposed agendas.

The second (as we have noted above) is that, far from abolishing quangos as promised in 1979, the Conservative governments have multiplied them and given them central roles in the provision of services and the regulation of activities that might have been assigned to or remained with more accountable public but non-state institutions. The top management of such quangos has been selected in the main on a highly partisan basis, creating a vast new domain of government patronage. Those affected by quangos' activities have been given no say over their policy and no means of democratic challenge, short of electing a non-Conservative government at Westminster. To take one example out of the vast number of these quangos that give cause for concern, the Urban Development Corporations have extensive discretionary powers, are independent of local authorities, and are not accountable to local residents.

The third tendency has been that central elements of the old system of self-regulation have been left undisturbed. This is the case even though in the financial sector the institutions in question handle billions of pounds of British citizens' and foreign investors' money. Lloyds, the London Stock Exchange, and the pensions and insurance industries have been left to govern themselves, despite pressing needs to meet international standards of public governance and disclosure. The government continues to treat as 'private' matters for company managements issues of major public concern such as the sale of Rover to BMW. In these cases the continuation of informality and self-regulation is indefensible and will ultimately undermine Britain's reputation for reliability and, therefore, its competitiveness in major international industries.

The central flaw in this approach to the governance of non-state institutions and publicly consequential activities is that it has not been shaped by a coherent model of how an advanced democratic market society should be run. Standards have been inconsistent and no explicit public debate about how to proceed has been encouraged by the Conservatives. Inconsistency is the rule, and ad hoc action and secrecy too often the norm. The Conservatives have been strongly interventionist in certain sectors and yet indulgently tolerant of continuing self-regulation in others. Powerful and undeclared vested interests, changing prejudices and fashionable theories, and the tendency of Whitehall to seek ever greater control, have all had a part in shaping the outcome.

The inconsistency of devising means for the governance for the whole of civil society by an exclusive party government elected on a minority of the votes cast and consistently minded to act in a highly partisan spirit should be all too obvious. To be effective, such forms of governance of public and private organisations need to be widely agreed, to follow clear and common models, and to be easily understood by those involved. The old informal system had at least the advantage that it was consensual and well-understood within the key elites. If the majority of the British public was excluded by the clubbyness of the old system, it is no less excluded by the complexity, haphazardness and insider dominance of the new. The new insiders are slightly different from the old, less cohesive in origins and more committed to manageri-alism. But they are no less members of an exclusive and unaccountable elite.

This is not just an issue of domestic political concern. How well British institutions work is also a matter of the country's long-run international competitiveness. This is obvious in the case of foreign investors, who want a well-run and secure financial system, but it is no less a matter of concern, for example, that British universities are seen to be free of unwarranted government interference if they are to gain a growing share of the market in foreign students. Building up democrat-ically accountable social institutions is part of being a modern open society, a necessity in an internationalising world where social efficiency is one of the key sources of competitive advantage. Complex, closed and capricious institutional cultures are both inefficient and a deterrent to foreign investors, consumers and internationally mobile talented professionals.

This last point is reinforced in its saliency because Britain is a member of the European Union. The Union is evolving common legal standards and regulatory practices that will have a major impact on British companies, organised markets, quasi-public institutions and the volun-tary sector. Just as the unwritten constitution makes it difficult to assess the impact of political change on Britain coming from the EU, so the incoherence of Britain's social constitution means that it will be in danger of importing a great deal of its standards of social governance piecemeal and without public debate. The UK can have little chance of a coherent policy on this issue whilst its social institutions remain in such a mess. It will have little idea of what to promote among its European partners or what it wants to resist at all costs becoming the European norm.[18]

Some of Britain's traditions of voluntarism and informality are genuinely valuable. Strictly voluntary associations, charities and clubs have played an important part in its social life and it is healthy that they should continue to do so. The point is not to insist that everything be legally regulated and bureaucratised, quite the contrary. Power, whether state, public or private must be clearly defined, its workings transparent, and it should be accountable to those affected by it. Voluntary organisa-tions, in particular, cannot prosper in a highly centralised state where power is concentrated in unaccountable government institutions and in quasi-public and corporate bureaucracies.

To achieve this transparency and accountability requires that the categories of state, public and private institutions be clearly defined and their powers circumscribed. The present system allows government and other powerful actors to play fast and loose with the categories of public and private. For example, monopolies and mergers, take-over rules, the operation of organised markets, and company governance generally, can all be presented as 'private' matters when it suits the government to do so. Similarly, the autonomy of quangos can be emphasised when the government wishes to avoid awkward issues, blaming job losses in the NHS on Trust managements, and yet as paymaster and standard setter it can direct the affairs of Trusts when it wishes. This gives government the discretion to intervene when it wants to and to let decisions happen by default when it does not. The situation is advantageous to ruling politicians and insiders, but it can hardly be in the interests of the public.

Britain has not resolved the conflicts that have arisen once the old informal system of self-regulation and elite control became obsolete. To do so will require extended public debate and the development of a model of how an advanced, open and democratic society should be run that is acceptable to a large part of informed opinion.

How can democratic accountability be enhanced?

The forgoing argument has made two points. First, that it is not a wholly effective response to the over-use and the excessive powers of quangos to reassert an established norm of representative democratic accountability. Quangos are part of a strategy of responding to those major problems of modern governance that also make democratic control by elected representatives increasingly difficult. Second, we can not treat the issue of quangos on its own, as if it were merely a matter of an ill-conceived policy on the part of the recent Conservative governments. Quangos are part of a much wider problem of the relationship between the state and civil society. Despite nostalgia for Britain's old social constition, its informal arrangements and unwritten understandings were no longer adequate in a world that demands openness and has rejected deference.

To raise the issue of the weakness of representative democratic accountability is to enter dangerous ground. Too often in the past the deficiencies of representative government were raised in order to argue that it be replaced by some other system that did not rely on multi-party competition for the votes of all adult citizens. Obvious examples are the marxist and radical advocacy of direct non-party democracy. Direct democracy has never been a viable option for democratic accountability in large and complex states and societies. For the purposes of giving all citizens power over their governors and of conferring legitimacy on core governmental institutions, there is no realistic alternative to representative democracy. However dissatisfied we may be with present forms of accountability, we shall have to adapt and supplement the institutions we have.

If radical direct democracy is no solution, then recent 'quick-fix' attempts to involve citizens in government through electronic referenda or citizens' juries are hardly a satisfactory solution either. The basic limitation of such solutions is that while they may involve citizens in some high-profile decisions and may involve the public in consultation on the formulation of some policies, they can not superintend the regular workings of modern large-scale government. Furthermore, electronic democracy is likely to be only partially inclusive. It will leave many citizens uninvolved and uncomprehending, especially those who currently under-participate in politics. The problem would be especially acute if these quick fixes were added to the present highly centralised state as a palliative, for it could just as likely enhance the power of the governors over the governed as it would increase democratic input. It could supplement government power with the gizmos of electronic legitimacy, enabling politicians to mobilise consent on certain key issues whilst leaving others unaddressed.

If the objective of reform is to be to renew democratic accountability, then we need to begin to tackle the problems of the current scale and complexity of government at root. Undoubtedly, short-term measures to make quangos more politically accountable in conventional ways and their personnel more broadly representative are necessary, though the sheer size of the quango state means that it can hardly be transformed overnight. But the way in which and the level at which governance functions are performed also needs to be changed. This would be necessary even if a strategy of increasing the existing powers of central government bodies had been followed instead of combining that with quangoism.

How might such reform be undertaken? Space forbids more than an outline here. I have tried to consider the issue in greater detail in *Associative Democracy*.[19] The essential task is to simplify government and devolve its powers so that the existing institutions of representative democractive accountability can begin to function somewhat as they were intended to do in the nineteenth century. The aim must be to simplify the core institutions of government and the role of legislation, without abandoning governance functions or reducing the public services or welfare provision that are essential to a well-managed modern industrial society.

This problem was perceived by the New Right in the 1970s in terms of governmental overload; their objective was to reduce the scale and scope of government by having it shed facilities and provision. This programme relied on giving publicly-provided services and regulatory tasks to markets. The market was seen as alternative to government, as a means of coordination and control in and of itself. The economic liberal diagnosis was partially correct; big government is unaccountable and unresponsive to citizens. On the other hand, weakly regulated markets cannot substitute themselves for the functions of government; they tend to undermine that minimum of social solidarity and economic security among citizens necessary to a cohesive and active democratic society. Worst of all, they tend to undermine the long-run capacity of the economy to promote investment and infrastructure.

The solution lies not with less government but with the restructuring of the state and the redrawing of the relationship between the public and the private spheres. This involves three distinct but complementary strategies of reform. The first is relatively conventional, if radical, in so highly centralised a state as the UK. That is political decentralisation, devolving powers to elected regional governments with legislative and fiscal powers. Regional governments are effective means of promoting local economic governance, as a great deal of international comparative evidence demonstrates that they are likely to have effective local knowledge and are able to promote consent and involvement through dialogue with local representative bodies such as trade associations and unions in areas like collective services to industry or and locally relevant education and training.

Regional governments are large enough entities to take over effectively many of the functions of economic regulation, social provision and planning currently performed by central government. Current local authorities are too small to do more than provide a limited range of local services. Regional governments could take over the responsibility for rendering key quangos like UDCs and TECs more accountable. If local democracy is to be restored, the chances are that regional governments are a better bet than existing local authorities. If they acquire major functions of central government, then they are more likely to attract the attention of voters; because they are bigger and more diverse, they are less likely to become single-party 'rotten boroughs' (especially if they are elected by proportional representation); and as they will be of some consequence, they are more likely to attract high-quality politicians than existing local authorities.

The second is radical and unconventional, that is to devolve functions to self-governing voluntary associations and to assist them by grants of public funds proportional to membership. Quangos are undemocratic organisations in receipt of public funds. In many cases they and government departments are pressing the voluntary sector to become more bureaucratic and managerial, more externally 'accountable' and less internally democratically accountable as a result. The voluntary sector remains one of the success stories in Britain. It is popular with and responsive to its members. The advantage of promoting the performance of governmental and public functions by voluntary associations is that they both reduce the administrative load on government institutions and can be directly accountable to their members, increasingly the decentralisation of democratic supervision. A radical shift in this direction would simplify the tasks of government, reducing its performance of now contradictory roles, that of service provider and that of overseeing the services provided.

The third solution is directly to democratise many quangos, like NHS Trusts, higher education corporations, locally-managed schools, and HATS, involving both their personnel and their consumers in their boards of management. This would return institutions to those involved in them rather than having them controlled by nominees who often do not use the services in question or know little about them.

If we accept that civil society is not just composed of private individuals but also consists of institutions of relevance to the public which receive public money, then we can see that 'publicising' civil society, by creating forms of democratic self-governance under the general superintendence of representative institutions, is a better solution than managerialising it and reducing the involvement of citizens in their services and institutions. This redrawing of the boundary between public and private, accepting democracy in civil society, also enables us to see a way of simplifying the scale and scope of legislation. If citizens are responsible for making their own rules for these activities of direct concern to them, then legislation need deal with fewer contingencies and guard directly against fewer risks and abuses. Legislation can be simpler if citizens have more remedies in their own hands. It can concentrate on protecting citizens from a more limited range of harms and act as a means of appeal, rather than as an initial remedy or all-purpose source of regulation.

Quangos are a means of farming out government functions based on distrust of the public, the belief that they are best left as passive consumers, and a belief that administrative accountability through management procedures is preferable to democratic control. Reform of the quango state offers a chance to enhance democracy by giving greater say back to citizens, thereby both increasing the scope for active involvement and countering the widespread feeling of alienation from politics. It would also make the institutions of representative democracy more effective by reducing the scale of the government activities they superintended.

1   E.g., Lord Hailsham, *The Dilemma of Democracy* (Collins, 1978).
2   'A new magistracy is being created in the sense that a non-elected elite are assuming responsibility for a large part of local governance' (J. Stewart, 'The Rebuilding of Public Accountability', European Policy Forum, 1992).
3   S. Wier and W. Hall (eds), *Ego Trip: Extra-Governmental Organisations in the United Kingdom and their Accountability* (Charter 88 Trust, 1994).
4   See D. Marquand, *The Unprincipled Society* Jonathan Cape, 1988).
5   See 'Reticulated Organisations . . .', G. Mulgan, *Politics in an Antipolitical Age* (Polity Press, 1994), ch. 8.
6   For an account of these changes see M. Piore and C. Sabel, *The Second Industrial Divide* (Basic Books, 1984).

7   It does not follow, of course, that national states are powerless in the face of globalisation. See e.g. P. Hirst, 'Why the National Still Matters' *Renewal* Oct. 1994.

8   For the role of regional governments see. C. Sabel, 'Flexible Specialisation and the Re-Emergence of Regional Economies', in P. Hirst and J. Zeitlin (eds), *Reversing Industrial Decline?* (Berg, 1989); and on industrial districts see J. Zeitlin, 'Industrial Districts and Local Economic Regeneration: Models, Institutions and Politics' in F. Pyke and W. Sengenberger (eds), *Industrial Districts and Local Economic Regeneration* (ILO, Geneva, 1992).

9   On why industrial districts have disappeared in Britain see J. Zeitlin 'Why are there no Industrial Districts in the United Kingdom', in A. Bagnesco and C. Sabel (eds), *Ce que petit peut faire: les petites et moyennes enterprises en Europe* (OCSEO, Poitiers, 1994).

10 See P. Hirst and J. Zeitlin, 'Flexible Specialisation and the Competitive Failure of UK Manufacturing', *Political Quarterly* 1988/2.

11 See A. Barnett, 'The Empire State' in A. Barnett (ed), *Power and the Throne*, (Vintage, 1994).

12 See A. Barnett, C. Ellis and P. Hirst (eds), *Debating the Constitution* (Polity Press, 1993)

13 The original edition of A. Sampson's *The Britain of Britain* conveys this informal elite culture very well.

14 See Marquand, *The Unprincipled Society* op. cit.

15 This approach is nowhere better conveyed than Hugo Young's *One of Us* Macmillan: London, 1989.

16 Hence the concern of intelligent economic liberals to have a written constitution in order to protect a market society; see F. Vibert (ed), *Britain's Constitutional Future* (Institute of Economic Affairs, 1991).

17 See P. Hirst, 'Labour and the Constitutional Crisis' in G. Andrews (ed), *Citizenship* (Lawrence and Wishart, 1991).

18 This is one of the reasons why intelligent Conservatives are concerned with constitutional reform; see F. Mount, *The British Constitution Now* (Heinemann, 1992).

19 Polity Press, 1993.

INDEX OF NAMES